perversions

deviant readings by

mandy merck

Published by VIRAGO PRESS Limited, February 1993
20–23 Mandela Street, Camden Town, London NW1 0HQ

*A CIP catalogue record for this book is available from the British
Library*

Printed in Britain by Cox & Wyman Ltd, Reading, Berkshire

contents

to partiality, irony, intimacy and perversity

acknowledgements

A great many people made this book possible. Parveen
Adams, Jennifer Batchelor, Clare Beavan, Tessa Boffin,
Charlotte Brunsdon, Lesley Caldwell, Jane Caplan,
Lindsay Cooper, Elizabeth Cowie, Sean Cubitt, John
Fletcher, Jean Fraser, Sunil Gupta, Matthew Hoffman,
Cora Kaplan, Mary Kelly, Annette Kuhn, Antonia Lant,
Susan Lipshitz, Sara Maitland, Biddy Martin, Laura
Mulvey, Constance Penley, Jean Radford, Jacqueline
Rose, Shirley Samuels, Anne Scott, Carolyn Steedman,
Barbara Taylor, Simon Watney, Margaret Williamson
and Sharon Willis solicited papers, suggested sources,
lent books, read drafts, wrote recommendations or
simply kept at me to keep at it. This support is characteristic of a certain kind of intellectual culture, with
roots in sexual and socialist politics, which reaches far
beyond the academy. For me, a longtime member of
what Terry Eagleton has called the lumpen intelligentsia, it has been crucial.

One of the most interesting (and influential) manifestations of that culture was the Society for Education
in Film and Television, an independent association of
people interested in media studies and the founding
publisher of *Screen*. SEFT perished some years ago in

what now seems an endless wave of cuts in radical arts expenditure. But its former officers and members retain my gratitude for choosing me to edit their journal, work with their staff and editorial boards, and in the process receive an invaluable education in contemporary theories of representation. For that education I must particularly thank Jennifer Batchelor, *Screen*'s deputy editor, and my unflaggingly generous teacher and collaborator.

This book was completed in Ithaca, New York, on a fellowship most unexpectedly provided by the Cornell University Society for the Humanities, in its 1991–92 programme on the Politics of Identity. I owe an immense debt to the Society and its director, Dominick LaCapra, its wonderful administrative staff Mary Ahl, Linda Allen, Pam Card and Agnes Sirrine, and the fellows of the academic years 1990–91 and 1991–92. I would particularly like to record my pleasure in attending Judith Butler's Society seminar on 'Phantasmatic Identification' and in working with a remarkable group of students busily 'Perverting the Academy'.

The following articles in this book are reprinted from journals and collections: 'The Train of Thought in Freud's "Case of Homosexuality in a Woman"' first appeared in *m/f* 11/12, 1986, and then in *The Woman in Question*, edited by Parveen Adams and Elizabeth Cowie (MIT Press, Cambridge, Massachusetts, 1990); 'A Case of AIDS' in *Ecstatic Antibodies: Resisting the AIDS Mythology*, edited by Tessa Boffin and Sunil Gupta (Rivers Oram Press, London 1990); '"Transforming the Suit": A Century of Lesbian Self-Portraits' in *Stolen Glances*, edited by Tessa Boffin and Jean Fraser (Pandora Press,

London, 1991); 'The Amazons of Ancient Athens' (under the title 'The City's Achievements') in *Tearing the Veil: Essays on Femininity*, edited by Susan Lipshitz (Routledge & Kegan Paul, London, 1978); '"Lianna" and the Lesbians of Art Cinema' in *Films for Women*, edited by Charlotte Brunsdon (BFI Publishing, London, 1986); and 'The Fatal Attraction of "Intercourse"' (under the title 'Bedroom Horror') in *Feminist Review* 30, Autumn 1988. I am grateful for permission to reuse this material.

Finally, my thanks to my publishers at Virago, my copy editor Gillian Beaumont, and most especially to my editor Ruthie Petrie, for her patience, encouragement, exclamatory faxes and a friendship now in its twentieth year.

introduction

This collection is titled *Perversions* for a number of reasons. It was begun in London in the late 1970s, an era of Queer Studies *avant la lettre*, when the work of Richard Dyer, Mary McIntosh, Simon Watney, Jeffrey Weeks and Elizabeth Wilson, among others, circulated in places like the National Film Theatre (where Richard curated its first gay film season), the feminist journal *Red Rag* (where Elizabeth memorably addressed the question of bisexuality), the men's collective Gay Left, and even – occasionally – in the classroom. (It's worth remembering that Mary McIntosh's pioneering analysis of the social construction of the homosexual identity[1] dates back to 1968, and the radical British school of sociology known as 'Deviancy Studies'.)

In those days I was employed by the London weekly *Time Out*, to which I contributed reviews of feminist and gay films, books, plays and other cultural objects. (For some time this included women's tennis: Billie Jean King, Martina Navratilova, *et al.*) As I became known as one of the few critics then willing to do this, I got commissioned to write longer pieces for journals and books. Thus, in 1976, when the Routledge collection *Tearing the Veil* was being planned to examine the many representations of the feminine, its editor asked me for an essay on the Amazon in pursuit of what she (and I) confidently assumed to be an image of the lesbian.

This is where another definition of perversion comes

1

in – not that of 'deviant sexuality', but of the broader opposition to what is expected or accepted (e.g. 'You're just being perverse'). As I read – or read about – Athenian literature, architecture and ceramics (a delightful project which occupied several months after work) it became apparent that the classical notion of the Amazon was very unlike that of the cultural feminists then donning their *labyrises*. Instead of commemorating a lost community of female love and sovereignty, these images warned of women's ferocity and unsuitability for power. Far from proving the existence of an ancient matriarchy, they seemed to have been constructed to justify an intensification of male dominance. As for 'lesbianism' proper, it simply didn't figure in these ancient evocations of the women warriors. (What they did after the battle, at night, under the wagons, etc., etc., seems to have been a more recent invention.) In broaching these observations, I broke the cardinal rule of essay collections organized around 'identity politics'. Then, as now, the responsibility of the individual (female/black/homosexual/whatever) contributor was to personify the identity assigned and present its claims for consideration. Instead, I argued that the ancient myth of the Amazon had nothing to do with lesbianism, and quite a lot to do with the patriarchal Athenian state.

Nevertheless, my first essay in what a friend now calls 'your killjoy criticism' did get published, but I doubt that it changed many minds. (After I offered its conclusions to the London Matriarchy Study Group, pointing out that Minoan frescoes of women being served by male attendants demonstrated little more in the way of women's rule than an ad for the local steakhouse, I was unceremoniously escorted from the room.) This reaction to my reading of the Amazon image points to a third meaning of 'perversion' – a defection from doctrine. If, as Jonathan Dollimore argues so vividly in his history of *Sexual Dissidence*,[2] the theological genealogy of perversion opposes it to *conversion*, these essays are, I hope, perverse. Still, it is the specifically sexual meaning of that term which is most likely to 'position' this book in the vast output of contemporary cultural criticism.

Only a century separates these *Perversions* from the constellation of texts which first sought to anatomize 'deviant' sexualities. In 1893, Richard von Krafft-Ebing published the earliest of what would become twelve editions of his medico-forensic study *Psychopathia Sexualis*. In it he distinguished between the 'perverse' (every sexual expression 'that does not correspond with the purpose of nature, *i.e.*, propagation'); '*perversion* of the sexual instinct' – 'disease'; and '*perversity* in the sexual act' – 'vice'.[3] In 1897 Havelock Ellis followed this triad of the unnatural, the pathological and the immoral with the (merely) abnormal. His second volume of *Studies in the Psychology of Sex*, 'Sexual Inversion', is described in its preface as 'a study of an abnormal manifestation of the sexual instinct'.[4] And in 1905, Freud defined perversions as:

> sexual activities which either (a) *extend*, in an anatomical sense, beyond the regions of the body that are designed for sexual union, or (b) *linger* over the intermediate relations to the sexual object which should normally be traversed rapidly on the path toward the final sexual aim.[5]

Such transgressions suggest an original sexuality, properly timed and located, which may then be perverted. But Freud's 'Three Essays on Sexuality' build to the opposite conclusion. 'Normal sexual behaviour'[6] is reached – and then perilously – only after an extensive opening discussion of the sexual aberrations (the first essay) followed by two more (on infancy and adolescence) elaborating the original perversity of childhood.

This genealogy is an early one, and it scarcely begins to anticipate the elaborate sexual aetiologies which Freud went on to devise for my favourite perversion, homosexuality, in the course of his researches. Judith Roof has plotted the turns and counter-turns which take Freud from *Dora* in 1905 ('heterosexuality masks homosexuality') to the 1914–15 'Case of Paranoia' ('heterosexuality masks homosexuality, which masks heterosexuality') to the *New Introductory Lectures* in the 1930s ('homosexuality masks heterosexuality').[7] Moreover, these manoeuvres intersect with Freud's repeated projection of male homosexuality back into a phylogenetic past before *Civilization and its Discontents*. Is it any wonder that critical theories of sexuality, confronted with accounts of object choice at once so authoritative and so inconsistent, have made the question of origins a central object of analysis?

This is the context of the opening essay in this collection, a consideration of 'The Psychogenesis of a Case of Homosexuality in a Woman' which examines Freud's contradictory attribution of both heterosexual and homosexual origins to lesbianism – a contradiction which is then resolved by a further contradiction, the resort to biology explicitly rejected at the outset of his case history. Freud's failure to keep his originals and his copies straight has attracted a number of astute responses, including a famous epigram I recently discovered as the caption of a painting – featuring the repeated motif of two dildo-wearing dykes frolicking across a leafy landscape – entitled 'Wallpaper for Judith Butler':[8]

> gay is to straight *not* as copy is to original, but, rather, as copy is to copy.[9]

Butler's challenge to the metaphysics of a 'true' sexuality, buttressed by two true genders, is part of a wider philosophical project, which has most insistently influenced our understanding of critical interpretation. Here too the title *Perversions* has a bearing, for it declares that these are *readings, versions*, for which the most appropriate dictionary definition is:

> an account or description from a particular point of view, esp. as contrasted with another account.[10]

That is to say: these readings are very often counters to other readings and do not themselves pretend to authority or finality, being in the main deliberate provocations to replies, retorts and further readings.

Readings imply, among other things, readers – 'narratees, actual readers, ideal readers, intended readers, superreaders, authorial audiences' – imagined interpreters who reply to one fiction with another; for, as Jonathan Culler argues, 'the reader's experience – at least in interpretations – is always a fiction: a narrative construction in a story of reading.'[11] If such experience is best described as hypothetical, lesbian and gay commentators have certainly multiplied the available positions since Culler propounded his own scandalous hypothesis, 'Reading as a Woman'.[12] Gloria Anzaldúa, for example, has called attention to 'Chicana, working-class, dyke ways of reading',[13] while Eve Sedgwick has proposed 'the omnipotent, unknowing mother' (your mother who mustn't know you're gay, but of course does) as the ideal reader of Proust's complexly closeted prose.[14]

Predictably, this proliferation of readings and readers has been condemned as (you guessed it) perverse. A recent denunciation of the 'Madonna Phenomenon' and its feminist and gay exponents in cultural studies rails against 'a state of intellectual anarchy that sanctions willfully perverse misreadings'. Goaded beyond endurance by Madonna theses titled 'Like a Thesis' and their offhand announcements that 'All readings, in some way, are misreadings', Daniel Harris decries the 'perversity in postmodernism'.[15] In so doing he handily points out another definition of 'perversion': the opposition to what is 'right, reasonable or accepted'.

Some would say that this is what political criticism has to be, particularly when reading as one whose views are so rarely deemed 'right, reasonable or accepted'. Writing about the arrival of lesbian and gay studies in the academy, John Fletcher observes that it is:

> openly and fiercely partial and necessarily so. Not
> because it is a form of apologetics that seeks
> narcissistically or self-consolingly to speak or hear

only good of itself, to confirm its own preconceptions or even to proselytise and in the words of Clause 28 to 'promote homosexuality'.[16] But because its very conditions of existence, both practically and epistemologically, are the sexual political struggles of lesbians and gay men, its relations to its object of knowledge are critical and transformative.[17]

One of the most dedicated exponents of this 'openly political epistemology' is Donna Haraway's figure of the cyborg, whose four commitments – to partiality, irony, intimacy and perversity – head this collection. A science-fiction creature, part machine, part organism, with scant regard for boundaries, blood ties or the fantasy of psychic wholeness, this hybrid is invoked as the presiding spirit of a politics 'completely without innocence'.[18] Its technologies 'are often stories, retold stories, *versions*'[19] – mutant mythologies which write the Garden out of Genesis and apologetics (to borrow Fletcher's term) out of politics.

The possibility of a sexual politics at once utopian and anti-idealist is crucial to these readings, which are as critical of the narcissistic projections of feminist and 'queer' cultures as those of their hegemonic counterparts. In particular (and guided from the outset by one of the most instructive films of the 1970s, Mulvey and Wollen's *Penthesilea*[20]) they reconsider a number of those cultures' 'positive images' – the Amazon of antiquity, John Sayles's *Lianna*, the rebellious patient Freud called 'Dora' – as well as less canonical figures like Duffy the activist bartender in the recent gay videoporn hit *More of a Man*.

7

Gay and feminist audiences are said to crave such characters for the purposes of self-recognition. But if we demand (under the heading 'positive') both resemblance and idealization, we function like our predecessors in Aristotle's *Poetics*, seeking identification *and* enhancement – someone like myself, only nobler. Of course, the pursuit of these ego ideals is not confined to oppositional cultures, as I argue in considering the heterosexual male narcissism of *Friendship's Death*. Indeed, such narcissism partakes of what Haraway describes as the Western imperative to make the revolutionary subject a mirror of its master – constructed along identical lines of nature, virtue and legitimacy.

Nevertheless, dominant culture's distribution of such ideals to some groups but not others (Hollywood's notorious reluctance to represent homosexuals at all, if not as butts or villains) presents strategic difficulties in the deconstruction of our hagiographies or (what often amounts to the same thing) our self-portraits. When a recent film festival advertised *Swoon*, a 1992 feature on the sexual relationship between the murderers in the Leopold and Loeb case, with the teaser 'Puts the Homo Back in Homicide', one gay critic replied with 'bored irritation':

> This is not to silence those voices among us who want to interrogate stereotypes by pushing them to the edge . . . But let's not be disingenuous about the times in which we live, or the fact that we are breathing in a bubble of freedom that is only 25 years old – historically speaking, a heartbeat. And

that nothing we throw into the discourse is without consequences.[21]

This raises, again, the question of reading, of how another of the cyborg's commitments – irony – gets understood. As Richard Dyer has argued, irony is a routine response of a cultural 'tradition which has always known, at least part of the time, the importance, nay inescapability, of performance'.[22] Yet other lesbian and gay critics have registered the historical ambivalence within homosexual cultures over their most pronouncedly ironic style: camp. Not only is camp often illegible to a wide range of readers (including homosexual readers), it may be – as it evidently was to Radclyffe Hall – utterly repellent to them. (Whether *The Well of Loneliness* could ever be deemed anything other than camp is another question.) But then camp, like other forms of irony, often cultivates both disguise and disgust. As a conspicuously non-proselytizing mode, it uses irony to secure distance *and* intimacy.

Irony is the medium of Haraway's political mythology because it resists resolution. Like her Santa Cruz colleague Teresa de Lauretis (whose refusal to foreclose the feminist debate on lesbian sadomasochism influences my own account of that conflict), Haraway stresses the importance 'of holding incompatible things together because both or all are necessary and true'.[23] This makes the ironist less an apostate, she argues, than a blasphemer, whose irreverence is itself an act of faith. In a similar way, these writings depend upon the sexual politics with which they so often argue. They may even have originated in my own anxiety about their possible disappearance (no small worry in this post-everything age). As Christian Metz maintains in defence of the sadistic pleasures of film theory: 'Lost objects are the only ones one is afraid to lose, and the semiologist is he who rediscovers them from the other side.'[24] And that, I suppose, is the place of these *Perversions* (from the Latin *perversus*, 'turned the wrong way, awry') – on the other side.

case histories

the train of thought in Freud's 'Case of Homosexuality in a Woman'

Nearly twenty years after the first of Freud's six celebrated case histories, 'Fragment of an Analysis of a Case of Hysteria' (completed on 25 January 1901), he wrote the final one – 'The Psychogenesis of a Case of Homosexuality in a Woman'.[1] 'The last case', notes Ernest Jones, 'resembled the first one in so far as the patient was a girl of eighteen and the analysis a short one. But this time it was Freud, more alive to the significance of resistance than twenty years earlier, who broke off the treatment.'[2]

The invitation to compare this analysis with the more famous case of *Dora* has proved 'irresistible' to commentators[3] – not least because of the much debated significance of Freud's own footnoted revision to the earlier study:

> The longer the interval of time that separates me from
> the end of this analysis, the more probable it seems to
> me that the fault in my technique lay in this omission: I
> failed to discover in time and to inform the patient that
> her homosexual (gynaecophilic) love for Frau K was the
> strongest unconscious current in her mental life.[4]

Freud's failure to discover Dora's homosexual tendency, 'which he none the less tells us is so constant in hysterics that its subjective role cannot be overestimated' – the exasperation is Lacan's[5] – seems difficult to detach from his own involvement with his patient, his famous counter-transference. The fact that nineteen years later he could break off the analysis of another 'beautiful and clever girl of eighteen' (Dora's 'intelligent and engaging looks' are also made much of) seems to support Jones's interpretation – that Freud had learned from a clear precedent. But as his analysis of the origins of homo-sexuality in this case suggests, there are many pathways for libidinal investment. It is upon these, particularly upon questions of identification, that I wish to focus here . . .

I

Like Dora, the young woman in this case was 'handed over' to Freud by her father – and also by her mother, slightly less the neglected party in this analysis than in Dora's. This was six months after an 'undoubtedly serious attempt at suicide' precipitated by a not-very-chance meeting of father and daughter while she was out walking with the woman she loved, an upper-class courtesan about ten years older whom 'the girl' (as Freud describes her throughout) 'pursued' with 'devoted adoration'. Although 'the lady', as Freud terms the courtesan, carried on numerous affairs with men, she lived with a woman lover, but her relations with Freud's patient were never more than friendly. Despite – or indeed, because of – this distance, the girl had become so infatuated with her that she had abandoned studies, social functions and most of her friends in order to conduct a courtship which seemed to consist of sending flowers, waiting at tramstops and occasionally taking walks 'in the most frequented streets' with her beloved. Here – inevitably – the pair were one day discovered by the girl's furious father, who had already become aware of her past and present attractions to women – including this woman of ill repute. 'Immediately afterwards', Freud writes, 'the girl rushed off and flung herself over a wall down the side of a cutting on to the suburban railway line which ran close by.'

Six months later, after an extended convalescence and a related softening on the part of her parents, the girl agreed to analysis for their sake – an unpropitious start, in Freud's view, for what he anyway saw as a difficult project. For he believed that the girl 'was not in any way ill' – not neurotic, but its negative, perverse. (As early as 1905, Freud had opposed the neuroses to the perversions, arguing that neurotic symptoms are formed at the cost of abnormal sexuality.[6] As Otto Rank reiterated in 1924, the neuroses can function to block the perversions.[7] This girl had no such block on her homosexual object choice.) And so, Freud speculated, unless the libidinal impulses which led the girl to mollify her parents were as strong as those invested in her consciously sexual objects, or unless she retained enough bisexual organization to provide compensatory heterosexual attachments, the prognosis wasn't good. Indeed, it was as bad as that for converting a convinced heterosexual to homosexuality, 'except that for good practical reasons the latter is never attempted'.

Thus Freud undertook a rather sceptical analysis of eleven weeks (Dora's also lasted eleven weeks), during which he nevertheless believed it possible to trace the 'origin and development' of female homosexuality 'with complete certainty and almost without a gap'. This 'remarkable' situation is explained by Jones as the result of the patient's determination 'to retain the sole "symptom" for which she was being analysed so that she could afford to let the analysis of it proceed quite freely: her resistance was not against the analysis itself, only against it having any effect.'[8] And in a fascinating comparison, Freud likens the process of analysis to the stages of a train journey to a distant country: the first, which this girl managed so well, is like the traveller's preparation – booking the ticket, acquiring a passport, packing, and finally arriving at the station (i.e. the analyst extracts the necessary information and interprets it to the patient). 'But after all these preliminary exertions one is not a single mile nearer one's goal.' The second stage of analysis requires the patient 'to make the journey itself'.

Before he relates the first stage of this analysis, Freud addresses himself to the 'fruitless and inapposite' question of the biological determination of homosexuality – a question to which, despite his own preference for a psychogenetic explanation, he will return in this case study. Here we are told that the 'beautiful and well-made' girl's appearance and menstrual cycle are feminine, although she is tall, sharp-featured, and conspicuously intelligent and objective (conventional, rather than scientific, signs of masculinity, argues Freud). More importantly – and this ostensibly non-physical evidence follows on immediately in the text – she takes the masculine part not only in her object (a woman) but in her attitude towards it (technically, her aim), greatly overvaluing the loved one and humbly renouncing all narcissistic satisfaction.[9]

II

Freud's account of his patient's psychical development is yet another of the frustrating consequences of his first theory of the Oedipus complex. (Lacan's commentary on this case refers to 'the . . . prejudice which falsifies the conception of the Oedipus complex from the start, by making it define as natural, rather than normative, the predominance of the paternal figure'.[10]) Although in his 1905 'Essays' Freud acknowledges the primacy of the mother's breast as an object for all infants, it is not until 1925 – five years after this case study – that the mother is posed as the original Oedipal object for both sexes.[11] Thus Freud assumes here that the father is the first normal Oedipal object for girls – including this one. After her father, in a trauma-free childhood, she turned to her older brother, with whom she compared genitals at the age of five – an event whose 'far reaching after-effects' Freud doesn't explain for several pages (in a writing strategy which effectively divides his patient's heterosexual history from her homosexual one). At five and a half a second brother was born, then at school the girl discovered 'the facts of sex' with the usual reactions of fascination and loathing. At thirteen to fourteen, she displayed a markedly maternal affection for a small boy in the local playground. But after a short time she grew indifferent to him and began to take a romantic interest in older women – mothers in their early thirties – and was chastized for this by her father.

Freud attributes this change in object to the birth of a third brother when the patient was sixteen, an affront to the girl's pubescent desire for a child of her own from her father. 'Furiously resentful and embittered, she turned away from her father and from men altogether. After this first great reverse she forswore her womanhood and sought another goal for her libido . . .' The consequent transformation, Freud points out, was severe: 'She changed into a man and took her mother in place of her father as the object of her love.'

This interpretation sets up several major themes which will reappear in the psychoanalytic literature on homosexuality:

1. its heterosexual origins (Jones refers to the 'discovery that homosexuals always have to begin with a profound fixation on the parent of the opposite sex'[12]);
2. the 'motive of evasion', or what Freud calls 'retiring in favour of someone else' – withdrawing from a painful competition for a heterosexual object into homosexuality;
3. and finally, the identification of the homosexual with the opposite sex ('she changes into a man').

In the girl's case, her renunciation of her father served to improve relations with her mother, a youngish woman who had hitherto favoured her three sons and treated her daughter quite harshly. And her blatant behaviour also produced a libidinal gain in regard to her father – namely, the pleasure of revenge for his betrayal of her.

III

The third section of this case study opens with the author's complaint about his previous linear presentation of the patient's development as an inadequate 'means of describing complicated mental processes going on in different layers of the mind'. The ensuing topographical digression (on the masculinity of the girl's attitude towards her objects and her resistance to the analysis) raises two more influential themes in the psychoanalysis of specifically female homosexuality – courtly love and the question of transference to a male analyst.

In describing his patient's attitude towards her lover, Freud repeatedly employs the terms of courtly love, at one point citing the Italian Renaissance poet Tasso's description in the *Gerusalemme Liberata* of a male lover who 'hopes for little and asks for nothing'. This idealization of the beloved and neglect for one's own satisfaction is a broadly masculine tendency, in Freud's scheme, which divided anaclitic and narcissistic object choice along gender lines. And courtly love, which places 'unsatisfied desire in the centre of the poetic conception of love',[13] also connects Lacan's analysis of female homosexuality to his theory of the excessive nature of all desire and the impossibility of its gratification. The homosexual woman, whose courtly love 'prides itself more than any other on being the love which gives what it does not have',[14] is phallic precisely in that lack. For it is lack, the threatened lack of castration, which constructs the masculine identity in Lacan's theory.[15] What neither Freud's homosexual patient nor Dora will accept is the mystery of the Raphael Madonna contemplated at such length by the latter in the Dresden Museum: that of accepting oneself as idol rather than idolator, as object of the man's desire rather than worshipper of woman.[16]

In Freud's view this homosexual girl's idealization of an unavailable woman of ill repute corresponds 'to the smallest details' with that special type of masculine object choice discussed in his 1910 essay[17] – the exclusive attraction to women who are both already attached and suffer from a dubious sexual reputation. This he traces to a profound mother-fixation challenged by the son's discovery of his mother's 'infidelity' with his father. Concluding 'that the difference between his mother and a whore is not after all so great', the boy elides their functions, combining genital desire and filial tenderness with phantasies of both rescue and revenge.

Now this allusion fleetingly reopens the question of early mother love only briefly mentioned thus far in the homosexual case study. But again it is deferred in favour of a discussion of the motives for the patient's suicide attempt – not simply the conscious despair she felt when the lady perceived her father's anger that day and broke off their relationship, but also, according to Freud, self-punishment and the fulfilment of a wish. The girl's fall on to the railway line, Freud argues, gratified her desire to 'fall' – to become pregnant – through her father's fault. (The pun works in both English and German.) Her own death-wish represented the turning against herself of her desire to punish her parents, and its coincidence with a fall indicated the girl's identification with her mother, 'who should have died at the birth of the child denied to herself'.

Underlying all this Freud perceives the girl's desire for revenge on her father, an emotion so strong that it actually permitted her coolly intellectual co-operation with the first stage of the analysis – while absolutely refusing to go further, and in particular to make anything but a negative transference on to the analyst. The patient's only ostensible gestures at a positive transference, a series of dreams which seem to suggest heterosexual wishes, are rejected by the analyst as lies – intended to deceive both father and father-substitute. And here Freud's own identification with his patient's father takes on an almost paranoiac tinge, as he speculates that the girl may have sought his good opinion of her 'perhaps in order to disappoint me all the more thoroughly later on'. His subsequent termination of the analysis has a strong emotional charge, as he accuses his patient of transferring to him 'the sweeping repudiation of men which had dominated her ever since the disappointment she had suffered from her father'. The parents are advised to take their daughter to a woman analyst and the case study moves on to its conclusion.

IV

In this final recapitulation of the psychogenesis of the girl's homosexuality, Freud notes the advantages of hindsight in tracing causation. Taken in reverse, no factor seems wholly determining, no result inevitable. So why were the patient's reactions to her mother's last pregnancy so extreme? The story of the girl's development is told again, but this time with an emphasis on the continuity of her homosexual attachments, which go

back from the courtesan, to one of her teachers, to a
number of young mothers, to a probable infantile
fixation on her own mother. Because this history is
conscious, Freud regards it as superficial, the surface
eddies of a river which also has its deeper – unconscious
– heterosexual current. And the fact that the deeper
current has been deflected into the shallower one,
rather than vice versa, seems to require an explanation –
the only one available being that of a congenital disposition to homosexuality.

To this end, albeit with some difficulty, Freud cites his
patient's early 'masculinity complex', her reluctance to
be second to her slightly older brother and her envy of
his penis upon the genital inspection conducted at age
five. But he also retains the belief of the term's origina-
tor – Van Ophuijsen – that the complex is the result of a
girl's sense of injustice at her parents' preference for a
son,[18] and he associates this sense of injustice with a
political protest:

> She was in fact a feminist; she felt it to be unjust that
> girls should not enjoy the same freedom as boys, and
> rebelled against the lot of women in general.

The notion of an inborn sense of injustice seems unten-
able, and Freud goes on to admit that the 'girl's behaviour . . . would follow from the combined effect in a
person with a strong mother-fixation of the two influences of her mother's neglect and her comparison of
her genital organs with her brother's'. But the explanation for the mother-fixation in the first place? Despite
the sophistication of Freud's final critique of the 'Third

Sex' theory of homosexuality in his conclusion to this study, the idea of a congenital – if not necessarily hermaphroditic – bias towards homosexuality is explicitly retained: 'on the other hand, a part even of this acquired disposition (if it was really acquired) has to be ascribed to inborn constitution.'

Afterword

The truncated character of Freud's analysis, and the ambiguous biologism with which the case study concludes, leave important questions unanswered. In the first place, the stated seriousness of the girl's suicide attempt, and the severity of her feelings about her father, do not fit comfortably with Freud's non-pathological diagnosis. Jacqueline Rose's discussion of this case argues that:

> his explanation of this last factor – the lack of
> neurosis ascribed to the fact that the object choice was
> established not in infancy but after puberty – is then
> undermined by his being obliged to trace back the
> homosexual attraction to a moment prior to the
> Oedipal instance, the early attachment to the mother,
> in which case either the girl is neurotic (which she
> clearly isn't) or all women are neurotic (which indeed
> they might be).[19]

But I wonder if there's a third possibility – which is to say that this girl may not suffer conflict about her object choice, but instead about the 'masculine' identification with which she carries it off, an identification presented in the case as a singular and unproblematic concommitant of that choice.

The question of whether a masculine identification is actually necessary to female homosexuality has preoccupied commentators from Havelock Ellis to Helene Deutsch. *Cherchez* the femmes, we might say, since the historical difficulty has been how to explain those 'feminine' women which the 'masculine' kind are supposed to desire. If a masculine libido is what produces female homosexuality, what makes these other women do it? Ellis's answer in 1897 was to distinguish the (masculine) 'actively inverted woman' from the (feminine) woman 'open to homosexual advances',[20] 'a womanly woman . . . not quite attractive enough to appeal to the average man'.[21] Thirty-five years later, Helene Deutsch solved the problem in a different way: while acknowledging the predominance of the 'phallic masculine form' of female homosexuality, she argued that this is often a cover for a joint infantilism reflecting a pre-phallic mother-fixation, which displays itself in reciprocal mother–child role play.[22]

In the 'Three Essays' Freud challenges Ellis's views on physical and psychical hermaphroditism in inverts, with one significant exception: 'it is only in inverted women that character-inversion of this kind can be looked for with any regularity. In men the most complete mental masculinity can be combined with inversion.'[23] Although this case study includes a general qualification of the view ('The same is true of women; here also mental sexual character and object-choice do not necessarily coincide'), it argues repeatedly for the masculinity of this patient's identifications. Indeed, Freud points out that the girl's masculine identification produced a 'gain from illness'; it improved the girl's relations with her mother, who evidently preferred to function as confidante to a homosexual daughter rather than competitor with a heterosexual one. He doesn't, however, count as related 'losses from illness' his patient's neglect of her own friends, her studies and her appearance; her attraction to impossible objects; and her 'undoubtedly serious' attempt to end her own life.

This may be the result of the positively narcissistic character of the girl's 'masculinity complex', with its suggestions of a robust refusal of inferiority. But this phallic identification, a five-year-old's rebellion against castration prior to the installation of mature gender identification at puberty, is not the only 'masculine' identification in this case. There is also the girl's psychical transformation 'into a man' after puberty, when her mother bore the child she desired from her father. This process corresponds to that described in 'Mourning and Melancholia', whereby the lost object is not relinquished, but instead absorbed into the ego through a process of identification.[24] Like the jilted melancholic, the homosexual girl could be seen to preserve her love for her father by this method. But in identifying with an object which she also hates for the pain it has caused her, she may suffer, like the melancholic, from an excess of self-denigration. Such a 'powerfully cathected and destructive' paternal introject is also remarked by Joyce McDougall in the clinical material presented by her analyses of four homosexual women.[25]

Thus we see, in an analysis structured on a simple masculine/feminine dichotomy, at least two different 'masculine' identifications: one with the father after puberty, the stage at which Freud would three years later identify the accession into the masculine/feminine division; and another, at five, via the masculinity complex, with a phallic principle which disavows castration and sexual division and may well be an identification with the 'phallic mother' – in short, a 'masculine' identification with a female *imago*.

This brings me to my second observation, which is that this case study closes where you think it really must continue, with the question of the girl's apparently fundamental (but largely unexamined) attachment to her mother. Delving into this area – that of Freud's 1931[26] and 1933[27] discussions of the pre-Oedipal development of girls – may not answer the question 'What does the little girl require of her mother?'. Especially if, as Jacqueline Rose points out – after Lacan – the answer is only the unanswerability of desire. But the hypothesis that girls do focus their early desires on their mothers, and refocus them with such difficulty, seems to contradict Freud's assumption of the dominance of the heterosexual current in his homosexual patient's psychical life. (It might also facilitate a less symmetrical account of male and female homosexuality than that in which both have an original love object of the opposite sex.) Furthermore, the 1931 essay's discussion of the active sexual aim[28] involved in early play with dolls (in which the little girl enacts the rituals which the mother performs on her – dressing, feeding, spanking, etc.) would also contradict the presentation of the homosexual girl's later interest in small children as her accession to a heterosexual passivity, which is then so thoroughly (and inexplicably) reversed.

Here it is instructive to compare Freud's famous comments in the 'Case of Homosexuality' with the relevant passage in 'Female Sexuality':[29]

> psychoanalysis cannot elucidate the intrinsic nature of what in conventional or in biological phraseology is termed 'masculine' and 'feminine': it simply takes over the two concepts and makes them the foundation of its work. When we attempt to reduce them further, we find masculinity vanishing into activity and femininity into passivity and that does not tell us enough. (1920)

> The fondness girls have for playing with dolls, in contrast to boys, is commonly regarded as a sign of early awakened femininity. Not unjustly so; but we must not overlook the fact that what finds expression here is the active side of femininity, and that the little girl's preference for dolls is probably evidence of the exclusiveness of her attachment to her mother, with complete neglect of her father object. (1931)

I should stress here that these references to the pre-Oedipal are not intended to propose it either as a possible place of refuge from the demands of mature womanhood or as the location of a 'true' femininity. I simply want to argue that it may offer an active sexual aim after the example of the mother, rather than the father, which may be preserved (along with others) into later life. Does the girl's impersonation of the courtly lover indicate a transformation of such early feminine activity into a masculine mode – and thus a recognition of bravado (and libido) as a male prerogative – at the expense of her own self-esteem? Does this amount to an inevitable splitting of the ego under the pressure of a conflict between a demand (to be active) and a threat (to relinquish her femininity in the process)? (In which case Lacan has the last word: 'in order to be the phallus, that is to say, the signifier of the desire of the Other . . . the woman will reject an essential part of her femininity . . . It is for what she is not that she expects to be desired as well as loved.'[30]) Or was there any therapeutic possibility of reconciling the girl's activity with her femininity?

I suspect that the failure to raise these questions makes this influential case study a somewhat less radical approach to female sexuality than its rejection of a 'cure' might suggest. Lacan argues that Freud played a part in this failure by not perceiving here, and with Dora, the identity of his patient's desire with that of the father, and her commensurate need to be seen as an 'abstract, heroic, unique phallus, devoted to the service of a lady'.[31] Yet, as we have seen, Freud seems to have no difficulty identifying his homosexual patient's 'masculine' ambitions (her desire *for* the mother) – the trick is to square them with her 'feminine' ones (her desire to *be* a mother). Does her mature homosexuality represent a displacement of an earlier heterosexual desire, or does the heterosexual episode (her desire for a child by her father) represent the usual displacement of what Freud sees as evidence of an early current of homosexuality? (The child as surrogate for the phallus which this patient, in her youthful 'masculinity complex', was so reluctant to relinquish.) Given the original 'bisexuality' of the infant, perhaps we should insist upon both.

As I pointed out above, the logic of his analysis leads Freud back to biology, and to his reflections at the end of this case on contemporary attempts to modify male inversion surgically (presumably through the replacement of 'hermaphroditic' testicles). Could an analogous ovary transplant be successful in cases of female homosexuality? Freud thinks the solution impractical, and his explanation is the final sentence of the case study:

> A woman who has felt herself to be a man, and has loved in masculine fashion, will hardly let herself be forced into playing the part of a woman, when she must pay for this transformation, which is not in every way advantageous, by renouncing all hope of motherhood.

Note here how motherhood has finally been gathered under the phallic aegis. In this strange hypothesis of biological causation, the subject's original – suspect – ovaries apparently enable both homosexual love ('in the masculine fashion') *and* heterosexual reproduction. On this assumption, female heterosexuality could be achieved surgically only at the price of one of its major compensations, motherhood. Without acknowledging it, this speculation inverts the equation heterosexuality = fertility/homosexuality = sterility ('at the time of the analysis the idea of pregnancy and childbirth was disagreeable to her') which has structured the entire case.

And this brings me back to an earlier point: the remarkable extent to which the homosexual patient has been masculinized. Might this say as much about the analyst as the analysand? In her discussion of *Dora* and this case, Suzanne Gearhart points out that Freud's solution for the homosexual girl – a woman analyst – is as biologistic as his solution for the hysteric – a husband. Neither analysis comes to terms with early bisexuality, and thus female homosexuality is assumed to present 'an absolute obstacle' to positive transference to a male analyst.[32] In insisting upon a woman analyst, isn't Freud acting precisely as he accuses his homosexual patient of doing? Retiring in favour of someone else when a rivalry for a loved object becomes intolerable? If this is so, it would suggest two things: that here, as in the case of Dora, countertransference is an important factor; and that in addition to Freud's conscious identification with the homosexual girl's father there is an unconscious one with the patient herself. (Similarly, Toril Moi has referred to Dora as both Freud's 'opponent and alter ego. She possesses the secret Freud is trying to uncover, but she is also a curious person in search of sexual information – a quest oddly similar to Freud's own quest for the secrets of sexuality.'[33])

Two aspects of Freud's own biography – if they are admissible to this sort of discussion – might support this argument. The first applies to his peculiar description of the surgical treatment of female homosexuality in the last sentence of the study: 'A woman who . . . has loved in masculine fashion, will hardly let herself be forced into playing the part of a woman . . .'. During the month that this study was written – January 1920 – and the previous December, Freud was visiting a dying friend every day. The friend was Anton von Freund, still in his early forties, a former patient and member of the private 'Committee' formed to support Freud's work. Freud had treated von Freund in 1918–19 for a severe neurosis which followed an operation for the cancer which eventually killed him. The operation which precipitated the neurosis involved the removal of a tumour of the testicle.[34] Could this contribute to the air of castration anxiety which pervades Freud's conclusion to this case?

The metonymical slide from castration to death (not so metonymical in the case of the unfortunate von Freund, who died on 20 January) brings us to the second biographical detail, an experience of the three-year-old Freud when his family was emigrating from Freiberg to Leipzig in 1859:

> the train passed through Breslau, where Freud saw gas jets for the first time; they made him think of souls burning in hell! From this journey also dated the beginning of a 'phobia' of travelling by train, from which he suffered a good deal for about a dozen years (1887–99) before he was able to dispel it by analysis. It turned out to be connected with the fear of losing his home (and ultimately his mother's breast) . . . Traces of it remained in later life in the form of slightly undue anxiety about catching trains.[35]

So . . . a man with an abiding fear of train travel undertakes the analysis of a woman brought to him because of her suicidal leap on to a railway line. After weeks of preparation, they reach what he terms the station — but then their reservation is cancelled. And who shall we say was more reluctant to make the journey?

the critical cult of *Dora*

The celebrated collection *In Dora's Case*[1] concludes with a bibliography listing some fifty articles on Freud's 'Fragment of an Analysis of a Case of Hysteria'[2] published in the previous thirty years, in addition to two other collections of articles on the case, plus a play and a film – and that's not counting the related pieces in the Institute of Contemporary Arts' *Desire* dossier, or Carolyn Steedman's consideration of '*the* story . . . of the bourgeois household' in *Landscape for a Good Woman*[3], or the twelve essays of *In Dora's Case* itself. So when the first note of the last article in this collection tells us that 'There is an extremely rich body of commentary on *Dora*' (p. 271), it seems a somewhat redundant remark, even in a history of work distinguished both for its repetitiousness and for its interest in repetition.

Almost every article in the collection opens with an acknowledgement of *Dora*'s key status in the psychoanalytic canon. To this the later commentaries (the second half of a chronologically organized volume) – after Steven Marcus's extremely influential 1974 reading of this case study as 'a great work of literature' (p. 57) – its status as a 'literary classic' (Maria Ramas,

p. 149) and as a feminist *cause célèbre* (Suzanne Gearhart, p. 105; Jacqueline Rose, p. 128; Toril Moi, p. 181; Jane Gallop, p. 200). Thus commentaries on *Dora* are characteristically also commentaries on its commentaries, a tendency from which *this* commentary will make no departure.

Moreover, many of these essays argue that this continual return to the case is itself worthy of interrogation. 'What would it mean', asks Jacqueline Rose, 'to reopen the case of Dora now?' (p. 128). Similarly, Claire Kahane, in her introduction to the collection, points out the author's own history of return to the case:

> Just as Freud could not let Dora go, at least imaginatively (as the text's history of delayed publication and added footnotes suggests), so analysts have continually returned to the case to account for the difficulties that Freud encountered . . . Why has this fragment commanded so much attention? Why do we now return to this failure of Freud's to complete his story of a sick girl in a sick milieu in *fin-de-siècle* Vienna? Why Dora now?

Having asked the question, Kahane then offers the by now routine answer:

> *Dora* stands in the middle of a contemporary, interdisciplinary questioning of the relation between interpretation and sexual difference, a questioning initially fostered by Freud's writings and given new energy by recent feminist criticism. Certainly it is no accident that the Dora case occupies this intersection,

34

for it was both the primary instance of the pitfalls of transference in interpretation and the only major case history that was the story of a woman. (pp. 19–20)

This answer also constitutes a set of instructions on how to read *Dora*, and these again are by no means the first. In his anxious preface to this study, Freud discussed the discretion required to keep a recent case of a Viennese resident away from 'unauthorized readers'. His solution involved four years' delay, changing the names, publication in a scientific journal. Still:

> I am aware that – in this city, at least – there are many physicians who (revolting though it may seem) choose to read a case history of this kind not as a contribution to the psychopathology of the neuroses, but as a *roman à clef* designed for their private delectation.[4]

Even if the early-twentieth-century Viennese medical establishment didn't read *Dora* this way, subsequent generations certainly have. In her contribution to this collection, Maria Ramas notes the study's potential both as popular romantic fiction and as soft-core pornography, and describes the jacket of a current US paperback edition: 'Its back cover bears the titillating heading, "Dora – her homosexual . . . love for Frau K. was the strongest unconscious current in her mental life."' The blurb goes on to advertise a 'cast of supporting characters' including '"an obsessive mother, an adulterous father, her father's mistress, Frau K., and Frau K.'s husband, who had made amorous advances to Dora"' (pp. 149–50).

Where Ramas sets such readings aside, others have pursued this talking cure as sexy conversation – specifically homosexual conversation, girl talk – on the premisses that Dora learned about oral sex orally, from discussions with her governess or Frau K., and that the continuation of these conversations in her analysis placed Freud in an uncomfortably feminine position. It is notable, however, that the reader's relation to this erotic discourse is not followed up. What of this case study's function in our own milieu, as – in the description of a friend of mine – 'the most legitimate sex literature for feminists'?

In their preface to *In Dora's Case*, Bernheimer and Kahane briefly sketch their criteria for choosing these twelve texts from the ranks of their competitors: Felix Deutsch's piece is selected because it records a psychoanalytic assessment of Dora in later life; Steven Marcus's for its pioneering literary approach; Lacan's because it's by Lacan – and also because of its subsequent influence; Erik Erikson's because he's also a major psychoanalytic figure. Beyond this, the choice seemed more difficult to the editors, but: 'assuming that our readers would have interests similar to our own, we decided not to reprint articles of a technical nature and to give preference to those analyses that question Freud's assumption about femininity and female desire' (p. viii).

Thus, our interest in this case is assumed to be political and aesthetic. Questions of illness, of the 'psychopathology of the neuroses', tend to be occluded. (Although Toril Moi does include an admonitory parenthesis on this subject in her contribution to the collection.) Or pathology is discovered in Freud, who is variously described in this collection as authoritarian, phallocentric (Moi), perverse, boastful (Hertz), neurotic in his forgetful and reticent presentation of the case (Collins *et al.*), callous, aggressive and anxious (Sprengnether). This displacement of pathology from the patient prompts me to register a question: Is it characteristic of the feminist appropriation of psychoanalysis that the more we embrace it as an account of gendered subjectivity, the more we escape it as an account of individual illness?

This lack of interest in the clinical aspects of the case seems particularly strange in a collection which opens with Felix Deutsch's description of Dora at the age of forty-two – bedridden with dizziness and insomnia due to unbearable noises in her ear, plagued with migraine, demanding, distrustful and downright malicious to friends and family: 'one of the most repulsive hysterics' (p. 43). In a sense, the project of this collection is to kiss this awful crone back into 'the first bloom of youth', when she came to Freud as an eighteen-year-old girl 'of intelligent and engaging looks'[5]. And this process of healing and rejuvenation is aided by the sequence of essays which construct the literary-political Dora.

The first of these is Steven Marcus's famous essay on the case study as a modernist masterpiece – involuted, reflexive, 'heroically unfinished' (p. 67); Ibsen-like in the daring of its subject matter; Proustian in the virtuosity of its multiple chronologies; Nabokovian in its use of framing devices; Borgesian in its studiously offhand address to the reader. One of the keywords of this encomium is 'richness', as in 'complexity, density and richness' (p. 56); 'fuller, richer and more complete than the most "complete" case histories of anyone else' (p. 65); 'inimitable richness' (p. 76). Marcus usually applies the term to the complex narrative technique employed in Freud's study, but sometimes it spills over on to his description of the 'actual case itself', and its themes of displaced sensations (a definition of hysterical symptoms) and deferred meanings ('the virtually limitless complexity of language' – p. 79). This incipient resort to semiotics (via the rather incongruous rhetoric of the ineffable) sets in train a process by which a text on hysteria will be transformed, in the course of subsequent readings, into a hysterical text. One by one, all the discourses of the case study are subjected to scrutiny and prove as symptomatic as Dora's 'own'. In this way hysteria is proposed as the disease of displacement, which is handy for would-be Derrideans, but not so useful for producing a definition of a specific neurosis. Thus Parveen Adams's complaint that it's difficult to relate the analysis of Dora to an understanding of 'what hysteria was for Freud'.[6]

The next stage of this transformation occurs in the collection's essays on the transference, which shift our attention from Freud's literary accomplishments to his analytic failure. Attention also shifts from the patient, who 'fades' (Rose) from the psychoanalytic 'scene' (Gearhart), displaced on the one hand by a concern with 'the prejudices, passions and difficulties of the analyst' (Lacan's definition of countertransference) and on the other by the problem of femininity. (Meanwhile, the displacement of pathology, the repulsive hysteric, is underlined by Rose's observation that Dora's 'symptoms are so slight, in a sense, that Freud feels it necessary to excuse to the reader the attention he gives to the case' – p. 130.) Despite their distance from Marcus's celebration of the 'richness' of Freud's study, these essays also insist upon the 'irreducible' and 'limitless' dimensions of the case. Notable here are the multiplication of analytic subjects proposed in Lacan's dialectical theory of transference, and Suzanne Gearhart's further elaboration of this dialectic of psychoanalysis into 'a series of conflicts that both define and put into question its limits' (p. 126).

The perfect complement to this mysterious process of analysis is its equally mysterious object, femininity. (Rose links the transference and the feminine as the 'two "vanishing points" of the case' – p. 141.) Ironically, Lacan proposes this 'mystery of femininity' as the resolution to the enigma which confronts Dora: somehow she must recognize herself as the erotic object which she perceives and desires in other women, notably in Frau K. and the figure of the Raphael Madonna which she contemplates in the Dresden Museum. The requisite bridging movement – from desire to identification, from activity to passivity – is read in these essays not so much as an answer to Dora's dilemma as a further question: 'women as object and subject of desire – the impossibility of either position' (p. 146). In contrast to other feminist accounts, Rose argues that the case study offers no definition of 'the feminine' as such, except perhaps the impossibility of defining it. It too is taken into the rich regress of displacements and enigmas which feature so strongly in Steven Marcus's literary appreciation.

The chronological structure of *In Dora's Case* elides this Lacanian critique of essentialist interpretations of

Dora into precisely its opposite, Maria Ramas's 'traditional feminist reading'. Where her predecessors reflect on the virtually limitless interpretations offered by the case, or on the futility of using it to fix the feminine as definable content or substance, Ramas insists that it is possible to identify its 'deepest level of meaning':

> Ida Bauer's hysteria [Ramas employs the patient's actual name throughout] was exactly what it appeared to be – a repudiation of the meaning of heterosexuality. (p. 151)

Ramas's Dora is real, rational and rebellious. Her 'ingenious', 'utilitarian', anti-patriarchal motives can be clearly read between the lines of Freud's case study. (She craftily chooses Herr K., Ramas argues, in order to comply with a heterosexual imperative that cannot be respectably consummated, while affording her access to his wife.) In so far as this Dora *has* an unconscious, it is structured like the language of a feminist manifesto, a 'belief that femininity, bondage, and debasement were synonymous' (p. 176). Mystery – whether it's Freud's final question about 'what kind of help she wanted from me' (p. 176) or a contemporary analyst's description of hysteria as posing 'the mystery of femininity' (p. 177) – is simply banished.

Yet this Dora, this resolute 'outlaw', as Ramas terms her, also exudes her own mystique – that of the resistant heroine who knows, albeit unconsciously, what isn't good for her. And despite the important differences between the essays in this collection, this portrait of a cult heroine is not wholly out of place. The narrative emphasized by the study's literary critics offers her a central dramatic role, while those who read it as an interrogation of femininity necessarily stress her typicality rather than her pathology. (As Jacqueline Rose concludes from her parallel reading of Dora with Freud's case of female homosexuality, perhaps 'all women are neurotic' – p. 136). In which case Ramas is only succumbing to the impulse which tempts so many of the contributors to this collection: that of producing a *Pan-Dora* for general feminine identification.

Jane Gallop's contribution to this question of identification is to restage a debate on Dora between two French feminists, Hélène Cixous – herself the author of a theatrical *Portrait of Dora* – and Catherine Clément. The issue, Gallop argues, is whether Dora is a heroine or a victim. If you identify, like Cixous, who writes 'The hysterics are my sisters' (p. 203), she is a heroine. If you don't, like Clément, who argues that hysterics are likeable but ineffectual and obsolete figures, she is a victim. But of course, heroism doesn't preclude defeat, and both situations invite identification.

This drive towards recognition, towards finding oneself in Dora, returns to Freud's fear that Viennese physicians would read his case study as a *roman à clef*. Gallop relates this key imagery to the skeleton key of vulgar psychoanalysis, 'a set system of interpretation, a ready-made symbolism to be applied to many cases' (p. 208). She does not reflect upon the term's more obvious literary reference – a story the reader already knows, a narrative which could confirm Viennese gossip about the Bauers and the K.s, or the ideas which we already possess about femininity, the place of women, female sexuality.

'I don't give a damn about Dora, I don't fetishize her' (p. 202), Hélène Cixous angrily protests in her debate with Catherine Clément. (And we know how psychoanalysis regards such denials.) Film theory has been preoccupied with the fetishistic propensities of the spectator for several years, notably in respect to the 'mysterious' figure of the castrated woman, which can be transformed into a fetish, Laura Mulvey writes in a famous essay, 'so that it becomes reassuring rather than dangerous'.[7] Because this threat can never be wholly abolished, only kept at bay, the fetishist oscillates between denial and recognition. And the fetish object may be subject to similarly oscillating treatment – both 'affection and hostility', Freud writes.[8] Perhaps we might add: both heroine and victim, both beautiful girl and repulsive hag?

This question of the visible brings me to the final essay in this collection, in which Madelon Sprengnether reflects on Freud's own analogy between the psychical investigations of the analyst and the visual investigations of the gynaecologist:

> Claiming that it is possible for a man to speak to young women about sexual matters 'without doing them harm and without bringing suspicion on himself,' he argues, 'A gynaecologist, after all, under the same conditions, does not hesitate to make them submit to uncovering every possible part of the body'. (p. 261)

Here is a rather different body from the 'rich body of *commentary*' which opened these remarks, but one no less rich in its implications. It sent me back to Lacan's interpretation of the 'mystery of her femininity . . . her bodily femininity – as it appears uncovered' (p. 98) in the second of Dora's dreams. This is the mystery which motivates Dora's 'idolatry for Frau K.' (p. 99): '"her adorable white body"', which Dora describes, Freud writes, 'in accents more appropriate to a lover than to a defeated rival'.[9] This bodily figure connects in Lacan's analysis with the painting of the Raphael Madonna which also fascinated Dora, and indeed with a whole history of feminine figuration – leading the eminent analyst to no less kitsch an emblem of enigmatic womanhood than the Mona Lisa, with whose smile, he writes, Dora withdraws from the case.

So, even if Dora is unable to compose herself out of the bodily fragmentation characteristic of hysteria, Lacan's commentary does it for her. This fetishistic portrait of Dora is not the French feminist body against which both Jacqueline Rose and Toril Moi warn in this collection. Set in perspective, with a vanishing point, the *Mona Lisa Dora* is composed rather than dispersed, narcissistic rather than autoerotic. This figure of the woman cannot be assimilated to some mysterious femininity outside repression and symbolization, yet she too vanishes with that notoriously mysterious smile – the smile that Leonardo took four years to paint, the same number of years Freud took to revise and publish this case; the smile whose fetishistic double meaning – 'of unbounded tenderness and at the same time sinister menace' – preoccupies his study of Leonardo.[10]

Eight years after his analysis of Dora, Freud published another case history, in which he argued that 'a thing which has not been understood inevitably reappears; like an unlaid ghost'.[11] And sixteen years after that, when Felix Deutsch's bedridden middle-aged patient discovered that he was an analyst and knew Professor Freud, she 'forgot to talk about her sickness, displaying great pride in having been written up as a famous case in psychiatric literature' (p. 38). She also got up: 'The next time I saw her,' Deutsch writes, 'she was out of bed and claimed that her "attacks" were over' (p. 39).

Which is only to conclude that ghosts may rise again out of unexhausted pleasure as well as unresolved pain. Our own involvement in the less licit of these pleasures – in the pleasures of mystification, and fetishism and narcissism – should be added to the infinity of answers to the question: Why Dora?

a case of AIDS

Thus, romances to some extent 'inoculate' against the
major evils of sexist society.

Tania Modleski

Sir Lucas Salik is a medical man, a glamorous heart
surgeon whose own is mortgaged to an indifferent
blond youth in the property business. This physician, we
are given to believe, is ill – a homosexual compelled to
love the coolly heterosexual Hal while seeking rougher
trade in the most dangerous haunts of the city. By his
own admission, Lucas cannot heal himself. He must be
rescued, twice over, from a brutal attack in a cruising
area near King's Cross, and from his own desires. For
homosexuality, as Judith Williamson has observed, can
threaten not only 'the family' but also its *narrative*: 'grow
up, get married, have children, repeat'.[1]

I write 'can' threaten, unlike Judith, in uneasy recognition of recent attempts by post-AIDS authors like
David Leavitt to *suburbanize* the gay novel, maintaining
its object choice while domesticating its stories and
settings. But the opposite obtains in the case of Sir
Lucas, who roams the exotic precincts of romantic

fiction – the operating theatre, the Bond Street furrier, the Scottish country house. Here, in Candia McWilliam's novel, homosexuality is appropriated to the conventions of the Betty Trask Award: our brooding dark-haired doctor, knighted for his services to small children, encounters a spirited single mother-to-be in the drawing room of Lady Cowdenbeath.

For a novel saturated in genre (the romance and its Gothic ancestor, as well as the crime thriller) *A Case of Knives*[2] executed an impressive crossover in the literary honours of 1988, copping half the riches of the above prize for romantic fiction and the kudos of the Whitbread shortlist. A less stolid critical culture might have found this an occasion for mirth, or at least introspection, but British reviewers played it straight.

Virtuosity (always noticed in a first novel) was their theme, and McWilliam's *writing* was singled out for its art, technique, accomplishment, brilliance, extravagance and ingenuity. Such controversy as there was clung to this problematic, with occasional dissenters complaining that the writing was *too* brilliant and extravagant, notably in its deployment of unfamiliar words and usages. The narrative itself, particularly its roots in the more vulgar genres, was given much less play, and indeed such attention might have compromised the novel's 'literary' success.

Interestingly, this success seems predicated not on any convincing naturalization of the creaking mechanisms of its plotting but on its opposite – the matching of a hyperstylized narrative with an equally stylized narration. The result is a surprisingly decorous melodrama, which presents its 'operatic' ironies as Destiny.

(The adjective, which is nothing if not solicited by the novel's own allusion to the ironic demise of Don Giovanni, comes from the *Sunday Telegraph* review.) The greatest of these ironies is sprung at the novel's finale, when we learn that Sir Lucas's backstreet assailant, who stabs him repeatedly and leaves him for dead, is none other than the young object of his love. The 'untroubled English boy' of his desires is finally revealed as a sadist, a social-climbing Jew . . . and a homosexual himself.

The three terms of Hal's transgression – violence, class counterfeiting and pathology – are invoked in the novel's title. For the knives will be out both as medical instruments (the surgeon's scalpels) and tableware (whose order of use – 'from the outside in' – Lucas teaches Hal) as well as weapons. Similarly, the 'case' refers at once to the object of a police investigation (the stabbing), a domestic container (the wallet enclosing a wedding gift of kitchen knives) and an illness (that of Lucas's patients, his own masochistic homosexuality). The arrangement of this triptych is indeed ingenious, but it is also compact with our most popular narratives of sex, class and disease.

Such subjects are the proper business of melodrama, with its perennial interest in family, death and inheritance, yet it is still surprising to see how closely this novel follows the rules of contemporary romantic fiction. As embodied in the works of Britain's Mills and Boon, and North America's Harlequin imprints, these include an extremely rigid story line, notoriously indebted to *Jane Eyre* and *Pride and Prejudice*:

> a young, inexperienced, poor to moderately well-to-do woman encounters and becomes involved with a

handsome, strong, experienced, wealthy man, older than herself by ten to fifteen years. The heroine is confused by the hero's behaviour since, though he is obviously interested in her, he is mocking, cynical, contemptuous, often hostile, and even somewhat brutal. By the end, however, all misunderstandings are cleared away, and the hero reveals his love for the heroine, who reciprocates.[3]

The *dramatis personae* of such tales are similarly formulaic, shaping into this familiar foursome:

THE HEROINE – young, pretty, virtuous (though she now may be sexually experienced), self-supporting but not highly ambitious, separated by death or geography from home and parents;
THE HERO – older, handsome, physically imposing ('big, hard and strong'[4]), socially superior, apparently distant or cruel, but also capable of strong feeling;
THE RIVAL WOMAN – older and more sophisticated than the heroine, often duplicitous in her pursuit of the hero and ultimately unsuccessful;
THE RIVAL MAN – younger than the hero and an ostensibly better match for the heroine until revealed as weak or immoral.

McWilliam's version of this quarter is faithful to the point of parody: Cora Godfrey evidences both the unconventional prettiness and the pluck of the genre's heroines, as well as their peculiar want of parents and professional ambition; Anne Cowdenbeath is all brittle sophistication and elegant *couture* as her rich rival for

Lucas's affection; and Hal Darbo is the perfect embodiment of the 'too smooth' rival man, 'egotistical, superficial, manipulative, unscrupulous, basically weak and, sometimes, physically violent'.[5] At times the characters themselves (all four of whom tell their version of the story in the first person) offer knowing observations about their own literary precursors. Thus the aristocratic Lady Cowdenbeath, mindful of other *Liaisons Dangereuses*: 'I would have been the Marquise de Merteuil for you, you know that, Lucas.' But the chief exponent of this self-reflexive style is the handsome hero, who certainly knows that he is:

I do resemble the surgeon of the nurse's comic-book
dreams. I am tall, dark, sad-eyed with a mien
combining that of television intellectual and Dracula . . .
Women fall in love with how I look. (p. 19)

Women fall in vain. Making both the hero and his rival homosexual might, you would think, put paid to the 'comic-book dreams' of romantic fiction, either by realist disillusion or by satirical excess. (Imagine how Joe Orton would have treated the story of a closeted doctor with a penchant for rough trade, a menopausal Scots noblewoman, a bottle-blond gay estate agent and his visibly pregnant fiancée.) Instead, for all its classy recalibration of the form, *A Case of Knives* never really rewrites the romance. Rather than upending the entire premiss of the genre, homosexuality is adapted to its requirements, functioning as a plausibly modern delaying device in the romantic narrative and a psychologically coherent explanation for the conventional ambivalence of the hero.

It is the mark of the romance's address to the woman

reader that it transfers that traditional attribute of our own gender, mystery, to the opposite sex. Much of these stories' narratives are occupied with the man as enigma and the heroine's attempt to figure him out. His provocative combination of attention and disdain, of piercing looks and complete indifference, drives her to distraction and the reader to a pitch of curiosity. At the same time, as Tania Modleski has argued, the optimistic tenor of this form reassures us that the hero's obnoxious behaviour must ultimately be explained in terms of love. Awaiting the inevitable happy ending, the veteran reader of romance comes to see misogyny as evidence of – indeed, inextricable from – male desire.

A Case of Knives opens with a rather different explanation for the hero's attitude, an apparently homosexual aversion to women which he is dismayed not to share with the young Hal:

> 'Oh God, Lucas, I want to get married. Married to a girl. You know, one of those things with two of one and one of the other, one of those things with dressing tables.'

> . . . How dare he? 'Dressing tables' was a code in our language; it stood between us for mess, screech, defilement, menses and powdery purses, habitual censorship and unnaked faces. Or so I had understood. (p. 24)

Such disdain for the opposite sex seems a bit categorical, even for the confirmed bachelors of the romance. Yet Lucas will marry at the novel's conclusion, a project of recuperation which requires an investigation of his homosexual milieu and his extraction from it.

There is another key character in this story, one who knows but does not speak. Unlike the members of the central quartet, Tertius is not given his own narration, or even much dialogue, and Hal compares him to a ventriloquist's dummy. We learn about him from the others, who have learned in their turn from his inveterate gossip. What Tertius knows about is evil, the hero's weakness for punishment, the villain's desire to mete it out. Unlike Lucas and Hal, who pass for straight, Tertius (the 'third sex'?) is an unregenerate old queen, an antique dealer who lives in the Albany. At the end of the book he is visibly wasting with suspected AIDS.

'The new Pink Death' [*sic*] hovers over this novel. It is named (along with cancer and coronaries) as the missing modern subject in a series of mosaics designed to illustrate disease in Lucas's hospital. It excites the jury's suspicions about the distinguished but unmarried victim in Hal's trial. It begins to infect Anne's (homosexual) friends, and Tertius's sudden weight loss provokes her concern. Hal equates this illness with guilt, Tertius's guilty reaction to Lucas's attack:

> he thought it was his fault. Perhaps that's what he's got, guilt, not the other thing, the disease, about as easy to cure as each other. Unhelpful, AIDS. (p. 260)

Guilt, of course, is also a risk in the romance, which must defend not only its apparently brutal heroes but the artless innocence of its heroines against their uncanny ability to marry rich and powerful men. (Cora

is saved from the accusation of Fielding's parodic
Shamela by the most worldly of narrative contrivances:
she *is* trying to make a suitable marriage for her unborn
child, but by cynically pursuing the fair Hal, not the
dark hero she really loves.) If the heroine is seen to
know what she's doing, to love to her conscious advantage, her virtue is compromised.

Cora escapes this culpability by what economists
would call 'uneven development'. Her sophistication –
enhanced by her incorporation into the authorial narration – impresses, but her naivety redeems. Her use of
the first person invites us into a rapport with her (as it
does with Lucas, Anne and even the cheerful psycho-
path, Hal); that of the three others reminds us that her
knowledge, and responsibility, are limited. Not so with
Tertius, who possesses a gossip's rich store of damning
information. He knows and he sickens.

This knowledge, and Tertius himself, must be kept at
a distance from the reader. Not only would it foreclose
the mystery, it might also produce an identification with
illness which the narration takes care to prevent. As
Erica Carter has argued about a similar mode of address
in British health education:

> On the one hand, the British public is charged to
> equip itself with the facts of AIDS and HIV infection:
> 'Don't Die of Ignorance,' says the billboard caption.
> But equally powerfully conveyed by this television
> advertisement's use of stock narrative and visual
> conventions – the AIDS sufferer as mute victim and
> vision of horror, the body positive as a man
> condemned – is the danger of identification with

those affected by HIV and AIDS. The hospital
narrative represents the dividing-line between the
sick and the healthy as immutable. Once the
hospital visitor becomes a patient, he is as good as
dead; now we recognise ourselves in him at our
peril.[6]

'The body positive as a man condemned': in precisely
that combination of juridical and medical discourses
we last see Tertius, 'so pale and thin now', preparing
to spend Christmas visiting Hal in prison. Tertius is
dying, but Lucas is saved. The novel's treatment of
death and sexuality strains for balance, with Anne's
lengthy parenthesis on AIDS a masterpiece of equivocation In it she considers how the epidemic has
reinforced the jury's prejudices at Hal's trial:

> These creatures of disease, thinks the heterosexual,
> so tenuously preserving his right to promiscuity,
> had it coming to them, for the way they looked, for
> the way they were . . . That the disease is shared by
> users of drugs, prostitutes, yes, and black men, puts
> power fair and square in the reins of the horsemen
> of the Apocalypse. Like all plagues, it gives work to
> liars and cowards and power to the bullies. (p. 239)

What follows is a remarkable attempt to reserve a safe
space for the straight liberal, uncontaminated by
bigotry *or* disease, with Anne's excursus shifting nervously between the admitted inevitability of heterosexual infection (but cast into an indeterminate
future); the moral paradox of the 'innocent' victim

53

('how do the righteous explain the babies?'); and the vexing question of the homosexual masochist:

> The dangers drawn by Lucas's black trysts were once rejection or attack. There was, he has told me, a thrill in the closeness to danger. It was a melodramatic, erotic danger, to be feinted but not fulfilled. There is no such frisson to the consideration of a more lingering and more painful danger. Yet Lucas and men like him need the anonymity, the lovelessness, like a fighter the fight. Should isolation hospitals become brothels? (p. 240)

Here the equivocation becomes ferocious. If 'Lucas and men like him' do not seek (and therefore do not deserve) slow death through immune failure, they are nevertheless proposed as the victims of their own compulsions. In true Wolfenden spirit, moralism is replaced by medicalization, and sexual transgressors are assigned to the contagion ward, brothel and hospital in one.

As the novel shifts between desire and disease, it is difficult to ignore the resemblance of the hero's name, 'Lucas Salik', to that of Jonas Salk – the real-life inventor of the polio vaccine, and even as I write this, a reported contender in the race to discover one against HIV. Thus the hero comes to us christened with intimations of an epidemic, but also of the prophylactic against it. This ambiguity structures his role in the story, which straddles sickness and health and their implied parallels – homosexuality and marriage. Lucas jokes about his resemblance to Dracula, another dashing object of female devotion, and the would-be seducer of that earlier estate agent, Jonathan Harker. In his perverse incarnation as a creature of the night, of exquisitely erotic violence, he stands on the side of contagion, blood to blood. But as Jonas Salk, vaccinator, saver of children, he is the heroic physician.

In *Mythologies*, Barthes employs precisely this figure – inoculation – to describe the process of limited acknowledgement through which mythic narratives engage with evil. If, through the administration of a small dose of the infectious agent, inoculation can prevent disease, our stories may adopt the same principle to forestall the forces of darkness. Tania Modleski reads a parallel strategy in the romance's acknowledgement of the hero's hostility, which is structured into both the characteristic enigma of the genre (is this man friend or foe?) and its equally characteristic vindication of the male sex:

> Men may appear moody, cynical, scornful and bullying, but they nevertheless provide romance and excitement.[7]

This tactic, which both allows and overrules female complaint, can also be compared to the treatment of sexuality in McWilliam's novel. Its homosexual hero, sophisticated milieu, and liberal asides against heterosexual bigotry are neatly offset – not only by the homosexual villain (villains, indeed, if we count Tertius and the bizarre lesbian animal-rights campaigner who incites the attack on Lucas) but also by a genre which identifies happiness with heterosexual romance and closure with marriage.

Why then, we might ask, is there any need to inoculate the straight love story? What is it about homosexuality which might, like HIV, be infectious?

Modleski's reading of the popular romance offers one
reply: while heterosexual love is its chief pleasure,
heterosexuality itself is its central problem. Similarly,
Ann Snitow has argued:

> these Pollyanna books have their own dream-like
> truth: our culture produces a pathological experience
> of sex difference. The sexes have different needs and
> interests, certainly different experiences. They find
> each other utterly mystifying.[8]

A Case of Knives makes use of this generic sex antagonism, notably in Lucas's abhorrence of female 'mess' and
the barbed badinage which accompanies his first
exchanges with Cora. But it can also escape it to suggest
an unusual understanding between straight women and
gay men (an impression enhanced by the styling of
Anne, Lucas and Cora's narratives in the same camp
idiom). And in a contemporary twist to the romance's
traditional interest in 'furniture, clothes and gourmet
foods'[9] it is the hero who is a fastidious cook and
decorator, as well as an intelligent observer of Lady
Cowdenbeath's extensive wardrobe. And she, if not
quite 'the type of woman who habitually fraternises with
homosexuals', enjoys something of a fag-hagging relation to him.

Cora's arrival, young and pregnant, adds further
possibilities to this sexual reconciliation. Like most of
her generic predecessors, she is conveniently orphaned,

and thus available for a lover *in loco parentis*, as Ann Snitow puts it.[10] Doubly so, since she also requires a father for her child. And this kind of fatherhood, offered without the inconvenience of physical passion, is admirably suited to a man of Sir Lucas's means. At the novel's close, we learn from Hal that the threesome have formed *a ménage* – indeed, that Lucas has married . . . but not which woman.

Such ambiguous conclusions are not unknown in narratives structured on sexual confusion or downright antagonism. (Consider the group engagements in *Twelfth Night* and *Calamity Jane*.) Never quite forcing the principals to commit themselves, they allow fantasies of the best of more than one world, in this case the simultaneous prospects of Lucas and Anne's mature rapport, a father for Cora's child, and the indulgence of her own youthful devotion to the distinguished older man. The varied possibilities seem quite to outnumber the problems which would beset any single solution.

But every marriage has its price. It is a truism that the romance settles its accounts with the powerful male by wounding him in a way which often seems castrating. If Rochester's mutilations level him with Jane Eyre, Lucas's injuries surrender him to the care of Anne and Cora. With the ties that bound him to his illusory 'English boy' well and truly severed, he can now take his proper place as father and husband.

In her reading of Henry James's *The Beast in the Jungle*, Eve Sedgwick considers the fate of another confirmed bachelor, one who does not desire to transform a long friendship with the woman who loves him into marriage. Her death brings him numbly to a cemetery, where he discovers another male mourner grieving over a fresh grave:

> The stranger passed, but the raw glare of his grief remained, making our friend wonder in pity what wrong, what wound it expressed, what injury not to be healed. What had the man *had*, to make him by the loss of it so bleed and yet live?[11]

James's description of this psychic wound – which Sedgwick identifies as the castratory threat which initiates the male into heterosexuality, 'into the status of fathers and into the control (read both ways) of the Law'[12] – returns us to our *Case*. To 'so bleed and yet live' is Lucas's literal fate, a violence which this romance would ascribe to the perverse underworld he leaves behind. Yet, as we have seen, McWilliam's novel carries its own, heterosexual, violence within its chosen form. Homosexuality may offer it – so to speak – new blood. The 'new Pink Death' may be brandished to restore the old straight imperatives. But as the romance continues to remind us, it is the problems between men and women which demand a cure.

portraits

Marilyn Monroe by Gloria Steinem, Brigitte Bardot by Simone de Beauvoir

In the 1960 film *la Vérité/The Truth*, Brigitte Bardot plays a brooding young beauty on trial for the murder of her lover. As the jury is about to be empanelled, counsel for the accused asks his female assistant if the defendant will appear in the dock dressed in 'too tarty' a manner. 'Not at all,' she replies. 'But it's hard to make her look ugly.' In response, the advocate instructs his assistant to challenge each of the women called for jury service. And so we are given a brief scene in which a woman lawyer objects to all the potential women jurors in defence of the woman accused. If I add that the murder victim was the fiancé of the defendant's sister, and the son of an anguished mother also present in the court-room, the spectacle of intra-female conflict comes into even sharper focus.

In the case of the cinematic sex goddess,[1] feminism has proved an ambivalent jury with an uneasy con-science. When Simone de Beauvoir (who will figure here on the libertarian side of the argument) dealt in *The Second Sex* with the female film star, she placed her in the chapter on Prostitution. There she is described as 'the latest incarnation of the hetaira',[2] the high-class courtesan who barters both body and personality into a saleable reputation. Like her predecessors (de Beauvoir mentions the flute-girls of Ancient Greece, Japanese geishas, Zola's Nana) the woman star relies upon male protectors and pursues male consumers, though the medium of her fame is no longer such an intimate one. She may never cross the ambiguous line dividing the display of beauty from its direct sale (here the symbiotic proximity of prostitution to show business is emphasized), but her function is no different: 'She yields Woman over to the dreams of man, who repays her with wealth and fame' (p. 579). The paradox of such a profession is, that its practitioners come to be active, independent subjects only through the strictures of self-objectification.

De Beauvoir argues that this bargain is a perilous one. The star's freedom depends upon the patronage of both male producers and the wider male public, and it rarely lasts longer than her youthful beauty. Nor is film acting itself, in de Beauvoir's assessment, a 'genuine project':

> The films, especially, where the star is subordinated to the director, permit her no invention, no advances in creative activity. *Someone else* exploits what she is; she creates nothing new. (p. 585)

> The subjection of Hollywood stars is well known. Their bodies are not their own; the producer decides on the colour of their hair, their weight, their figure, their type. . . .. The prostitute who simply yields her body is perhaps less a slave than the woman who makes a career of pleasing the public. (p. 583)

The equation of Hollywood with whoring was hardly a new one, even forty-four years ago when *The Second Sex* was published. It relies upon assumptions about the cinema, and mass culture generally, which are all too familiar. In the studio's grooming of the contract player ('dieting, gymnastics, fittings'), in the artistic authority of the director, in the boredom built into production schedules, de Beauvoir rediscovers the alienation remarked upon by commentators since Pirandello – whose lament for the work of the silent film actor, exiled not only from the audience 'but also from himself', was imported into Benjamin's formulation of the loss imposed on performance by its mechanical reproduction.[3]

These assumptions might apply to any screen worker, and the novelist who 'prostitutes' his art to write for the movies is a much-mythologized example. But they tend to cluster around the figure of the sex goddess, who is characteristically cast in the role of the prostitute or her metonymic sisters – the showgirl, the model, the loose woman, the gold-digger. My intention here is to tease out the application of such assumptions by two noted feminists, both 'stars' in their political firmaments, to two emblematically erotic actresses. These two encounters are separated – by time (twenty-seven years), politics, and the circumstances of the stars in question. No one will be surprised that Gloria Steinem's posthumous account of Marilyn Monroe assumes a gravity entirely absent from Simone de Beauvoir's profile of the then twenty-five-year-old Bardot, or that the latter piece exudes an enthusiasm about sexual honesty which now seems somewhat dated. In many ways, these two readings of the sex goddess represent the furthest poles of feminist response. Yet both remain available for contemporary appropriation, and neither is quite what it seems.

Marilyn Monroe

Where the woman star has been accused of pandering to male desire and betraying her own sex, the central figure in the demonology has undoubtedly been Marilyn Monroe. For many feminist critics she has functioned as the right-hand column, so to speak, of an entire taxonomy of the female screen star. This classificatory system owes a lot to Molly Haskell's influential mapping of 1950s screen personae in *From Reverence to Rape*, which counterposes Monroe both to 'wholesome' 'girl next door' types like Doris Day and Debbie Reynolds, and to the 'aristocratic and independent' Grace Kelly and Audrey Hepburn:

> They never swallowed their pride, exploited their
> sexuality, or made fools of themselves over men.
> Marilyn did, and she aroused our jealousy and
> contempt. (p. 253)

Writing in the early 1970s, a decade after Monroe's death, Haskell is careful to qualify these observations by distancing them in the faraway 1950s:

> Women, particularly, have become contrite over their
> previous hostility to Monroe, canonizing her as a
> martyr to male chauvinism, which in most ways she
> was. But at the time, women couldn't identify with
> her and didn't support her . . . women hated Marilyn

64

for catering so shamelessly to a false, regressive,
childish and detached idea of sexuality. (p. 254)

Such contradictions, it has been suggested, still
inform many women's responses to Monroe's star persona. Graham McCann's survey of the posthumous
commentaries on the actress by women writers finds
them surprisingly condescending. Whether by separating the performer from her work to denounce it, if not
her, as grossly sexist (Joan Mellen); by inflating Monroe's death to a meta-statement on Western civilization
(Diana Trilling); or by seizing upon the star as an
all-purpose figure of female victimhood (Gloria
Steinem), such readings, he argues, deny Monroe both
agency and specificity.[4]

McCann rarely attempts to explain these attitudes
towards Monroe – indeed, all too frequently his own
account of her star image collapses back into the discourses of Victimization ('inside she was bruised and
broken, increasingly forced to use drugs to assuage her
agony') and Inflated Cultural Significance ('Marilyn
Monroe epitomizes the ambiguities in modernity').
More helpful is Richard Dyer's ascription of this uncertain handling of Monroe to the contradictions in her
own negotiations with the ideological imperatives of the
1950s. As he argues, feminists have criticized the star's
exhibitionism at one juncture and saluted her protests
against 'sex roles' at another precisely because Monroe's
representation (that is to say, the representation of and
by Monroe) involved both strategies. Dyer exemplifies
this duality in the star's appearance in extremely décol-
leté gowns to make serious political statements at press

conferences, as well as the unusual point-of-view structures of films like *Bus Stop*. Here he notes how the camera's look at Monroe's body is often framed by the shabby *mise en scène* of her dressing-room – a contradiction (between aspiring glamour and actual frustration) which informs many of Monroe's showgirl roles.[5]

Such observations speak to the polysemic possibilities of Monroe's image, as well as to the varied reactions it has provoked. But what of the feminist critic herself? What investments does she bring to her encounter with the sex goddess?

If, as a writer, lecturer and campaigner, Gloria Steinem became – as the blurb for a 1984 collection of her writing reads – 'the most visible and persuasive advocate of the women's movement in America', she was already a journalist of some renown before the launch of *Ms.*, the glossy US monthly which she co-founded and edited from the early 1970s to 1987. As early as 1963, Steinem attracted considerable notice by infiltrating the Manhattan Playboy Club as an undercover Bunny Girl. Her report on this legendary bastion of the sex industry established certain concerns which reappear in her later, feminist writing, including that on Monroe. In the 1970s Steinem became a leading activist in the US anti-pornography movement, and *Ms.* one of its major platforms.

Steinem's first article on Marilyn Monroe was published in the August 1972 issue of *Ms*. Writing to commemorate the tenth anniversary of the star's death, she recalls her teenage repugnance on viewing Monroe as Lorelei Lee in the 1953 musical comedy *Gentlemen Prefer Blondes*:

> I walked out on Marilyn Monroe. I remember her on
> the screen, huge as a colossus doll, mincing and
> whispering and simply hoping her way into total
> vulnerability. Watching her, I felt angry, even
> humiliated, but I didn't understand why.[6]

(And it *is* difficult to understand why this of all Monroe's
films should have produced that reaction. Lorelei Lee is
one of the actress's least dumb blondes, and the contradiction between her presentation as spectacle and her
knowing commentary on just that phenomenon has
animated an extensive critical debate.[7])

Twenty years later, Steinem explains her humiliation
in terms of identification. Like Monroe, she was raised
in a working-class neighbourhood where girls fantasized
escape in 'show-business dreams'. If her teenage years as
an aspirant dancer in Toledo culminated in college
entrance rather than nude calendars, 'there's not much
more confidence in girls who scrape past college boards
than there is in those who, like Marilyn, parade past
beauty contest judges' (p. 234).

Just a few years after her fateful departure from
Gentlemen Prefer Blondes, Steinem happened upon the
real-life Monroe when the two took classes at the Actors
Studio in New York. Although the actress was then at
the height of her celebrity, Steinem recalls that 'her
status as a movie star and sex symbol seemed to keep her
from being taken seriously' in the American headquar-
ters of the Stanislavski Method. And this again offers
scope for a memory of mutuality in the experiences of
the stagestruck student and the dumbstruck star:

So the two of us sat there, mutually awed, I think, in
the presence of such theatre people as Ben Gazzara
and Rip Torn, mutually insecure in the masculine
world of High Culture, mutually trying to fade into
the woodwork. (p. 234)

Elsewhere in her writing, Steinem suddenly attempts
to check this tendency to identification with a quick
corrective. 'I don't mean to suggest', she cautions the
reader of another profile, 'that the Most Famous
Woman in the World is just like everyone else' (p. 257).
Since the subject of this caveat is Jacqueline Kennedy
Onassis, I am inclined to abide by it. Those who might
do otherwise, however, would not be entirely discour-
aged by the intimate style of Steinem's *Ms.* profiles,
whose knowing anecdotes and present-tense narration
foreground the author's familiarity with her subjects.
These are basic procedures of what in the 1970s was
called the New Journalism, and they fit surprisingly well
into a certain notion of 'sisterhood' – sisterhood as
shared experience. The 1972 memoir concludes with an
attempt to recruit the star posthumously to this ambit,
imagining her as a newly confident beneficiary of a
feminism posed both as politics and as 'the support and
friendship of other women'. It is the fantasy of rescue
repeated in so many accounts of the doomed actress,
and I shall return to it below.

In 1986 Gloria Steinem enlarged upon her earlier
article in an illustrated collaboration with George Barris,
who had photographed Monroe during the last two
months of her life for an uncompleted biography. The
resulting study, *Marilyn* – like so many other lives of this

star – is an exemplary tale. 'Few', Steinem writes, 'become parables.'[8] The author's exegesis of her own parable returns to the *Ms.* profile of 1972, and the readers' responses which followed its story of sexual assault in childhood, overmedication by physicians, the anxieties of the glamour industry, repeated marriages in pursuit of identity or caring, failure to bear a child. The *via dolorosa* of this exemplary sufferer attracted a vast correspondence of identification, and the feminist rehabilitation of Marilyn Monroe had begun.

As a vehicle for this rehabilitation, *Marilyn* is a strange hybrid, a sort of consecrated coffee-table book. Its philanthropic designation (Steinem's fee and portions of Barris's and the publishers' earnings were earmarked for children's charities) is declared early on, in compensation for its status as just another piece of Monroe merchandise, and to carry out the imagined bequest of its subject:

> she remained loyal and protective toward the
> children of her friends, and got special satisfaction
> from giving to an orphanage like the one where she
> had felt abandoned. Probably, she would have
> contributed more if she had paid attention to
> money . . . (p. 2)

Note how this double act of penance – for the commercial prospects of the book and the neglectfulness of its namesake – is focused on children, whose redemptive characteristics will also be imported into its portrait of the star: 'the endlessly vulnerable child who looked out of Marilyn's eyes' (p. 3).

As we shall see, this infantilization solves several problems for Steinem, absolving her subject from adult responsibility and calculation, particularly in matters sexual, while discovering a true self beneath the star image. (Barris's photographs – a set of rather contrived candids employing natural light and beach and bungalow locations – also give the rounded features of the thirty-six-year-old Monroe a childish cast.) Here childhood is marshalled to its traditional associations with psychical truth and interiority, figured in the star's given, 'real' name, the 'Norma Jeane' inscribed in cursive script over the title page's 'Marilyn'.

This splitting is a marked feature of *Marilyn*, allowing at once both critique and hagiography, as well as a fantasy of reintegration all the more poignant for its impossibility:

> If acting had become an expression of that real self, not an escape from it, one also can imagine the whole woman who was both Norma Jeane and Marilyn becoming a serious actress and wise comedienne who would still be working in her sixties, with more productive years to come.
>
> But Norma Jeane remained the frightened child of the past. And Marilyn remained the unthreatening help-person that sex goddesses are supposed to be. (p. 180)

Steinem elaborates this split in the traditional dichotomies of the star biography: 'the woman behind the mask' (p. 23); 'the public artifice and the private Norma Jeane' (p. 154); 'her external self [versus] some real identity' (p. 158). Conventionally, these structured oppositions locate sex and the body with the private self, counterposed to the rational and the social. But the erotic celebrity forces a reversal of this pattern, identifying individuality with intellect and externalizing sexual attractiveness into 'glamour' and sexual intercourse into performance. Thus, if sex for Monroe was a commodity exchanged for love or company or professional advantage, it could not also be a source of personal pleasure: 'Sex was less a reward to herself than a price she paid gladly' (p. 141).

This separation of sex from the self encourages the figurative decapitation of the sex goddess – a fate notoriously realized in the actual death of Jayne Mansfield. The face, and particularly the eyes, are severed from the corrupt body beneath:

> in these photographs, the body emphasis seems more the habit of some former self. It's her face we look at. Now that we know the end of her story, it's the real woman we hope to find – looking out of the eyes of Marilyn. (p. 23)

In Steinem's account, Monroe's 'magic' body becomes real only through pain and dysfunction. Her drug-taking, headaches, rashes, weight gains and numerous operations – even a burn from bleaching her pubic hair – are lovingly catalogued in a litany of suffering. Particular emphasis is laid on the star's reproductive failings: miscarriages, menstrual pain, abortions. The traces of a bartered sexuality scar her beauty in a retribution which her biographer seems almost to relish.

The victim of 'uncaring guardians, rapacious suitors, thoughtless and prodigal husbands and fathers, and the general vicissitudes of a hostile and selfish world'[9] has been a central figure of melodrama since its origins. In appropriating its conventions to write this life, Steinem effectively displaces both Monroe's professional achievements and her personal beauty – for suffering, in melodrama, is itself evidence of merit. Thus the star becomes, in Steinem's description, 'a minor American actress' who is repeatedly – almost obsessively – characterized in terms of her awkward bosom:

> the big-breasted woman in a society that regresses men and keeps them obsessed with the maternal symbols of breasts and hips. (p. 15)

This inversion of the infantilization developed so often elsewhere in the biography makes the star symbolically a mother – 'older and more experienced' (p. 3) than the teenage spectator of *Gentlemen Prefer Blondes*. It begins to explain the ambivalence which informs this sadistic tribute, as well as the themes of maternal melodrama – of failed, lost or self-sacrificing mothers (Monroe is quoted comparing hers to Stella Dallas) – which thread through it.

If we consider Freud's work on the 'rescue motif' in erotic fantasy, it seems likely that it is the maternal adult Marilyn, not the child Norma Jeane, whom Steinem imagines saving. And this returns us to the figure of the prostitute, for Freud is considering 'a special type' of object choice, the compulsive desire for women of ill repute. This he traces back to the pre-pubescent boy's jealous realization that his parents are no 'exception to the universal and odious norms of sexual activity', which makes his beloved mother . . . very like a whore. The subject's subsequent fantasies, driven both by 'desire and a thirst for revenge', lead him to fallen women, whom he invariably seeks to rescue from their immoral ways.[10] And who better to inherit their mantle than the erotic women of the cinema, styled for the jealous consumption of each spectator, yet shared – necessarily – with millions?

Brigitte Bardot

My reading of Steinem's *Marilyn* suggests that an unacknowledged desire for the Sex Goddess as Mother may lie beneath the more polite feminist identification with her as Sister. Simone de Beauvoir's 1959 essay on Brigitte Bardot reverses those terms, flaunting its erotic appreciation of the star, while also constructing her as an object of identification. 'Brigitte Bardot and the Lolita Syndrome' was written for the American monthly *Esquire* in 1959, just after de Beauvoir had read Nabokov's novel. Surprisingly, for an occasional piece scarcely noted by her biographers, it was among those cited by the author at the end of her life as an important source 'for any interpretation or evaluation of her *oeuvre*'.[11] In a rare attempt to deal with the essay at any length, Claude Francis and Fernande Gontier situate its writing in a period of depression exacerbated by the waning of the fifty-one-year-old writer's affair with the thirty-three-year-old Claude Lanzmann.[12] The intimations of old age prompted by this parting were

73

intensified by Sartre's own collapse in the wake of the Left's defeat in a constitutional referendum over the Algerian crisis. His illness, and the couple's increasing personal and intellectual estrangement, condemned de Beauvoir to a solitude in which all these factors seemed to merge, producing in *Force of Circumstance* a strangely eroticized account of her political disappointment:

> The result of the referendum had severed the last
> threads linking me to my country. There were to be
> no more trips through France . . . From that time on I
> lived through the pride of our autumns in
> humiliation, and the sweetness of summer in
> bitterness. Sometimes I still feel a catch in my throat
> at a landscape's sudden grace, but it is the memory of
> a love betrayed, it is like a smile that lies.[13]

And in a dream recorded in this period, the abused Republic itself appears in the traditional guise of a woman, underlining the author's personal sense of betrayal: 'they were drowning a naked woman, half flesh, half statue, who was the Republic' (p. 412).

De Beauvoir never mentions her essay on Bardot in *Force of Circumstance*, but she does allude to the star herself, midway through a denunciation of the French indifference to the torture of Algerian nationalists:

> I had been labelled, along with several others, anti-
> French. I became so. I could no longer bear my fellow
> citizens. When I dined out with Lanzmann or Sartre,
> we hid away in a corner; even so, we could not get
> away from their voices; amid the malicious gossip

about Margaret, Coccinelle, Brigitte Bardot, Sagan,
Princess Grace, we would suddenly hear a sentence
that made us want to run for the door. (p. 381)

So the naked star – like the Republic, like the Algerians,
like the author herself – is a victim of the French. At a
New Year's Eve party in 1959, de Beauvoir watches her
on television in the company of a hostile audience: 'Only
two or three of us, among thirty or so spectators,
thought her charming . . . Once again I could observe
that Brigitte Bardot was disliked in her own country.'[14]
De Beauvoir opens her essay with this anecdote,
effectively establishing the star (then at the height of her
early celebrity) as a personal cult object, retrieved from
a national opprobrium not wholly unlike that which had
greeted the author of *The Second Sex* ten years before:

To say that 'BB embodies the immorality of an age'
means that the character she has created challenges
certain taboos accepted by the preceding age,
particularly those which denied women sexual
autonomy. (p. 58)

This is not, apparently, the dubiously acquired autonomy of the Hollywood stars decried in *The Second Self*.
De Beauvoir is careful to concentrate on the persona
rather than the person ('If we want to understand what
BB represents, it is not important to know what the
young woman named Brigitte Bardot is really like' p. 8)
and to attribute its creation to her directors, particularly
Vadim. But BB's star image seems impervious to the
splitting which characterizes Marilyn/Norma Jeane.

Unlike the painfully groomed courtesans of the studio system, de Beauvoir's Bardot is what she appears to be. Where Garbo's face launched a thousand interpretations, hers defies the hermeneutic impulse: 'It is what it is. It has the forthright presence of reality' (p. 34). De Beauvoir invokes the *nouveau roman* to explain the star's physical presence, a sexuality which, she maintains, is too 'precise' to sublimate or fetishize. In her refusal to transform herself 'into a remote idol', Bardot becomes a symbol of female emancipation, the free woman. Here, as in Steinem's writing on Marilyn, the star's childishness signifies innocence, naturalness, honesty – to de Beauvoir, that is. Its appeal to men takes on a rather more sinister tone in her description of 'the Lolita syndrome'.

'Bardot', de Beauvoir maintains, is simply 'the most perfect specimen' in a series of cinematic types adjusted to maximize both sexual difference and box office receipts. In her argument, Hollywood's postwar economic crisis can be blamed on the girl next door: as the Jean Arthur figure replaced the vamp, the cinema lost its appeal. The 1950s arrival of Sophia Loren, Gina Lollobrigida, and – indeed – Marilyn Monroe represented the first steps in Hollywood's campaign to retrench: the signs of physical difference magnified in a crude attempt at mystery. With child-women like Audrey Hepburn and Leslie Caron, this difference was extended to age, a ploy with particular allure for fragile American manhood. In Bardot, writes de Beauvoir, the process reached its apotheosis. Young and voluptuous, both nymphet and *femme fatale*, she triumphantly doubled the difference. And Cinema Re-created Woman.

De Beauvoir's attempt to justify Bardot's paedophiliac appeal to American men, in terms of a New World sexual egalitarianism which somehow leads them to respect – and therefore shun – their female contemporaries, is one of the oddest pieces of a logic in an argument not distinguished by its rigour. Frenchmen, by contrast, are accused of such an overweening sense of superiority that they find BB's youthful insouciance intolerable. But if her 'haughty shamelessness' threatens them, why doesn't it perturb their US counterparts, who are said to cower under the dominance of Momism? De Beauvoir does not (indeed, cannot) explain this distinction any more than she can explain her gendered definition of the cinema-going 'public' – particularly after noting that Bardot receives fan mail 'from boys and girls alike'. To pose the question asked so often since: Where is the female spectator in this account?

If we go to de Beauvoir's own appreciation of her subject, we receive an interesting answer:

Brigitte Bardot is the most perfect specimen of these ambiguous nymphs. Seen from behind, her slender, muscular, dancer's body is almost androgynous. Femininity triumphs in her delightful bosom. The long voluptuous tresses of Mélisande flow down to her shoulders, but her hair-do is that of a negligent waif. The line of her lips forms a childish pout, and at the same time those lips are very kissable. She goes about barefooted, she turns up her nose at elegant clothes, jewels, girdles, perfumes, make-up, at all artifice. Yet her walk is lascivious and a saint

would sell his soul to the devil merely to watch her
dance. (p. 14)

This female spectator first beholds her subject from
behind – a familiar angle on Bardot at this time (when
her posterior was as celebrated as frontal nudity was
forbidden), but one singled out in *The Second Sex* as a
particularly shaming supervision: 'Many adult women
hate to be looked at from behind even when dressed' (p.
402). De Beauvoir's ascription of an objectifying force to
this look is derived from Sartre's famous observations in
Being and Nothingness. But it was she who proposed its
heterosexual dynamic, which Sartre then elaborated in
his discussion of the incriminating gaze which interpo-
lates Genet:

> This first rape was the gaze of the other, who took
> him by surprise, penetrated him, transformed him
> forever into an object . . .. Undressed by the eyes of
> decent folk as women are by those of males, he carries
> his fault as they do their breasts and behind. Many
> women loathe their backside, that blind and public
> mass which belongs to everyone before belonging to
> them . . .[15]

In assuming the position of voyeur, de Beauvoir takes
the place which she herself has designated masculine.
This masculinization of the look would later become one
of feminism's most influential – and contested – premisses. In particular, and most relevant here, it has
haunted descriptions of erotic looking by and between
women.

How, then, should we understand de Beauvoir's *blazon* of BB? As a parody of a certain style of erotic appreciation, *roué*'s rhetoric and all? As a knowing assumption of a masculine attitude? Or as a homoerotic tribute unbounded by the binarism of gender? Similar questions confront critics contemplating the erotic ensemble of de Beauvoir's first novel, *She Came to Stay*.

Commentators have noted the Oedipal figurations which structure this *roman à clef*, with the Sartrean male 'Pierre' as the paternal apex or 'père' of a triangle which pits the autobiographical figure of an older woman in desperate rivalry with a younger. Not surprisingly, the positions in this triangle are never stable. Judith Okely argues that the heroine (named Françoise after de Beauvoir's mother) oscillates between identification 'with her childhood self as daughter and her adult wish-fulfillment as mother',[16] while Jane Heath emphasizes the 'unresolved'[17] homosexuality of 'the older woman's attraction to her rival.

> She felt Xavière's beautiful warm breasts against her, she inhaled her sweet breath. Was this desire? But what did she desire? Her lips against hers? Her body surrendered in her arms? She could think of nothing. It was only a confused need to keep for ever this lover's face turned toward hers and to be able to say with passion 'She is mine.'[18]

Both this interrogation of desire and the acknowledgement of its many positions survive into de Beauvoir's study of Bardot. They enable her to dissect the peculiar antagonism generated by the star's most famous film,

Et Dieu créa la femme/And God Created Woman (directed by Roger Vadim, 1956).

Created as a vehicle for Bardot (then languishing as a starlet signifying 'French spiciness' in pictures like Dirk Bogarde's *Doctor at Sea*), the film was calculated to identify the performer with the role of the impulsive, sensual, animal-loving Juliette. ('Never have I been so much at ease,' she declared to *Cahiers du Cinéma*. 'Vadim knows me so well. All the lines were so natural.') Erotic sequences and Mediterranean *mise en scène* were emphasized at the expense of psychical plausibility or narrative congruence. (Eighteen-year-old Juliette departs unloving step-parents in pursuit of passion in a Provençal fishing village.) The result was the presentation of the star as sheer spectacle, 'la femme' at her most abstract, in the simplest chain of associations:

> Brigitte Bardot makes the most of sun and sex in St. Tropez.

Dilys Powell's laconic *Sunday Times* notice was not untypical of the film's critical response, for which de Beauvoir offers an astute explanation. The film's unconvincing story line, its 'background of fake colours', the 'discontinuity' of love-making and performance sequences presented like musical 'numbers' – all are adumbrated as an 'analytical' strategy which 'desituates' sexuality, uncomfortably alerting the spectators to their own voyeurism. And de Beauvoir, unlike Steinem, is able to acknowledge one consequence of the desire laid bare by this device:

> When BB dances her famous mambo, no one believes in Juliette. It is BB who is exhibiting herself. She is as alone

on the screen as the strip-tease artist is alone on the stage. She offers herself directly to each spectator. But the offer is deceptive, for as the spectators watch her, they are fully aware that this beautiful young woman is famous, rich, adulated and completely inaccessible. It is not surprising that they take her for a slut and that they take revenge on her by running her down. (p. 46)

As the erotic admirer of Bardot, who – like the heroine of *She Came to Stay* – loves 'to look on', de Beauvoir is able to catalogue her subject's charms in the most conventionally voyeuristic style. But as the object of a similar resentment, the antagonism reserved for the woman whose fame is associated with sexual freedom, the critic – as we have seen – can also make common cause with the movie star. ('It is no new thing for high-minded folk to identify the flesh with sin and to dream of making bonfires of works of art, books and films that depict it complacently or frankly': p. 6.)

It is difficult to ignore the narcissistic gratification available in the implied comparison between the ageing intellectual at the end of her active sexual life and the young actress who had come to represent active sexuality. Nor is it easy to reconcile (except in the most ambitious dialectic) Bardot's dual status as both the *epitomé* and the deconstruction of cinematic femininity. But de Beauvoir's ambivalence has the happy consequence of offering a reverse angle on its subject – allowing us to see not only the star but her audience, and the mechanisms of cinema itself. In this respect, as well as in her gendering of *le regard*, de Beauvoir

81

anticipated the feminist criticism which would come after her, particularly its interest in films which 'foreground' relations of spectatorship.

But the imbrication of the rebel writer with the rebel star had further consequences, literally inscribing the critic in the cinematic text. The year after the *Esquire* profile saw the release of Bardot's most serious drama, *la Vérité*. The story of a young bohemian accused of the murder of her former lover, it was co-written and directed by Henri-Georges Clouzot, a close friend of de Beauvoir. A courtroom drama with flashbacks to the events in question, *la Vérité* includes a scene in which the Bardot character, Dominique Marceau, is interrogated about her early delinquency in the provincial town of Rennes. After establishing that Dominique destroyed her sister's doll at the age of eight, 'dismembering it with alarming ferocity', the examination turns to her teenage years. Was it usual, the Judge asks, to take a book 'as indecent as *The Mandarins* to school'? When the *blasé* defendant replies that she found de Beauvoir's novel 'boring', a dispute erupts in the courtroom between Eparvier, counsel for the prosecution, and Guèrin, Dominique's attorney:

Judge: And didn't this book surprise or shock you?

Eparvier: (*to judge*) Here, your honour, at random, page 74. (*Reads*) His lips teased my breasts, slipped down over my belly, and on . . . (*gasps*) I surrendered to the pleasure he gave me.

Guèrin: No, no, your honour! Three carefully chosen lines from a 600 page novel!

Eparvier: They're in it though!

Guèrin: That didn't stop the book from winning
             the Prix Goncourt.

Eparvier: So you'd give it to your daughter to read,
             would you?

Guèrin: Is Mme de Beauvoir on trial here?

This tribute to de Beauvoir – if tribute it is – presents a rather strange account of her most celebrated novel. Although *The Mandarins* was, with *The Second Sex*, placed upon the Vatican Index of prohibited books for traducing 'the good character and sanctitude of the family', it was almost universally praised when it appeared in France in 1954. Its love scenes, although shocking to some readers, did not provoke the kind of reaction which occurs in Clouzot's courtroom – a reaction (and a setting) much more appropriate to a contemporary event in Britain, the 1960 *Lady Chatterley* trial, whose prosecuting counsel memorably asked the jury if Lawrence's novel was a book that they would 'wish your wife or your servants to read?'. *La Vérité*'s allusion to literary censorship (French, British or both) can be seen as a bid for seriousness in its own fidelity to 'the truth' of passion. And while endowing Dominique's crime with a similar intellectual dimension, it simultaneously renders *The Mandarins* (and its author) sexy.

'Young women', de Beauvoir observed in *Force of Circumstance*, 'have an acute sense of what should and should not be done when one is no longer young. "I don't understand", they say, "how a woman over forty can bleach her hair; how she can make an exhibition of herself in a bikini; how she can flirt with men. The day I'm her age . . ." That day comes: they bleach their hair;

they wear bikinis; they smile at men' (p. 291). By 1959 Claude Lanzmann had left de Beauvoir. For seven years their affair had postponed a final renunciation of this narcissism. ('When I had first known him, I was not yet ripe for old age; he hid its approach from me,' she wrote [p. 480] with the melodramatic intensity with which she contemplated ageing.) Now, when it beckoned at last, de Beauvoir composed her celebration of a star who bleached her hair, wore bikinis, flirted with men. Moreover, this was a star who signified narcissism, who was forever photographed checking her make-up or kissing her own image, filmed sunbathing in the nude and dancing alone ecstatically (in *Et Dieu créa la femme*) or fatally wounding herself (in *la Vérité*) with a shard of broken mirror. 'You're just a kitten,' she is told in the former film, where she displays that intense self-absorption which Freud noted in those classic narcissists: cats, children, and beautiful women.

'Another person's narcissism has a great attraction for those who have renounced part of their own,' Freud observes,[19] pointing to the desire which animates de Beauvoir's profile of Bardot and its final, projective, wish: 'I hope she will mature, but not change.' But even de Beauvoir's benediction could not forestall the traditional fate of the sex goddess. Like Monroe, Bardot was to endure the broken marriages, suicide attempts and early retirement reckoned to be the routine hazards of her career. Despite the warning implicit in her own invocation of the 'Lolita' syndrome, de Beauvoir ignored the destiny of Nabokov's nymphet: to outgrow her youthful beauty. It's not surprising that she did so, since de Beauvoir's project is, at bottom, no more biographical than Steinem's. Whatever the real differences between their subjects, these essays diverge most profoundly in their attitude not to the sex goddess but to sex itself. Where Steinem's tragic parable is essentially one of sexual abuse, de Beauvoir celebrates women's pursuit of sexual pleasure.

Those opposing attitudes towards sex have coexisted within feminism for the last two centuries, with the modern Anglophone movement currently sustaining a strain of almost nineteenth-century social puritanism (presented most forcefully in the polemics of Andrea Dworkin and Sheila Jeffreys) together with a vocal libertarian opposition. In its midst arrived the latest sex goddess (who modelled her 'Material Girl' video and her delivery in *Dick Tracy* on Monroe's own performances). If, as Sheryl Garrett announced so memorably, feminists have learned to 'stop worrying and love Madonna',[20] this may reflect the fluctuations of the movement even more than the canny mutations of the star herself (the hints of bisexuality, the statements in support of feminism, the AIDS campaigning, the songs about Mum and marital violence). Madonna may seem to be the most self-authored sexual artifact of this (or any other) time, but her career coincides with the feminist revaluation of long-held positions on pornography, fashion and sexual conduct. Consciously or not, such changes will rewrite our narratives of the stars, for the story of the sex goddess can never be entirely her own.

'Transforming the Suit': a century of lesbian self-portraits

'But what about those old photographs?' asks Esther Newton in a pioneering essay. 'Was the mannish lesbian a myth created by "the [male] pornographic mind" or by male sexologists intent on labelling nineteenth-century feminists as deviant? Maybe the old photographs portray a few misguided souls – or perhaps those "pre-movement" women thought men's ties were pretty and practical?'

Newton describes what 'you see' in these photographs: a female figure 'with legs solidly planted, wearing a top hat and a man's jacket, staring defiantly out of the frame, her hair slicked back or clipped over the ears'.[1] The ontology of the photograph, its relation to a 'real' referent, is her first piece of evidence in a historical account of the 'new social/sexual category "lesbian"' (p. 10). So unproblematic is this ontology – the photograph as visible proof of the subject's existence – that it needn't be put to the test. No actual photograph is illustrated or even cited by Newton. Instead, photography's power – what Barthes described as 'the power of authentication'[2] – is harnessed to a less evidential medium, the novel.

The novel in question is Radclyffe Hall's *The Well of Loneliness* (1928), and as Newton's essay demonstrates, it is *about* visibility. Indeed, it can be seen as the textual culmination of an entire sociomedical tradition which sought to 'embody' sexual deviance. Hall's lesbian heroine is born a 'narrow-hipped, wide-shouldered' baby, whose infant features include an incipiently cleft chin.[3] Throughout the novel she is subjected to the frequent, invariably productive, scrutiny of others as well as herself:

'Doesn't Miss Stephen look exactly like a boy? I believe she must be a boy with them shoulders, and them funny gawky legs she's got on her!' (p. 16)

That night she stared at herself in the glass; and even as she did so she hated her body with its muscular shoulders, its small compact breasts and its slender flanks of an athlete. (p. 187)

People looked at Stephen curiously; her height, her clothes, the scar on her face, had immediately riveted their attention. (p. 352)

In the massively influential first volume of his *History of Sexuality*, Foucault attributes the invention of this homosexual body – and that of the homosexual soul, or psyche – to the taxonomical impulses of the nineteenth century.[4] Among its categories were those pertaining to the origins of the orientation – 'innate' and 'acquired'. From Leopold Casper's development of this distinction at mid century flowed a vast literature, in which the reader of *The Well* will recognize three names: Karl Heinrich Ulrichs, the German lawyer and writer who proposed a theory of homosexual development in the embryo brain; Richard von Krafft-Ebing, the Austrian psychiatrist whose vast *Psychopathia Sexualis* numbered '238 histories and 437 pages by the 12th edition of 1903';[5] and Havelock Ellis, the English social reformer whose study *Sexual Inversion* argued for legal tolerance on behalf of an incurable minority. All three espoused (in different ways) a theory of congenital homo-sexuality, or 'inversion', with associated cross-gender characteristics. And all three names figure in the novel: Ulrichs as the author of the mysterious text pored over by young Stephen's father; Krafft-Ebing as the source for her own later discoveries; and Ellis as the contribu-tor of the novel's foreword.

It is with the last that Hall's work is most associated, not least because his arguments combined biological determinism with moral exculpation, attributing to female inverts a degree of moral sensitivity in direct proportion to their homosexual predisposition. From his six case histories of female homosexuality, Ellis fashioned a 'portrait' of the female invert neatly synthe-sized by Hall's biographer, Michael Baker: 'a nervy artistic type, boyish in manners and looks, deep-voiced, capable of whistling, and prone to deeply felt attach-ments'.[6] It is an image which – as Newton revealingly argues – Hall and many of her contemporaries 'embraced' – a term which suggests the eroticized intro-jection of an external ideal. Such a process is readily equated with 'identification' or 'self-recognition,' but its dynamism, the required transposition from outside to in, belies any simple idea of a reflection or pre-existing equivalence. As both Newton and Baker observe, Hall's life was in many ways different from that of her martyred heroine (the author being both less aristocratic and more successful with women). If Stephen Gordon is an effort at lesbian self-portraiture, she serves to remind us just how constructed such portraits are.

This brings us back to photography, and Hall's efforts to construct her own image (efforts which extended to having the luxuriant curls of her childhood portrait obliterated in conformity with Ellis's theory of congenital gender reversal).[7] Hall was never reluctant to involve herself in the marketing of her books, and she furnished *The Well*'s American publisher, Blanche Knopf, with photographs for its launch there. Among her stipulations to Knopf are directions to avoid a publicity photograph used by her previous publisher, a silhouetted image which, she wrote, resembled a 'middle-aged gent who is given to imbibing, or worse still a stout old lady masquerading' (p. 208). Some images of the mythic mannish lesbian were clearly more acceptable than others, even to the legendary progenitor of that figure.

The recurrence of the 'mannish' figure in lesbian self-portraits has elicited a variety of explanations. Newton herself moves between simple verisimilitude – 'Many lesbians *are* masculine' – and the cultural masculinization of sexual desire between women. Teresa de Lauretis raises in reply the question of visibility. Lesbian representation, she observes, is 'still unwittingly caught in the paradox of socio-sexual (in)difference . . . (homo)-sexuality being in the last instance what can not be seen'.[8] But if what she terms (after Newton) 'male body drag' does confer visibility, it does not confer meaning. We are still left with Newton's opening question: What *about* such photographs?

Consider, for example, case number 160 of the twelfth edition of *Psychopathia Sexualis*, 'Mrs von T'. Krafft-Ebing reports that this patient had been brought to him by her husband 'because after a banquet she had fallen upon the neck of a lady guest, covered her profusely with kisses and caressed her like a lover, thus causing a scandal'.[9] Her case history records sufficient evidence of both homosexual practice and masculine identification to elicit the diagnosis of 'Homosexuality in Transition to Viraginity', one of Krafft-Ebing's subcategories of congenital inversion:

Her love for sport, smoking and drinking, her preference for clothes cut in the fashion of men, her lack of skill in and liking for female occupations, her love for the study of obtuse and philosophical subjects, her gait and carriage, severe features, deep voice, robust skeleton, powerful muscles and absence of adipose layers have the stamp of masculine character. (p. 278)

Mrs von T offers the first portrait for our consideration. Among her affairs with women the case history notes a liaison 'with a dressmaker's model with whom she had herself photographed in man's attire, visited, in the same costume, with her places of amusement and was finally arrested on one of these occasions. She escaped with a warning and gave up male attire out-of-doors' (p. 277).

Had Krafft-Ebing commissioned that photograph, it would have admirably illustrated one function of the newly invented medium, the visualization of socio-sexual deviance as an image of the body, whose every feature –

from carriage to clothing – is biologically ordained and medically legible.[10] But this portrait was ordered by its subject, which calls to mind another function of the nineteenth-century photograph.

In his account of the parallel rise of the photographic portrait and the middle classes, John Tagg characterizes the medium as 'a sign whose purpose is both the *description* of an individual and the *inscription* of a social identity'.[11] The latter function, Tagg argues, is performed both by the photograph's replacement of the earlier portrait media by which the rising classes claimed their social place – the painted miniature, the silhouette and the engraving – and by its role as a commodity in itself, an object whose very purchase conferred a certain status upon the purchaser. From its invention, then, photography registered an ontological split, between a claim to record the sitter's 'nature' and a promise to advance his (the gender is deliberate) rank. Somewhere along this faultline, Krafft-Ebing's patient posed 'in man's attire' with her woman lover, an image which might well have confirmed a diagnosis of 'congenital inversion', but which also, of course, represented the social mobility traditionally afforded the 'passing' woman.

During the period which saw Krafft-Ebing compile his case histories and Ellis embark on *Studies in the Psychology of Sex*, another woman pictured herself 'in man's attire'. In 1891–2, Alice Austen, an American of independent means who photographed the domestic life around her Staten Island home, undertook a number of self-portraits which still survive. Among them is *Julia Martin, Julia Bredt and Self Dressed Up as Men 4.40 pm, Thursday October 15th, 1891*. Unlike the masquerade of Mrs von T, this photograph has been read as an attempt to parody the male prerogative rather than lay claim to it. The broad poses and highly typified dress-styles (capped respectively by the deerstalker, boater and top hat), the 'ridiculously phallic umbrella', the sheer amusement suggested by Austen's smiling stance (one which reveals, as Susan Butler notes, both a feminine bosom and the fringe beneath her hat) – all have been adduced to suggest high jinks rather than hysteria:

Julia Martin, Julia Bredt and Self Dressed Up as Men 4.40 pm, Thursday October 15th, 1891. Photograph by Alice Austen (Staten Island Historical Society).

> For if these women steal the attributes of masculinity,
> as the central axis of the umbrella leaves no doubt,
> they hardly do it in a spirit of aspiration. Their theft
> and their playacting serve rather to reveal patriarchal
> postures precisely as such: a series of assumed
> poses.[12]

By making representation – the patriarchal pose – its subject, Austen's photograph seems to resist the continuity of image and identity assumed by the medical gaze. The suited bodies cannot be read symptomatically, as forensic evidence of some transgressive identification, nor as actual disguises. In short, these women look neither butch nor male, particularly in the context of the other two Austen photographs from the 1987 exhibition *Staging the Self*. *Self-Portrait, Full Length with Fan Monday September 9th, 1892* discloses the photographer in evening dress, her hair formally coiffed, neck bared, arms gloved. She is seated on a high-backed chair whose wooden carvings repeat the insistent patterning of her lace-collared dress and the greenery in the background – palm fronds, leaves and a curtain of ivy. Her flounced skirt rests on a carpet whose pattern multiplies the motif. Upon it lies a casually splayed bouquet.

Susan Butler notes that the loosely-clad figure of the previous photograph is now tightly corseted in the style of the time. This, and the photographer's hyperdetailed *mise en scène*, in which virtually every organic form is doubled by its artificial equivalent (the fan splayed like the flowers, the jardinière and its pedestal decorated in ceramic vegetation, the lace trim filigreed like the ivy), might suggest another masquerade, one which leads

Self-Portrait, Full Length with Fan Monday September 9th, 1892.
Photograph by Alice Austen (Staten Island Historical Society).

Butler to register 'a reverse Pygmalion effect . . . of woman become sculpture'.

Ironically, this statuesquely 'feminine' portrait may accomplish the phallic imposture parodied in the previous photograph. As Freud reminds us of another scene of multiplied symbols and bodies turned to stone, the threat of castration can be warded off by the stiffening of the flesh. And art has often assigned this consoling erection to the original source of the horror, the figure of the woman.[13] If this interpretation holds for Austen's *Self-Portrait . . . with Fan*, it reminds us of one of the many paradoxes in the relation of visibility to sexuality: the artistically perfected 'feminine' figure may be more phallic than any woman in male attire.

It is questionable whether one would even hazard these speculations about Austen's work without the 'evidence' provided by her third photograph in *Staging the Self*. In this surprisingly surreal image, two masked women face each other in identical poses, identically clad in white petticoats which reveal their bare arms and stockinged calves. Both hold cigarettes which almost touch, in this evocation of the female figure and her mirror image in the intimacy of the boudoir. The symmetry of the pose and the artifice of its staging are emphasized by the theatrical curtains which border the pair, and apparently enclose the alcove in which they stand. The photograph's title – *Trude and I Masked, Short Skirts 11pm, August 6th, 1891* – records the lateness of the hour, while a description which accompanies the glass negative identifies the setting as the bedrom of Gertrude Tate, 'the woman

with whom [Austen] was to share her life and work for
over forty years'.[14]

Trude and I Masked, Short Skirts 11 pm, August 6th, 1891. Photograph
by Alice Austen (Staten Island Historical Society).

The time, the place, the partial undress of these
women and their gaze at each other offer an irresistibly
erotic reading. This photograph, Butler notes, 'speaks
of desire'. But whose desire? And for whom? The very
doubling that implies a sexual pairing also denies it in a
repetition too exact to suggest an encounter rather than
a reflection. Two women, two cigarettes, two curtains,
with that endlessly repeated floral pattern – the signs of
intimacy proliferate indifferently, to suggest desire
without identity. These figures, after all, are *masked*. If

this anonymity is required by the transgressive circumstances (signalled by the cigarettes and the short skirts as well as the pose), then it presents a problem for self-portraiture. Homosexual desire may be representable, but not the homosexual 'self'. Or again, if the doubling works to represent the homoerotic as fundamentally narcissistic – the desire for the same – identity collapses in a crisis of liminality. Which is self and which is other?

'Or perhaps the question is rather, is there a "true" Alice', Susan Butler concludes in response to this bewildering trio of self-portraits, 'one that could be singled out from the multiple selves or aspects Alice Austen confronts us with?'

We are now a century on from these photographs, a century which has made the deconstruction of the 'true' self one of its central critical projects. But the problems which confronted the representation of homosexuality then still remain. Jean-François Chevrier may consign 'the idea that some reflection of a psychological truth may be recognised in a person's bodily form' to a dark age of Positivism, but in the case of homosexuality the notion of a visible psychology displayed on the body persists.[15] Spurred by the discourses surrounding AIDS, a new generation of taxonomists reconstruct an old anatomy of desire, discovering in every weakened body the predestined consequences of perversion. Meanwhile, we negotiate the contradictions of 'identity politics' in an era which privileges subjective experience even as it declares the crisis of the subject.[16] The recent efforts of the British photographer Rosy Martin to take on both imperatives furnishes us with a final sequence of self-portraits.

Martin's work on lesbian representation emerged from a project of 'phototherapy' developed with Jo Spence. In a joint essay they distinguish the practice from traditional portraiture, 'typified by the notion that people can be represented by showing aspects of their "character" . . . In the course of this work, we have amply demonstrated to ourselves that there is no single self but many fragmented selves, each vying for conscious expression, many never acknowledged.'[17]

To represent this fragmented identity, and its challenge to the historical iconography of lesbianism, Martin returns us to the 1890s and Ellis's characterization of the female invert: 'a disdain for the petty feminine artifices of the toilet' . . . 'masculine straightforwardness' . . . 'a decided taste and toleration for cigars' . . . 'nothing of that sexual shyness and engaging air of weakness and dependence which are an invitation to men'.[18] These phrases accompany a five-panel 1986 project entitled *Extract from Transforming the Suit*. Martin is the model in all the photographs, which can be read from left to right, from long shot to medium close-up, from phallic (the admonishing finger and brandished cigar) to vaginal (the lily), from domineering to withdrawn.

Transforming the Suit – What Do Lesbians Look Like? Rosy Martin, Sitter/Director; Jo Spence, Photographer/Therapist.

This spectrum of psychical identities anticipates a prominent new current in the theorization of lesbianism, to judge not only from the 'Perverse Politics' issue of the British journal *Feminist Review*, but also recent philosophical studies like Judith Butler's *Gender Trouble*. While the latter poses the homosexual as the postmodern Proteus, whose 'sexual nonidentity' exposes 'the illusion of an abiding gendered self',[19] the contributors to the former issue queue up to formulate a definition of lesbianism 'based on a mobility of desire, an oscillation of identifications':[20]

> Today's lesbian 'self' is a thoroughly urban creature who interprets fashion as something to be worn and discarded. Nothing is sacred for very long. Constantly changing, she dabbles in fashion, constructing one self after another, expressing her desires in a continual process of experimentation.[21]

It isn't inappropriate to characterize this model Ms in the rhetoric of the fashion spread, since she seems subject to a process of idealization not wholly unlike that which led Hall's readers to 'embrace' Stephen Gordon. So self-conscious a celebration of evanescent selfhood brings to mind Laura Marcus's reservations about the recent vogue in psychoanalytic autobiography: 'the autobiographical self can remain intact while gesturing towards and remaining in authority over structures which could disrupt this position'.[22]

A similar reluctance to de-centre the subject is detectable, I would argue, in *Transforming the Suit*. 'Many fragmented selves' may be on display, but they are not ordered arbitrarily. Both the title and the traditional direction of reading draw us away from the severely tailored figure of Ellis's description, while a similar pull is exerted by the successive reframings, which build to the alluring intimacy of the close-up. But the coy femme at the extreme right is as stylized as the bossy butch opposite, and the sense of exaggeration sends us back to the median figure, whose centrality, scale and apparently uninflected pose mark it as the apex of the series. This symbolic midpoint coincides with a direct gaze (emphasized by the spectacles), unfussy hairstyle, softly tailored suit . . . and the flower, now worn as a boutonnière: a combination of gender signifiers to be sure, but organized into a single, intact (and historically recognizable) 'identity'.

The paradoxical project of *Transforming the Suit* – the simultaneous assertion and deconstruction of identity – provoked these thoughts on the lesbian self-portrait. Indeed, all the images here could be exhibited under Martin's title. My concern in tracing such transformations across a century of photographic practice is not to document a succession of lesbian identities so much as to register that paradox, and the problems it presents to photography's promise to record identity. If these photographs 'show' us anything, it may be only this: that the lesbian self-portrait is as persistent as it is impossible.

portrait of a marriage?

I

If one liked him, was it marriage? If one liked other
people, was it marriage?

(Virginia Woolf, *Orlando*)

When the *Guardian* previewer blandly noted that the
BBC's *Portrait of a Marriage* might have been better titled
Portrait of an Affair,[1] he struck a sore spot in current
'queer' criticism – the heterosexualization of the homo-
sexual romance. If the screens of the 1980s suddenly
featured that romance to an unprecedented extent
(*Lianna, Another Way, Personal Best, Making Love, Parting
Glances, Kiss of the Spiderwoman, My Beautiful Laundrette,
Another Country, Prick Up Your Ears, Maurice, Desert
Hearts, Torch Song Trilogy* in the cinema; *Brideshead
Revisited* and *The Rainbow* on television), its specifically
homosexual character seemed to be qualified at every
turn. While film-makers nervously insisted upon the
'universality' (i.e. heterosexuality) of titles as various as
Lianna ('people I knew, both gay and straight, have been
through the same experiences': director John Sayles[2])
and *Prick Up Your Ears* ('a universal story': producer

Andrew Brown[3]), lesbian and gay critics began to conclude that they were absolutely right. As Simon Watney
observed about *Making Love*, the film is no more
interested in homosexuality than it is in lovemaking
itself:

> That is to say, it carefully avoids the whole messy
> business of sex. Love is about 'feelings'. As Roberta
> Flack croons in the film's title song, 'there's more to
> love than making love'.

In this case – and it isn't the only one – that surplus
turns out to be marriage: '*Making Love*', Watney argues,
'explores the meaning of marriage in today's middle-
class America.'[4]

Mark Finch comes to a similar conclusion in his
reading of *Prick Up Your Ears* as not only 'a relationship
movie' (in the wilfully ambiguous phrase of its American
publicist) but one centrally focused on marital relationships. The characterization of Joe Orton's lover, Ken
Halliwell, as a 'neurotic wife-figure gives the film its
central metaphor. The difficulties of heterosexual marriage are both explored and relieved through this
analogy.'[5]

If marriage is the theme of these homosexual scenarios, melodrama is their appropriate form. As Watney
notes, *Making Love*'s publicity slogan ('After eight happy
years of marriage Claire Elliott is discovering there's
someone new in her husband's life') sets up both the
viewpoint and the dilemma typical of the woman's film.[6]
Similarly, Finch identifies Halliwell as only one of *Prick
Up Your Ears*'s unhappy housewives – parallel roles are

assigned to the patient spouse of Orton's biographer and to Orton's sister, shown quarrelling with her husband. (If there are any doubts about the film's intended genre, Finch clinches his argument by noting that Alan Bennett's original script is introduced by Elizabeth Hardwick's observations on the disadvantages of the marriage contract for women and closes with an [abandoned] final scene showing yet another unhappy heterosexual couple later residing in the Islington flat where Orton and Halliwell lived and died.)

Finch's reading of *Maurice* (written in collaboration with Richard Kwietniowski) elaborates the symbiosis of homosexuality and melodrama. This, after all, is a genre with a past. Historically, Hollywood melodrama has been saturated with homosexual associations arising from its 'exaggerated' performance style and actual personnel, as well as the gay following generated by 'an empathy with melodrama's painful impossibilities, and also an ironic appreciation of the genre's excesses, or camp'.

But even these associations cannot withstand the heterosexual bias of the form. Homosexuals appear in these texts 'not as subjects', warn Finch and Kwietniowski, 'but as symptoms, effects of disorder'.[7] And as a modern melodrama, *Maurice* (whatever its art cinema inscriptions) is again preoccupied by marriage, with the familiar figure of the wife torn between duty and desire literally divided into two – Maurice (who risks everything for a romance with his best friend's under-gamekeeper) and Clive (who renounces Maurice for an evidently undesired spouse and a safe seat in the shires). As Finch and Kwietniowski conclude: 'The film brings together the impossibility of Maurice and Scudder as a sunset romance, and Clive's unhappy sublimation. The happy homosexual is, then, apparently a contradiction in terms, like the fulfilled woman.'[8]

And so, warned of the screen's predisposition to make homosexuality mean marriage, wifehood, infidelity, lost youth, confession, class privilege – anything but itself – lesbian and gay critics came to the BBC dramatization of *Portrait of a Marriage* (serialized in four weekly parts, 19 September–10 October 1990) sadder but wiser. Thus Elizabeth Wilson's response to the drama in a piece on the 'intense cultural ambivalence' suggested by the 'higher visibility' of homosexuality in the British media at a time of anti-homosexual repression:

> But if everyone hates lesbians, why screen it at all? We never discover . . . what Vita Sackville-West's affair with Violet Trefusis was supposed to tell us either about marriage or about itself.
>
> But, could it be that gay love is the lens through which heterosexual society is desperately peering at its own problematic practices?[9]

II

An important piece of advice to wives is: Be always escaping.

(Marie Stopes, *Married Love*)

Those who turn to Nigel Nicolson's *Portrait of a Marriage* for the book of the film will scarcely recognize it. The

1973 volume is divided into five sections, only one of which contains Vita's account of her affair with Violet Trefusis. The rest includes an autobiographical sketch which moves from the author's ancestry to her own early married life, and three substantial sections of commentary by Nicolson himself. Without these, he maintains in the volume's foreword, publication of the memoir would have done 'my parents less than justice, for it was written in the eighth year of a marriage which lasted forty-nine'. And he describes his final commentary (which takes us from the waning of the Trefusis affair in 1920 to his father's death in 1968) as 'a justification for the whole book and of its title, for it summarizes the remaining years of her marriage, and shows . . . how my parents' love for each other survived all further threats to it, and made out of a non-marriage a marriage which succeeded beyond their dreams'.[10]

Vita's marriage to Harold Nicolson is not the only unorthodox one in this *Portrait*. Her memoir recounts her grandfather's liaison with the Spanish dancer who bore him five illegitimate children, the extra-marital attachments of both her parents, and a similar *ménage* in the family of her schoolmate Violet, whose mother was the mistress of King Edward VII:

> Often when I went to their house I used to see a
> discreet little one-horse brougham waiting outside
> and the butler would slip me into a dark corner of the
> hall with a murmured, 'One minute miss, a
> gentleman is coming downstairs.' (p. 26)

Vita Sackville-West grew up, then, in a world of complicated marriages, in which legitimacy, property and
propriety were frequently in crisis. Her memoir in
Portrait of a Marriage may be brief, but it includes the
lawsuit her uncle brought against her father for succession to the Sackville title, and another celebrated court
case in which the family of Sir John Murray Scott
contested his will, which named Vita's mother as chief
beneficiary. (It is worth noting that Vita's parents won
these cases, establishing in the process both her mother's
illegitimacy and her intimacy with Scott – to great
publicity but little disapproval.)

In the light of these Edwardian arrangements, the
successful marriage of two people who were 'constantly
and by mutual consent unfaithful to each other' (p. 3)
may seem less surprising than it would otherwise. (So
might Vita and Violet's conviction that they would be
freer to continue their affair if Violet married.) But by
the end of the War (and the beginning of that romance)
new ideas about marriage had begun to circulate – ideas
which also encouraged greater freedom between
spouses, not for aristocratic convenience but as 'the only
secure basis for a present-day State'.[11]

In the winter of 1918–19, when Vita was travelling in
France with Violet, Harold Nicolson read *Married Love*.
Marie Stopes's 'new contribution to the solution of sex
difficulties' had been the sensation of 1918, reaching six
editions by its close. Victoria Glendinning notes that
Harold 'rushed' to write to his wife about it:

It is wonderful: it goes into every detail. There is a
whole chapter which explains why Hadji goes to sleep

and Mar doesn't. I find I am the *rule* and not the exception . . . But I am appalled at my own ignorance . . . I know that you must have suffered terribly – and that only a splendid character like yours could have kept from hating me.[12]

Stopes's remedy for this wifely insomnia was orgasm, for which she offered husbands both a schedule ('three or four days of repeated unions, followed by about ten days without any' (p. 78)) and a map:

> Woman has at the surface a small vestigial organ called the clitoris, which corresponds morphologically to the man's penis and which, like it, is extremely sensitive to touch-sensations. This little crest, which lies anteriorly between the inner lips round the vagina, erects itself when the woman is really tumescent. (p. 87)

This stress on the phallic attributes of female sexuality is an important theme in *Married Love* and, I will suggest, in the television *Portrait*. Despite Stopes's description of the man as 'still essentially the hunter, the one who experiences the desires and thrills of the chase, and dreams ever of coming unawares upon Diana in the woodlands' (p. 114), her prescription for companionate marriage relies upon the reduction rather than the enhancement of sexual difference. 'Marriage', she argues, 'can never reach its full stature until women possess as much intellectual freedom and freedom of opportunity within it as do their partners' (pp. 156–7). To those freedoms she adds that of

107

association, decrying the cramped spaces and conventions of middle-class marriage, which encourage the couple to sleep, dress and entertain together at all times. In defence of extra-marital friendship she cites no less an authority than Edward Carpenter on 'that excellent dual love of man and wife . . . fed also by the love they give to others' (p. 146).

Marriage, Stopes maintains, requires 'complete and unquestioning trust', with each partner free to go on 'visits, week-ends or walking tours' (p. 154) without the other. The recreative powers of separation are stressed, as are the damaging effects of close cohabitation, particularly the 'unbeautiful trivialities' (p. 113) of the shared bathroom. In the interest of maintaining the fragile ardour of their hunter husbands, wives are advised to 'be always escaping. Escape the lower, the trivial, the sordid . . .' (p. 115).

It wasn't only Harold who took Stopes seriously. Both he and Vita spent a good deal of their subsequent careers propagating views like hers via the wireless and the printed page. In 1929, the couple conducted a scripted discussion on 'Marriage' for the BBC. In it they advised husbands to cultivate 'the feminine qualities of gentleness, sensitiveness and intuition'[13] and wives to develop the masculine virtues of reason and detachment. Harold stood up for mutual esteem, and Vita for women's careers. 'The caveman plus sweet-little-thing theory', she observed, 'is long past.'[14] The producer of this programme was one Hilda Matheson, then BBC Director of Talks. The BBC's listeners might have been surprised to learn that she was also at that time Vita's lover. If this is an irony, it is one which is repeated in

Vita's final novel, and her most sustained discussion of marriage.

The story of a shipboard romance between a beautiful widow and a distinguished journalist with only months to live, *No Signposts in the Sea* seems an apt choice for its serialization in the 1961 *Woman's Own*. As Laura and Edmund cruise the south seas, they discuss marriage in precisely Stopesian terms, even to Laura's aversion to connubial 'hair-combings floating in a basin of soapy water'.[15] At times their dialogue echoes Harold and Vita's radio talk:

> 'And what about community of interests?'
> 'Nice, but not essential. What *is* essential, is the same set of values.'
> 'Meaning that one must be shocked, or otherwise, by the same things?'
> 'Exactly. And amused by the same things too.'
> (p. 87)

Despite all this heterosexual harmony, *No Signposts in the Sea* is the only novel in which Sackville-West actually discusses homosexuality. Both main characters, in the course of their conversations, find it necessary to deny that they are 'that way inclined', and Laura comments at length on the pleasures and perils of lesbianism:

> Then, or so I have been given to understand, the concord may approach perfection. You see, there is a kind of free-masonry between women – and no doubt between men also – which makes up for the elemental excitement of the sex-war.' (p. 135)

Are Laura's observations on this subject (which go on for nearly as long as her views on marriage) a 'red herring', as Edmund concludes afterwards? Or are they in some way important to a novel about 'workable marriage', a novel in which the principals never *do* marry, or even confess their love, before Edmund's sudden demise? Nor, despite its theme, is this novel dedicated to the author's husband, but to 'Edie' – Edith Lamont, a widow herself at the time of the book's writing, and Vita's last lover.

III

Brideshead for dykes

(Elizabeth Wilson, *New Statesman*)

Seventeen years separate Nigel Nicolson's *Portrait* and that of the BBC. Predictably, the television dramatization was preceded by precisely the sort of denial recorded by gay critics. 'Portrait of a Marriage', its producer solemnly informed the *Radio Times*, was about 'a human triangle . . . To get sidetracked on issues of lesbianism is irrelevant. It's the story of a woman torn between two lovers, one of whom happens to be a woman.'[16]

In one sense the script (by Penelope Mortimer, the former wife of *Brideshead Revisited* adaptor John Mortimer) contrived to create that impression, if only by concentrating on the most easily dramatized episode in Nicolson's text, the Violet–Vita–Harold conflict. As Mortimer herself admitted,[17] this was accomplished by sacrificing Vita's numerous other lovers, with the exception of a brief name-check for Rosamund Grosvenor, the object of her adolescent passion. Meanwhile, Harold's lifelong homosexuality was consigned to even greater ignominy, being figured in the first instance as disease, the venereal infection which prompts him to confess his 'diversions' to Vita, thus setting off Mortimer's plot and the bizarre sexual aetiology summarized by the television critic of *Today*:

> First Harold told Vita he was gay. Then Violet
> Trefusis confessed her love for Vita. All of which left
> poor old Vita feeling terribly confused.[18]

This truncated narrative may offer the advantage, within the terms of heterosexuality, of presenting the heroine's passion for another woman as a largely reactive affair, a matter of circumstance rather than conscious intent, but its sheer concentration on that episode also produced a counter-effect. As Nigel Nicolson was to complain in *The Times*, Mortimer's adaptation was not 'the portrait of a marriage, but the portrait of an affair'. The BBC had ignored his written (but not contractual) stipulations that the drama show the lesbian relationship as 'a crazy escapade, from which Vita just recovered in time, largely owing to Harold's extraordinary gentleness and understanding . . . the triumph of love over infatuation'. And contrary to his insistence that there be 'no pawing or mutual undressing', the couple were 'filmed semi-clothed or naked in and out of bed, writhing in passionate embraces'.[19]

Comments like these ensured the BBC a *succès de*

111

scandale even before their *Portrait* was transmitted. The tabloids immediately dispatched their representatives to Sissinghurst, where officials of the National Trust were said to be holding an 'emergency briefing' on the 'awkward questions' likely to be asked by inquisitive visitors.[20] And indeed, by the drama's fourth and final week, *The Times* Diary reported 'hundreds' of queries to Sissinghurst staff about the precise location of 'passionate female embraces', and the official reply that 'nothing like that happens on National Trust property'.[21] British viewers might be forgiven for assuming that something like that seems to happen rather often on National Trust property, or its stage lot equivalent, since the *Brideshead* genre now rivals the stately home as a leading heritage industry. (Quentin Crisp's coinage – 'the stately homos of England' – was surprisingly absent from reviews of this drama.) But the problem of this *Portrait* – marriage or affair? heterosexual or homosexual? – is not easily resolved by referring to its conventions.

As a sub-genre of the classic serial introduced on British television with Trollope's *The Warden* in 1951,[22] the 'white flannel'[23] drama has traditionally associated homosexuality with youth, the upper classes and the past. But the youthful characterization of its lovers also corresponds to wider presentations of the subject, for the homosexual romance is frequently written as a *Bildungsroman*, with that form's emphasis on the young individual seeking personal happiness. (Lesbian fiction is replete with autobiographical novels in this vein: *Rubyfruit Jungle* is *Not the Only Fruit*, one might say.)

Franco Moretti associates this personal temporality with that of history: in the late-eighteenth-century novel, he suggests, youth comes to represent *modernity*, even *modernization*.[24] The combination clearly survives in contemporary fiction, with its linking of the central figure's assumption of homosexuality to the new politics of feminism and gay liberation.

But the 'white flannel' film undercuts that equation by placing its youth in the *past* – making homosexuality a sort of phylogenetic phase on the way to a more mature culture. This, together with the remote class location of its characters and the overtones of gentility bestowed by the drama's literary antecedents and museum *mise en scène*, puts its homosexual romance at what is often seen to be a safe distance from contemporary appropriation.

Ironically, Nicolson's protests served to drag this costume drama briskly into the present. Where he maintained – at the age of seventy-three – that neither audiences nor actresses were ready 'for scenes of explicit sexual love between women',[25] both the players and the producers could respond that these presented no problems to contemporary standards. As producer Colin Tucker argued to the *Daily Mail*, 'We think we got it right for 1990'.[26]

In another sense, Nicolson's own status as the son of Harold and Vita also contributed to the latter-day relevance of the BBC *Portrait*. Here, in the face of the notorious Section 28 of the Local Government Act, was living proof that homosexuality need not 'pretend' to family relationships – indeed, that perverts could produce children. And his much-reported horror at the drama's 'pawing' and 'mutual undressing' – 'Naturally, no son likes to see his mother portrayed in these circumstances'[27] – offered viewers the *frisson* of a real primal scene – enacted in the past, perhaps, but witnessed in the present by both the television audience and the affronted child.

IV

VITA SEEKS HADJI . . . Looking for tolerant, quiet, intelligent man with whom to grow beautiful life together.

(Personal ad, *City Limits*)

The autumn 1990 transmission of *Portrait of a Marriage* could not have been more timely. In Bournemouth, the annual Conservative Party Conference railed against the vast increase in divorce and single motherhood. Meanwhile, the Department of Health and Social Security was preparing a White Paper providing for greater powers to extract maintenance payments from absent fathers (while deducting any such receipts from the state benefits currently paid to two-thirds of single mothers). At the same time the Law Commission was drawing up proposals to retard divorce, described by a study published that autumn as 'now as central to our culture and experience as death and taxes'.[28]

In the midst of these events, David Haig, in the guise of Harold Nicolson, drank whisky in a panelled drawing-room with a sympathetic companion played by the actor previously cast as the homosexual Viscount Risley in *Maurice*. To Nicolson's hesitant confession of misery at his wife's new-found passion and his fears that he is 'no ladies' man', 'Risley' (now 'Reggie') replies: 'But

Vita's very much what they call a man's woman . . . a woman who's tough and honourable. Female rather than feminine . . .'. The exchange occurs in the middle of the drama's second part, the drag episode which opens with Violet spending the night in a lodging-house with Vita dressed as her soldier husband. It moves to the couple's scandalous first sojourn in France (Vita alternating men's dress with the most fetishistic female costumes of the drama – towering hats and furs, glittering dresses and jewelled hairpieces). As Harold pens rapt accounts of *Married Love* to a *poste restante* in Monte Carlo, the two women tango in a local bar stocked – in the iconographic overkill of prestige drama – with refugees from Grosz and Brassaï. The episode closes in Paris, with Harold arriving for the Peace Conference in the midst of marital war (a martial motif signalled in the first episode by the opening shots of a German bomber squadron flying over Sissinghurst). There he discovers, in the couple's discarded luggage, another portrait – Violet and Vita, posed for a souvenir photograph before a painted backdrop of the Eiffel Tower. In an agony of revulsion he recognizes the suited figure leaning against the lady and tears the picture apart.

That final sequence furnishes an easy emblem for a reading of this *Portrait*: to restore his marriage, Harold must tear the lesbian couple apart. But I think we should resist this conclusion until we consider the episode's reference to *Married Love*. In his letter to Vita, Harold cites the study on the restlessness of the unsatisfied wife: 'Now I know why Hadji goes to sleep and Mar doesn't' (a line which is quoted in Mortimer's script). Stopes's remedy for that restlessness, we may recall, was the recognition of the phallic organ of female sexuality, the clitoris, 'which corresponds morphologically to the man's penis'. Similarly, her recipe for marital harmony required that wives be afforded the masculine prerogatives of privacy, opportunity and freedom. In place of the ladies' man of patriarchal chivalry, companionate marriage raises up the man's woman, tough and honourable, female rather than feminine.

In their different ways, both the literary and the television *Portrait* seem to be meditations on this theme. With the new man (and here the casting of both Harold and Denys Trefusis departed from verisimilitude to make them both smaller and less imposing than all the commentaries suggest) goes the new woman. Thus the emphatic role reversal of Part II, in which Harold's exemption from military service is juxtaposed with Vita's uniform, and his 'fin-de-siècle' reserve with her disguise as a working-class husband. (The point is extravagantly underlined in her announcement to Violet – while the two lie naked together in bed – 'If I were a man and he were a girl, I would have married him just the same.')

But this phallicization of the heroine plunges this drama into the quandary from which it cannot escape, for the logic of its marriage settlement is precisely perverse. If the wife is really to be assigned the masculine prerogative, why should it stop at sex with other women? Heterosexual amity would seem to require the very homosexuality which threatens to destroy it. Or as Harold writes to Violet after Vita's death (a complete Mortimer invention voiced over a reprised shot of the young couple arm in arm, her greater height emphasized by her upswept hair): 'One cannot expect to have fifty years of such companionship and not have to pay for it one day.'

In his critique of films like *Prick Up Your Ears*, Mark Finch argues that 'although they sustain narratives of homosexual passion and romance, their ultimate allegiance is to heterosexuality'. One doesn't need the testimony of this *Portrait*'s producer – 'living a respectable mortgaged life and then thinking, hang on, isn't there something else?'[29] – to suspect that its allegiance is at least strained.

As if in anticipation of Elizabeth Wilson's optical metaphor – that homosexuality functions transparently, like a lens through which heterosexuality may study itself – the *Daily Telegraph* reprovingly headlined its preview of this drama 'Marriage Viewed from a Perverse Perspective'.[30] That vantage point is anything but neutral, but it may always be a logical place from which to view the drama of modern marriage. As Judith Butler reminds us, the failure of heterosexuality to secure its status as a compulsory system undermines the boundaries – marriage *or* affair, heterosexual *or* homosexual – it would enact in law.[31] It may not always avail the homosexual critic to rebuild them – not even in pursuit of portraits of ourselves.

heroines

the Amazons of ancient Athens

But it seems to me fitting that I should speak also of the
city's achievements against the barbarians . . . Now,
while the most celebrated of our wars was the one
against the Persians, yet certainly our deeds of old offer
evidence no less strong for those who dispute over
ancestral rights. For while Hellas was still insignificant,
our territory was invaded by the Thracians, led by
Eumolpus, son of Poseidon, and by the Scythians, led by
the Amazons, the daughters of Ares.

(Isocrates, *Panegyricus*, 65–8)[1]

As the women's movement debates its own cultural
feminism, it seems appropriate to reconsider that ideology's signal motif – the image of the Amazon. Beneath
the welter of contemporary mythographies lies, as
Adrienne Rich has observed, a valid purpose:

Today, one quest of women is a search for models or
blueprints of female power which shall be neither
replications of male power nor carbon-copies of the
male stereotype of the powerful, controlling
destructive woman. The resurgence of interest in the

121

work of J.J. Bachofen, Robert Briffault, Joseph
Campbell, Robert Graves, Helen Diner, Jane
Harrison, the response generated by E.G. Davis's
'The First Sex', has been in part a search for
vindication of the belief that patriarchy is in some
ways a degeneration, that women exerting power
would use it differently from men: nonpossessively,
nonviolently, nondestructively.[2]

A feminist history, a meditation on life unstructured by
patriarchy – these are important, if not necessarily
similar, projects. But the Amazon myth stands at a
stubborn distance from them, mediated by successive
generations of analysis which have come to be conflated
into the semblance of a single story.

Here Rich's bibliography is in itself revealing, combining as it does mythographies of very different purpose.
Can we resort indiscriminately to a contemporary radical feminist like Davis ('Only the overthrow of the
three-thousand-year-old beast of masculinist materialism will save the race'[3]) and a nineteenth-century evolu-
tionary patriarchalist like Bachofen ('The triumph of
paternity brings with it the liberation of the spirit from
the manifestations of nature, a sublimation of human
existence over the laws of material life'[4])?

If commentators as disparate as Davis and Bachofen
have anything in common, it is literalism – their reading
of myth as an actual record of the past. Shackled by the
nineteenth-century's fundamentalist antiquarianism,
their inquiries fail to consider myth (whatever its connection to history) as ideology, and mythmaking as itself
a historical event.

Davis prefaces the final chapter of *The First Sex* with a citation from Edward Carpenter celebrating 'the new young women of today who, as the period of feminine enslavement passes away, send glances of recognition across the ages to their elder sisters'. If we take this as her – and our – purpose, we must be doubly wary of any uncritical appropriation of the Amazon myth. Across the ages our glance is met, not by our elder sisters, but by their several images in a hall of distorting mirrors. The Amazon myth flourished, after all, in ancient Greece, particularly the state of Athens – a patriarchy which extensively mythologized women, but recorded first few – and then none – of their words, a culture distinguished both for its unusual degree of female subordination and for its fascination with female dominance.

However feminists choose to recover the tradition, it seems essential to examine its first political uses. Contemporary commentators may argue for the actual existence of the warring tribes, or simply for the importance of the myth as a postulate of female power in Antiquity. Neither view is politically adequate without an understanding of how the Greeks actually employed the image of 'the daughters of Ares'.

First, this essay considers the historical construction of the myth of the warrior women by the Greeks. The Amazons, I would argue, are introduced into myth not as an independent force but as the vanquished opponents of heroes credited with the establishment and protection of the Athenian state – its founding fathers, so to speak. Patriotism reinforces patriarchalism to define the tribeswomen as opponents of the state, an image potent enough to be invoked by aspirant politicians.

Second, it locates the myth within the context of Athenian misogyny, where it may have functioned as a justification of that culture's radical subordination of women.

Finally, this essay questions the contemporary appropriation of the myth by feminists. Is the image of the warrior women severable from its originating context? Does it discourage or inspire our struggle against a constraining definition of femininity?

Early sources

The earliest known references to the Amazons occur in the *Iliad*. Five times the warrior women, or one of their number, are named, twice at some length: in Book 2 (lines 189 ff.) Priam, the King of Troy, recalls a youthful military campaign in Phrygia:

> and there I saw in multitudes the Phrygian warriors, masters of glancing steeds, even the peoples of Otreus and godlike Mygdon, that were then encamped along the banks of the Sangarius. For I, too, being their ally, was numbered among them on the day when the Amazons came, the peers of men . . .

In Book 6 (179 ff.) they are named as one of the epochal foes killed by the Greek hero Bellerophon:

> first he bade him slay the raging Chimaera. She was of divine stock, not of men, in the fore part a lion, in the

hinder a serpent, and in the midst a goat, breathing
forth in terrible wise the might of blazing fire. And
Bellerophon slew her, trusting in the signs of the
gods. Next fought he with the glorious Solymi, and
this, said he, was the mightiest battle of warriors that
ever he entered; and thirdly he slew the Amazons,
women peers of men.

Here the Amazons already have a mythic status – peers
not just of men but of the great heroes – and a firm
place in the epic catalogue of legendary warriors. The
oldest references are already allusive, although in a
sense this is true for all the matter of the early epics,
proceeding as they do from oral tradition. The problems of their dating and authorship are immense, but it
is generally agreed that Homer, or whoever wrote the
Iliad, must have lived before 700 BC (probably sometime
in the eighth century), and that the nearest approxi-
mation of the Troy of the poem is the archaeologically
designated Troy VIIIa, which flourished for about forty
years before its destruction by fire in the first half of the
thirteenth century BC.

This casts the historical basis of the *Iliad* into the
Mycenaean Bronze Age, a civilization which antedated
that of Homer by half a millennium. But Mycenaean
Greece's relation to the later Iron Age civilization of the
epics is extremely vague, not least because much of its
history, and that of the intervening 'Dark Age', is
unwritten.

Another suggested point of origin for the myth is the
Hittite civilization, which dominated Asia Minor in the
second millennium and came in contact with the Greek

colonies in the eastern Aegean around the twelfth century. There is a great deal of rather fanciful debate about whether the Amazons were really clean-shaven Hittites, or whether their costumes in later vase-paintings include items of Hittite apparel.[5] More interesting is Mina Zografou's suggestion that the term 'Amazon' refers to a mixed-sex ethnic group who lived in Asia Minor during the era of Hittite dominion:

> what the Greeks considered as an Amazonic way of
> life and where the women fought in the wars . . . the
> inexistence of the concept of marriage and
> fatherhood . . . the custom of child-production
> through ritual promiscuity and . . . the resistance . . .
> to adopt the patriarchalistic customs that were
> brought and imposed by the peoples who placed Zeus
> at the head of the hierarchy of the gods detronizing
> [*sic*] the old Mother-Goddess.[6]

Unfortunately, Zografou's work at transliterating Homeric names and comparing them to contemporary Hittite records yields no more than a very speculative account of some possibly matrilineal Asian societies possibly involved in the political and ethnic upheavals which shook the thirteenth-century Aegean.

However, this essay does not purport to investigate the historical reality of the Amazon myth, but that of its application. In this I am encouraged by Martin Nilsson's observations on the subject:

> It is uncertain what real fact underlies the myth of the
> race of warlike women, the Amazons. The opinion

has been brought forward that they are a reminiscence of the Hittite empire, but that cannot be proved conclusively, though it may be possible. If this is so, the myths originated in the Mycenaean age. I am not able to make any decision, but I should like to observe that this myth was so famous it was sooner or later applied to the most famous hero, Heracles.[7]

It is how the myth was 'sooner or later applied', its ideological uses in patriarchal society, which concern us here.

The next source for the Amazon myth is a post-Homeric epic by Arctinus of Miletus (eighth century BC). His *Aethiopis* does not survive, but we know from a summary in Proclus' (AD 410 or 412–485) *Literary Chrestomathia* (a handbook of classical Greek literature) that it was part of an eight-section Trojan cycle which included the *Iliad* and the *Odyssey*.[8] Proclus' work, and other writings of post-Homeric and even post-classical authors, suggest a much broader body of sources than are available today. Even allowing for embellishments and plain inventions by later authors (and I will argue that these were extensive and often done with specific political motivations) the Amazon corpus seems to have been well established, and available for allusion, by the eighth century. Gradually additional details were invented and/or written down, but most of what remains dates from long after the Homeric era, and is imbued with a sense of the subject's already mythic status.

The eighth-century *Aethiopis* takes up the story of Troy after the killing of Hector by Achilles. Proclus' summary of the episode includes the arrival of the

Amazon queen Penthesilea and her army from Thrace. This is already a departure from Homer (and an anomaly in the tradition generally, which tends to place the tribes-women in the eastern or north-eastern Aegean) and one historian suggests a political reason for this location: 'The change by Arktinos from Asia Minor to Thrace perhaps reflects increasing Ionian interest in the northern Aegean coasts and the Thraceward regions about 700 BC.'[9]

Penthesilea allies her army with the besieged Trojans, confronts the Acheans, and dies at the hands of Achilles. A later account by the Byzantine scholar Photius simply says:

> In the pride of her valour Achilles slays her, and the Trojans bury her. Achilles destroys Thersites for speaking slander against him and carping at his alleged love for Penthesilea; whence there is a division among the Greeks in regard to the murder of Thersites.[10]

The Heracles theme

About the time of the *Aethiopis* another Greek hero, one who shall have even greater implications for the patriotic application of the myth, joins Achilles and Bellerophon in the story. Much of the Heracles myth is already present in the *Iliad*, but not his conquest of the Amazons. It is in his *Catalogue of Women* that we find Hesiod (born sometime before 700 BC) referring briefly to:

> the mighty Herakles, when he was journeying in quest of the horses of proud Laomedon – horses of the fleetest of foot that the Asian land nourished – and

128

destroyed in battle the tribe of the dauntless Amazons and drove them forth from all that land.[11]

This is the earliest available text of a story better known to us in subsequent versions.[12] In it the heroic strong-man, a son of Zeus and the mortal Alcmene, is forced by Zeus' jealous wife Hera to serve his elder cousin Eurystheus through a series of heroic deeds. These twelve labours, the popular subject of legend and art, include a voyage to the Amazon capital Themiscyra on the river Thermodon. There he was to secure for Eurystheus' daughter the golden girdle given by Ares to the Amazon queen. Accounts of what resulted vary (with another hero, Theseus, taking a greater part as he superseded Heracles in Attic cult) but the burden of the tale has Heracles eventually take the trophy by force, sometimes killing or kidnapping the queen or her sister, and returning with it to Greece.

Like Achilles, Heracles is associated with a complex sex antagonism (initiated by Hera literally in the womb when, hearing Zeus announce that on that day a child of his would be born who would rule the land, she arranged for the earlier birth of another of his descend-ants) and legendary martial success.[13] But typologically he is far closer to Bellerophon – like him obliged to perform a series of heroic tasks to expiate crimes (Bellerophon's murder of Bellerus and his own brother Deliades; Heracles' insane killing of his children, two nephews and – in some versions – his first wife Megara). It may be these similarities that permit him to supplant Bellerophon, while the Achilles–Penthesilea story main-tains a lateral popularity.

Where literary sources are missing we have the evidence of Greek ceramics. The first recognizable Amazons, on a terracotta votive shield found at Tiryns, probably date from the eighth century. But it is in the second quarter of the sixth century (575–550 BC) that the subject becomes popular with vase-painters, 'arriving suddenly and in force, without any apparent

The first recognizable Amazons, on a terracotta votive shield found at Tiryns, probably eighth century BC.

antecedents'.[14] Almost all of it is Attic – produced, that is, in Athens or that city's surrounds.

From the beginning the dominant theme is the battle between the Greek heroes and the warrior women (known as 'Amazonomachies' from the Greek root 'machy' – 'struggle'). The subject had obvious compositional advantages for the silhouette style of black-figure painting, but the abundance of martial episodes in Greek myth negates this as the explanation of its popularity. ('The fight is second in popularity only to the Lion and better represented than most Labours in the second quarter of the century.'[15]) Nor does it explain the frequency with which Heracles figures as the Amazons' named or iconographically identifiable opponent.

We do know that Heracles is a central icon of the period, accounting for some 44 per cent of all mythic representations on Athenian vases, He often appears in conjunction with his patron, the city's eponymous deity, Athena (an association which goes back to even non-Athenian art in the seventh century). Belief in such patronage not only canonized mythic figures, it was also used to legitimate the claims of aspiring rulers.

Victor Ehrenberg reminds us how important the local heroes were in a region of culturally homogeneous but competitive city-states:

> The heroes had their special importance . . . they were by their graves and by the character of their cult more closely bound to the soil than most of the gods; they represented a strong element of intense religious life, and their cult formed the centre of many small associations . . . [which] could also grow into a kind of

representative of the state. The majority of the heroes had once been great men of the epic stories and thus were intimately associated with the form of life which belonged to the times of the clans and their contests. They did their part in breaking Greece up into its many political units; in the mythical contests between heroes the actual fights between states found both model and expression.[16]

Interestingly, Heracles' Panhellenic importance exempts him from Ehrenberg's observations (although it may make his cult that much more appealing to an aspiring imperial power). And indeed, he may have been introduced into Athenian veneration through his mythic connections with the city's goddess rather than any local association of his own. But however his cult was established, it was sufficiently representative of the Athenian state to interest the sixth-century politician Pisistratus.

In staging his repeated coups, this tyrant was rather given to the *beau geste*. (When we consider how important popular support was to the tyrant's challenge to the aristocratic oligarchy, this is not surprising.) Pisistratus' first seizure of power involved his capture of the Acropolis, the city's citadel and its sacred precinct. In attendance was a bodyguard armed with clubs, the traditional weapon of Heracles in contemporary painting. A deliberate reminiscence of the hero's much-represented 'Introduction to Olympus'? 'Promoting himself', John Boardman argues, 'to be a neighbour of the gods, of Athena in particular, might well appear a form of apotheosis to the myth-minded.'[17]

After a brief reign, the tyrant was exiled. But his return to Athens in the 550s was, if Herodotus is to be believed, even flashier. This time the allusion to Athena's presentation of her ward to the Olympians took the form of a charade: the politician arranged for an unusually tall and comely woman to dress in full armour and mount a chariot.

> Then having rehearsed her in the most impressive pose to adopt, they drove to the city where heralds who had been sent ahead announced, according to their instructions, 'O Athenians, receive Peisistratos with friendly spirit. For Athena has favoured him above all men and herself leads him to her acropolis.'[18]

Herodotus' account indicates Heracles' civic importance and the way a politician might invoke his prestige. Since Pisistratus also extensively patronized the arts, the abundance of visual motifs representing 'his' hero's exploits, and perhaps even associating them with his own achievements, is a logical development of the period.[19]

But Heracles' dominance in this black-figure ware suggests a subordinate role for the Amazons. Admittedly the subject must have held its own fascinations for artists, and the women are often represented alone – but the coincidence of their popularity with the Heraclean cult cannot be ignored. Without concluding that the production of the image is entirely dependent on interest in their mythic male adversaries, we must note that the first important era of Amazonian art occurred in a state which extensively venerated and depicted their conqueror.

Black-figure painting of the Athenian patron Heracles battling the Amazon Andromache.

Pisistratus' administration of Athens was, despite its absolutism, relatively humane and efficient, and he was finally able to establish a degree of dynastic control. His sons ruled the city from his death in 528 BC until 510, when the Spartans invaded to restore oligarchy. The Pisistratids' deposition, like their rise, seems to have coincided with changes in Attic iconography. In the first quarter of the fifth century the predominance of the Heracles image lessens significantly in black-figure ware and that of a parallel hero, Theseus, increases (19.4 per cent and 13.2 per cent of total mythic scenes respectively versus 44 per cent and 5 per cent before 510).[20] (The final Heraclean Amazonomachy in Attic art occurs on a 'metope' [a stone block with relief sculptures] in the mid-fifth-century Hephaisteion.) Perhaps Heracles was tainted with the unpopularity of the deposed tyrant. More probably the newly established Athenian democracy (c. 507 BC) and the rising threat of Persian invasion encouraged the development of a more peculiarly Athenian cult. And certainly Heracles had a rustic impetuosity less and less suitable to a population rapidly becoming urbanized. As Isocrates (436–338 BC) notes in his *Helen* (X, 24): 'It came to pass that Heracles undertook perilous labours more celebrated and more severe, Theseus those more useful, and to the Greeks of more vital importance.'

Did the Athenians find it necessary to replace their hero with a 'negative idealisation', in Philip Slater's terms, 'a kind of pastel Heracles'?[21] The stylistic changes of the period, including the opportunities for detail offered by the development of the red-figure technique and the general adoption of classical illusionism, could be argued to encourage a change to prettified and less totemic heroes.[22]

The Theseus variant

It may simply be our clearer vision of the later era, but Theseus seems a remarkably synthetic figure, plucked from relative mythic obscurity and fixed up with a retrospective genealogy in the traditional way. Nilsson

suggests his importance to the fictive continuity of the
Athenian state:

> the aspirations of which were, as usually happened,
> projected back into the mythical age . . . during its
> heyday in the fifth century BC, he is made the hero of
> the Athenian democracy, the founder of the
> Athenian state through the synoecism (the unity of
> the Attic peoples) and of the democratic institutions
> of Athens.[23]

About 520 BC a poem was written (perhaps by the
constitutionalist Cleisthenes) attributing specifically
Heraclean feats to the new hero, making him a companion of the older figure in the Trojan War, confronting
him with giants on his journey from Troezen to Athens,
etc. Among these was his accompaniment of Heracles
on the expedition against the Amazons.

Accounts of this episode again vary, moving from
Theseus' lieutenancy on the voyage (Heracles sometimes awards him a captured Amazon bride in thanks
for his aid) to command of one of his own. The wedding
of the two traditions is graphically evident in the
metopes of the Athenian Treasury at Delphi, built
sometime after the establishment of post-Pisistratid
democracy (*c*. 505 BC).[24] The subjects of the metopes are
threefold, and evidently interconnected: the labours of
Heracles, the labours of Theseus, and the battles of the
Greeks and the Amazons. The Amazonomachy is the
unifying device. Its position on the eastern face of the
Treasury links the easternmost metopes of the north
and south – each showing an Amazon, the former with

Heracles, the latter with Theseus. The theme may well be their joint expedition to Themiscyra.

Neither this iconography nor the Treasury itself can be precisely related to Athenian politics, especially if it is too early to have been built in commemoration of the Greek victory against the Persians at Marathon in 490. But the newly propagandist direction of these sculptures is significant, notably in one of the few non-combatative metopes: 'Theseus and his patron Athene standing quietly, as if in conversation'.[25] Another hero is promoted to the Athenian pantheon, and the warrior women are conquered anew. The patriotic theme circumscribes – and reconstructs – the myth.

The salient difference in the two heroes' campaigns against the warrior women is that where Heracles returned with the queen's stolen girdle, Theseus returns with the queen herself – a crucial link to the new myth's centrepiece, the Amazons' retaliatory attack on Athens. The original amatory adventure yields to an emphasis on patriotic endeavour and local defence.[26]

By at least as early as the fifth century, the Theseia – the Athenian festival honouring the hero's rescue of the citizens marked for sacrifice to the Minotaur – was coupled with a memorial recalling his defeat of the Amazons. And soon the logistics of the tribeswomen's attack on the city were written into the historical record. Plutarch (born before AD 50 – died after AD 120), citing the fourth-century historian Cleidemus, reports:

> the Amazons' left wing extended to what is now called the Amazoneum, while their right rested on the Pnyx, at the point where the gilded figure of Victory now

stands . . . the Athenians engaged the left wing,
attacking it from the Museum, and . . . the tombs of
those who fell are on either side of the street leading
to the gate near the shrine of the hero Chalcodon,
which is now known as the Piraeic gate. On this flank,
he [Cleidemus] tells us, the women routed the
Athenians and forced them back as far as the shrine
of the Eumenides. But on the other side, the
Athenians who attacked the Amazons from the
Palladium and Ardettus and the Lyceum, drove their
right wing back to the camp and killed great numbers
of them. Cleidemus adds that after three months a
peace was arranged through Hippolyta.[27]

How did this tradition of Amazon attack arise? The
Athenians may, for various political and demographic
reasons, have enjoyed something of a siege mentality.
They also had a propensity to mythologize unascribable
graves or monuments. But if any historical event
encouraged their elaboration of mythology, it was the
Persian Wars. From the mid-sixth century the Greek
colonies in western Asia (Ionia) were threatened by the
rising strength of the Persians, who took over and
enlarged the empire of the Medes from 550 BC. In 499
BC Athens and Eretria aided an unsuccessful Ionian
rebellion. Nine years later the Persians sent a punitive
invasion across the Aegean, Eretria was sacked, but the
Athenians were victorious at Marathon. (And a rumour
spread of Theseus' ghostly deliverance of his country-
men: 'Many of the men who fought the Medes at
Marathon', writes Plutarch, 'believed that they saw the
apparition of Theseus, clad in full armour and charging

ahead of them against the barbarians.'[28]) A decade later, in 480, Xerxes mounted a larger invasion, reaching Athens and securing the entire eastern part of continental Greece. Attica was evacuated and its capital sacked by the invaders. Yet somehow in the following year the weak and divided Greek states managed to rout the invaders decisively.

Athens, with Plataea and Megara the only states to refuse submission from the outset, saw the victory in literally epic terms. The defeated power joined the catalogue of heroic enemies overcome by the state, and Robert Drews notes that 'Later orators who spoke in praise of Athens included as a standard "topos" the recital of Athens' defence of Greece against the Amazons, Eumolpus' Thracians and Xerxes' Persians.'[29] Thus Isocrates' (436–338 BC) *Panegyricus*, cited at the beginning of this essay.

As the historic attack by one group of Asiatics was assimilated into the record, it had a reciprocal effect on the myths about another. One explanation is that both parties came to be identified with a barbarism deservedly crushed by civilization, but this is probably an overstatement. Certainly the Persians were not treated contemptuously in the resulting commemorations. Their triumphs over the era's major civilizations were soberly respected. 'It was precisely because the Greeks appreciated the significance of the fall of Lydia, Babylon and Egypt that their own victory over the Persians stood out as an event not paralleled since the Trojan Wars.'[30]

If anything, both Xerxes' invaders and their mythic Asian counterparts may have consolidated each other's place in the enemy pantheon. From the second quarter of the sixth century (i.e. long before the invasion) Amazons in black-figure painting are sometimes kitted out in fanciful elements of 'oriental' costume: wicker shields, Phrygian caps, geometric motley. With the development in detail offered by the red-figure technique, this practice was intensified, and then transferred back to the Persians. The first half of the fifth century sees Xerxes' warriors in costumes by that time associated with the Amazons.

This new heroic configuration was again invoked by Athenian politicians. A decade after the Persians' defeat, Cimon, a general in the Athenian-led Delian League, bid for the leadership of what was by then an imperial power. His rival, Themistocles, derived his prestige from his participation in the naval victory against the Persians at Salamis. Cimon (who had also distinguished himself in this battle) could counter with his father Miltiades' generalship at Marathon, a heritage which he sought to make good by an even more explicit identification with that battle's patron, Theseus. Recalling an oracular injunction to return the hero's remains to the city, he sought out the island of Skyros while on a naval patrol. The traditional burial place, Plutarch tells us, providentially yielded up some unusually imposing remains – a very large skeleton interred with a bronze spear and sword.

> He had the bones placed on board his trireme and brought them back with great pomp and ceremony to the hero's native land, almost four hundred years after he had left it. This affair did more than any

other achievement of Cimon's to endear him to the people.[31]

The result was the eclipse and eventual ostracism of Themistocles, the rise of his rival and the consolidation of Theseus' place in the city's devotions. The hero's return to his city was annually celebrated in a state festival (the Theseia referred to above) and a memorial erected to house his bones. Again political purposes were to shape Amazon iconography.

The commemorative Theseion was a large public assembly place, serving as a council chamber, armoury, and refuge for slaves and the poor. The decorations included a trio of wall-paintings by Micon, a painter and sculptor associated with the pro-Cimon party. These no longer survive, but Aristophanes alludes in the *Lysistrata* to Micon's painting of mounted Amazons, and the second-century-AD guidebook of the Greek geographer Pausanias describes the scenes on each wall: Athenians fighting Amazons, Theseus battling with the Centaurs, and his recovery of a ring which King Minos, challenging his descent from Poseidon, had thrown into the sea.

A decade after Themistocles' exile, Cimon too grew unpopular and was finally forced to leave the city. But an upswing in his political fortunes returned him to power and stimulated a spate of even more explicitly political mythmaking, once again featuring the Amazons. At this time (*c.* 460 BC) Cimon's brother-in-law Peisianax erected the 'Stoa Poikile' or Painted Portico in Athens.[32] It was decorated by a contemporary of Micon's, the muralist Polygnotus of Thasos. The painter's associations with Cimon were considerable –

enough for him to be the rumoured lover of his sister Elpinice (whose features supposedly found their way into one of the Portico's paintings), although Plutarch argues that there was no personal commission; Polygnotus 'undertook the work for nothing, simply out of the desire to honour his city'.[33] In any event, the civic-spirited painter honoured Athens' leading citizen: the murals, Pausanias reports, juxtaposed (1) combat between the Athenians and the Spartans; (2) the Greeks after the capture of Troy; (3) Theseus leading the Athenians against the Amazons; and (4) the Battle of Marathon, featuring Theseus and a prominently displayed figure of Cimon's father, Miltiades.

These monumental Amazonomachies both re-affirmed and modified the traditional images. The theme of conflict with the state and its founding fathers was evidently maintained, but stylistic and technical developments wrought significant changes.

Polygnotan classicism – developing perspective, a denser and more 'realistic' composition – is thought to have directly influenced the art of ceramic painting. So, perhaps, did Polygnotan iconography. As Giovanni Becatti argues:

> In the fervid pictorial climate of the Athens of
> Cimon, it is no wonder that Attic vase painters,
> working to renew their own language, should have
> drawn inspiration from the rich figurative world of
> the Polygnotan school. It therefore seems legitimate
> to look for ideas and motifs from Polygnotos' and
> Mikon's painting in the enormous corpus of vases. A
> whole group of red-figure vases which develop the

theme of the Amazonomachy show compositions of Amazons on horseback, or on their knees, or retreating. The fact that these motifs constantly recur in similar forms bears witness to their derivation from a common archetype, diversely transmitted and reformulated; this archetype could indeed have been the painting of Mikon.[34]

The red-figure technique, as noted above, permitted a richer detail than its black-figure predecessor – a richness sometimes heightened in the mid-fifth century by the use of added colour. The Amazonomachies on the vases of the period may result from the convergence of such technical opportunity, the stylistic influences of the monumental muralists, and the political and artistic suitability of these combat scenes. Thus, commentators argue, the rocky terrain where the Amazon battled on the Areopagus could now be effectively rendered by a change from a single baseline to an uneven ground.

This tendency to elaboration had other effects on the motif: it permitted the painter further to characterize his subjects as foreign, female, and – though here commentaries have oversentimentalized – erotically conquered.

Perhaps the fullest treatment in this vein is the 'Penthesilea' cup-tondo by the artist known today as the Berlin painter. The expressiveness of this painting has prompted a great deal of comment, much of it highly speculative – notably the ascription of its subject to Achilles' fatal wounding of the Amazon queen. If, as Dietrich von Bothmer maintains, its unusual size and colour are owed to the Polygnotan murals, might it not

Red-figure painting of the Greeks fighting the Amazons. Note the uneven ground made possible by the red-figure technique.

also derive its subject from them? (In which case the cup depicts the Amazons against the Athenians, not the Trojan Wars.)[35] And if the cup is, in some sense, related to a project celebrating the Athenian state, what does that suggest about the phallocratic possibilities in the patriotic theme?

Compared with the severe silhouettes of the black-figure period, the Penthesilea scene seems like a close-up, its depiction both emotionalized and, despite the gravity of its subject, somehow 'decorated'. The protagonists' costumes, for instance, have been richly – and most fictively – exoticized. Charles Martin Robertson notes that the painter has combined Greek and 'alien' fashions to achieve the colourful Amazon ensembles, and 'is not concerned with actual practice either in his own day or in the supposed time of the heroic scene. To enrich his design he rings the changes in Greek and foreign costume.'[36]

Then there is – given the painting's vivid physicality – the subject of the protagonists' confrontation. Is this the poignant exchange of a victorious Achilles ruefully contemplating his reproachful foe, or simply an evocative movement of conscious victory and conscious defeat? However we interpret it, there is no ignoring the deliberation with which the painter focuses on the subordination of the Amazon – not just as foe, but as woman. If previous Amazonomachies brought patriotic concerns to an image of sexual conflict (and in so doing provided the impetus for that image's dissemination), the Penthesilea cup returns the sexual to the military episode with a vengeance.

145

Detail from the cup-tondo said to be of Achilles' fatal wounding of the Amazon queen Penthesilea.

The Parthenon Amazonomachies

The apotheosis of the patriotic Amazonomachy occurs in the Parthenon – itself the apotheosis of Athenian state art. In size, in situation and in subject, the temple of the city's presiding deity was designed to proclaim Athenian power.

Begun in 447 BC, at the instigation of Cimon's successor Pericles, the Parthenon was part of a massive building (and public employment) programme financed largely by tribute from the Athenian-led Delian League. The cult to which it was dedicated, that of Athena 'Parthenos', or virgin, can itself be interpreted as a strident expression of patriarchal ideology. Not only is Athena the inveterate ally of Greek heroes against her Olympian sisters, not only does she abjure the 'feminine' functions of coupling and childbirth, not only is her physical sexuality swathed in male armour – but her mythic parentage (portrayed on the temple's east pediment) presents her as born only of the Father:

> Zeus married Metis (Wisdom), got her with child, and then swallowed her, fearing a prophecy that she would later bear another child who should be stronger than he. After a period of gestation, seized with a fearful pain in the head, he called on Hephaestus (or in some versions Prometheus) to split it open with axe or hammer, which performed, out sprang Athene armed 'cap a pie'.[37]

The temple of this patroness was decorated with images so explicitly and unusually secular in their concerns as to provoke charges of impiety. Around the wall of the interior building, or 'cella', ran a frieze portraying the annual Panathenaic procession of the citizens honouring their goddess, 'the first and one of the very few surviving cases where a mortal activity is represented on a Greek temple instead of something from divine or heroic mythology'.[38]

The outside of this temple was decorated with metopes depicting combat with the traditional enemies – (1) the Greeks against the Centaurs; (2) the Gods against the Giants; (3) the sack of Troy; and (4) the Greeks against the Amazons – opponents which at least one commentator has described as 'variously superhuman, inhuman, subhuman, or non-human . . . a general background of conflict for the human state'.[39]

Two of these images – the Gigantomachy and the Amazonomachy – were also inscribed on the shield of the temple's cult statue, a huge ivory and gold colossus of the armed deity brandishing an image of Victory. The sculptor was Phidias, the director of the entire project and a friend and supporter of Pericles. Phidias' Amazonomachy, like the Polygnotan murals, is thought to have explicitly identified the Athenian leadership with the victorious Greeks. Plutarch writes:

> in the relief of the battle of the Amazons, which is represented on the shield of the goddess, he carved a figure representing himself as a bald old man lifting up a stone with both hands, and also . . . he introduced a particularly fine likeness of Pericles fighting an Amazon. The position of the hand, which holds a spear in front of Pericles' face, seems to have been ingeniously contrived to conceal the resemblance, but it can still be seen quite plainly from either side.[40]

Neither the Parthenon colossus nor its accoutrements survive, and extant copies do not correspond precisely to Plutarch's description. Among these, however, the Lenormant copy does bear a figure hurling a rock with both hands, while the Strangford shield includes a warrior with a spear. The latter figure's dominant place in the composition has also prompted an identification with Theseus. 'Is it he, or is it Pericles? Or is it both, Theseus appearing as, and identified with, Pericles?'[41] The evidence is inconclusive but, perhaps it can be little else. As the city's 'past' was constructed in opposition to such as the mythic heroines, its historical personages became ineluctably mythologized.

The Parthenon Amazonomachies may seem, in their conscious contraposition of the forces of the state and its female enemies, to be the climax of the genre. They are anyway among the final works their kind. The fourth century saw the decline of Athens from imperial preeminence and its artistic celebration. But the traditional encounter between Greek patriarch and female warrior did not yet pass out of currency. It would find its way into the exploits of still another mythologized leader, the Macedonian conqueror, Alexander the Great.

The Athenian patriarchy

We have seen how the myth of Athens' triumph over the Amazons was used to historicize the claims of that state. In his 'Funeral Oration' the Athenian orator Lysias (c. 459–380 BC) joins that patriotic theme to another:

> They [the Amazons] would not return home and
> report their own misfortune and our ancestors' valour:

for they perished on the spot, and were punished for
their folly, making our city's memory imperishable in
its valour; while owing to their disaster in this region,
they rendered their own country nameless. And so
these women, by their unjust greed for others' land,
justly lost their own.

As victory thrust the Athenian state into immortality, so
defeat removed the Amazons from history altogether,
effectively expunging them from the record.

In the light of the former's concern to construct just
such a record, the condemnation of the warrior women
to literal – and literary – extinction seems pointed. And
the provocative phrase 'they rendered their own country nameless' suggests an expulsion from a symbolic
order (the named, or spoken, past) consonant with the
Lacanian view of the patriarchal control of (history as)
language. But the burden of Lysias' argument – and the
one I wish to pursue – is that these women deserved it.

In her survey of the myths of female rule, Joan
Bamberger challenges Bachofen's famous reading of
the Amazon story as 'real and not poetic'. As she argues:

Myth may become through repeated recitation a
moral history of action while not in itself a detailed
chronology of recorded events. Myth may be part of
culture history in providing justification for a present
and perhaps permanent reality by giving an invented
'historical' explanation of how this reality was
created.[42]

Bamberger's study of a group of South American myths leads her to observe:

> the ideological thrust of the argument made in the myth of the Rule of Women, and the justification it offers for male dominance through the evocation of a vision of a catastrophic alternative – a society dominated by women. The myth, in its reiteration that women did not know how to handle power when in possession of it, reaffirms dogmatically the inferiority of their present position.[43]

The Amazon tradition offered the Athenians precisely such a justification, and they needed it. For economic, political and demographic reasons, the women of that state suffered an institutionalized subordination radical even by the standards of their Greek predecessors and contemporaries.

Perhaps the best expression of their plight remains Lewis H. Morgan's writing in *Ancient Society*:

> It still remains an enigma that a race, with endowments great enough to impress their mental life upon the world, should have remained essentially barbarian in their treatment of the female sex at the height of their civilization. Women were not treated with cruelty, nor with discourtesy within the range of the privileges allowed them; but their education was superficial, intercourse with the opposite sex was denied them, and their inferiority was inculcated as a principle, until it came to be accepted as a fact by the women themselves.[44]

But Morgan overemphasizes the enigmatic character of this oppression, contradictory as it may seem in such an enlightened culture. In the same work he speculates on the influence which the accumulation of private property may have had on the gentile (tribal) organization of archaic Athens:

> The growth of the idea of property, and the rise of monogamy, furnished motives sufficiently powerful to demand and obtain this change [from the female line to the male] in order to bring children into the gens of their father, and into a participation in the inheritance of his estate . . . The pertinacity with which the principle was maintained down to the time of Solon, that property should remain in the gens of the deceased owner, illustrates the vitality of the organization through all these periods. It was this rule which compelled the heiress to marry in her own gens to prevent a transfer of the property by her marriage to another gens. When Solon allowed the owner of property to dispose of it by will, in case he had no children, he made the first inroad upon the property rights of the gens.[45]

Solon's sixth-century reforms reorganized Athenian society to meet the demands of a new economy founded on maritime and monetary supremacy and the labours of an increasingly large slave class. This legislation included the licensing of state brothels staffed by slaves, the abolition of the sale of children into slavery – excepting those of an unmarried non-virgin woman by her male guardian, and severe penalties for adultery. It was aimed, argues historian Sarah Pomeroy, 'at eliminating strife among men and strengthening the newly created democracy. Women are a perennial source of friction among men. Solon's solution to this problem was to keep them out of sight and to limit their influence.'[46]

The effect of this legislation persisted, even intensified, in the next century. As Athens grew into an imperial power, its population (the largest of the Greek states) was further stratified into a dominant layer of some 300 wealthy families; a nominal citizenry of 30,000–40,000 (the majority of these, the much poorer 'hoplite' and 'thete' classes, comprising urban craftsmen, poor peasants and the like); a large number of 'metics' or non-citizen foreigners, who were forbidden land-ownership but permitted to engage in the city's trading and industrial enterprises, and some 80,000–100,000 slaves, performing fieldwork, domestic service, and artisanal functions.[47]

The chief obligation of citizen women in these circumstances was the production of male heirs to meet the demands of war and familial continuity (the citizenry was seen to be composed of the 'oikoi', its family units) without exceeding the already overstretched resources of an enlarging leisure class. Heiresses of families without sons were deemed 'attached to the family property', which went with her to her husband, and thence to their child. Widowed heiresses were obliged to marry their nearest male kinsman.

Conjugal sexual abstinence, female infanticide, male homosexuality (but not female; neither opportunity nor ideology supported such a practice) and rigorous penalties for adultery were established features of such a situation. So was a dowry to ensure a daughter's marriageability, and responsible fathers did not raise more daughters than they could adequately provide for. Marriages were arranged by fathers for political and economic considerations, the optimum age being considered fourteen for the bride and thirty for the groom. The bride could then look forward to passing from the guardianship of her father to that of her husband (legally, women never came of age) and a short, arduous and secluded life.

In the home women's work was often performed by – and associated with – slaves. To a leisured male ruling class which condemned most manual labour as 'banausic' (unfit for citizens) this lowered female status went even further, condemning even the spinning and household administration of upper-class women to servility.

The resulting tension between the Athenian state and its female members found its way into artistic expression:

Many tragedies show women in rebellion against the established norms of society. As the 'Oresteia' of Aeschylus makes clear, a city-state such as Athens flourished only through the breaking of familial or blood bonds and the subordination of the patriarchal family within the patriarchal state. But women were in conflict with this political principle, for their interests were private and family-related. Thus, drama often shows them acting out of the women's quarters, and concerned with children, husbands, fathers, brothers, and religions deemed more primitive and family-oriented than the Olympian, which was the support of the state.[48]

Read in such a context, the Amazon myth can be interpreted as an expression of this unease. Their threat, like that of the adulterous Phaedra or the homicidal Deianara, was a reversal of the extremity of their oppression: 'that some day the vanquished would arise and treat their ex-masters as they themselves had been treated'.[49]

The Amazon myth resolved this tension by representing such a rebellion as already concluded in deserved defeat. Lysias suggests that greed for land was the source of the tribeswomen's downfall. The association of their image with primitive, chaotic or alien forces (the Centaurs, the Giants, the Trojans and the Persians) produces similar justifications. So, interestingly, do the folk etymologies invented by the Greeks in explanation of a name whose derivation was already lost.

Perhaps the most famous of these is 'a-mastos', variously translatable as 'breastless', 'not brought up by the breast', 'beings with strong breasts', and 'with one breast'. This has been suggested as the source of the tradition that the Amazons excised one breast to further their military prowess (a tradition notably absent from both Greek art and myth; although the physician Hippocrates does say that the women of the Sauromatae, identified by his older contemporary Herodotus as the descendants of Amazons and Scythian men, seared the right breast of their female infants to divert strength to the right arm and shoulder).[50]

Other retrospective etymologies include 'a-maza', 'without barley bread'; 'azona', 'chastity belt'; and 'ama-zosas', 'opposed to man'. What is significant in these inventions is their characterization of the warrior women as anti-feminine, self-mutilating, man-hating and technically underdeveloped. (The suggestion that they could not grow barley is not atypical: another account suggests that they had to detour hundreds of miles overland on their expedition from Asia Minor to Athens because they had no knowledge of sailing, and usually the women are presented as virtually without culture.)

Where the Greeks could not christen their enemies, they invented etymologies; where they could – in the individual Amazon names inscribed on vases or in the myths – the choices are again significant. Several of these names link the women with their traditional animal, the horse: 'Hippolyte', 'of the stampeding horse'; 'Melanippe', 'black mare'; 'Alcippe', 'powerful mare', etc. Others convey a homicidal threat: 'Molpa-dia', 'death song'; 'Penthesilea', 'compelling men to mourn'.[51] Did such bestial, murderous beings deserve better than annihilation at the hands of civilization?

The inimitable heroine

A peculiar thing has happened in the case of the account we have of the Amazons; for our accounts of other peoples keep a distinction between the mythical and the historical elements; for the things that are ancient and false and monstrous are called myths, but history wishes for the truth, whether ancient or recent, and contains no monstrous element, or else only rarely. But as regards the Amazons, the same stories are told now as in early times, though they are marvellous and beyond belief. For instance, who could believe that any army of women, or a city, or a tribe, could ever be organised without men, and not only be organised, but even make inroads upon the territory of other people, and not only overpower the peoples near them to the extent of advancing as far as what is now Ionia, but even send an expedition across the sea as far as Attica? For this is the same as saying that the men of those times were women and that the women were men. (Strabo, *Geography*, 11.5.3)

The dilemma of the Greek writer Strabo (*c.* 64 BC – AD 21) still perplexes us. In part, it can be resolved by the reading of Athenian history suggested here – a reading which leads us to conclude that its object was not 'truth', but the construction of a periodicized basis for the hegemony of the patriarchal state. But if we could somehow ignore this 'history', and its inbuilt lesson of female inferiority, what of the Amazon triumphant? Is the idea of 'autonomous warrior women' invariably paradoxical in patriarchal culture? Can it resolve itself only in the reversal of the sexes, making the heroines into their opponents, men?

As victor or vanquished, feminists have argued, the Amazons are structured within the same terms of dominance and militarism:

If a matriarchy did develop . . . it would necessarily have been a society based on the exchange of men and probably on their exploitation and oppression as well. Consequently the Amazons, as an antidote for female subservience, are not as attractive as some feminists have assumed.[52]

In 'The Guerrilleres' (a contemporary reworking of the Amazon theme) Wittig retains the martial ideals of epic, wrongly, I think: no struggle is as glorious or as triumphant as that. To suggest it is to accept male values.[53]

Nor was Strabo alone among the ancients in relegating the achievements of the Amazons to the sphere of the marvellous, the supranatural. [54] In his fourth-century-AD 'Posthomerica', the Byzantine poet Quintus Smyrnaeus describes a debate among the Trojan women as they watch the exploits of Penthesilea from their city's walls:

>   Suddenly
> A fiery passion for the fray hath seized
> Antimachus' daughter, Meneptolemus' wife
> Tisiphone. Her heart waxed strong, and filled
> With lust of fight she cried to fellows all,
> With desperate-daring words, to spur them on
> To woeful war, by recklessness made strong:
> 'Friends, let a heart of valour in our breasts
> Awake!' Let us be like our lords, who fight
> With foes for fatherland, for babes, for us.
> And never pause for breath in that stern strife!
> Let us too throne war's spirit in our hearts!
> Let us too face the fight which favoureth none!

For we, we women, be not creatures cast
In diverse mould from men: to us is given
Such energy of life as stirs in them.
Eyes have we like to theirs, and limbs: throughout
Fashioned we are alike; one common light
We look on, and one common air we breathe:
With like food are we nourished: – nay, wherein
Have we been dowered of God more niggardly
Than men? Then let us shrink not from the fray!
See ye not yonder a woman far excelling
Men in the grapple of fight?

But the poet, aware as Tisiphone is not of the doom impending upon both the Trojan men and their Amazon allies, posits a prudent intervention by 'one voice of wisdom', the dissuasive Theano:

                     For your strength
Can never be as that of Danaan men,
Men trained on daily battle. Amazons
Have joyed in ruthless fight, in charging steeds
From the beginning: all the toil of men
Do they endure, and therefore evermore
The spirit of the War-god thrills them through,
They fall not short of men in anything;
Their labour-hardened frames make great their
    hearts
For all achievement; never faint their knees
Nor tremble. Rumour speaks their queen to be
A daughter of the mighty Lord of War.
Therefore no woman may compare with her
In prowess – if she be a woman, not

159

A God come down in answer to our prayers.
   Yea, if our blood be all the race of men,
Yet unto diverse labours still they turn.
And that for each is evermore the best
Whereto he bringeth skill of use and wont.
Therefore do ye from tumult of the fray
Hold you aloof, and in your women's bowers
Before the loom still pace ye to and fro;
And war shall be the business of our lords.'

Here the exploits of the Amazons serve only to confirm sexual dimorphism and the sexual division of labour. Their successes literally remove them from female comparison, rendering them either masculine or divine. Nothing of the real oppression of their sex is challenged by these mythic heroines, it is merely transcended. As the lecture sequence of Laura Mulvey and Peter Wollen's film *Penthesilea* observes: 'their weapons and strategy are men's weapons and strategy. They offer a solution which is magical not political.'[55]

This said, is it none the less possible to extract a kernel of female potency from the patriarchal shell? Can the Amazon myths, like Engels's postulation of a communistic past in which 'the position of women is not only free, but honourable', function as an historical white lie, freeing our aspirations from a legacy of unvaried defeat? Can we break with history, remaking its images as we choose?

In her preface to *The Lesbian Body*, the novelist Monique Wittig compares two autonomies, that of the contemporary women's movement and its mythical precursors:

We already have our islets, our islands, we are already in process of living in a culture that befits us. The Amazons are women who live among themselves, by themselves and for themselves at the generally accepted levels: fictional, symbolic, actual. Because we are illusionary for traditional male culture we make no distinction between the three levels. Our reality is the fictional as it is socially accepted, our symbols deny the traditional symbols and are fictional for traditional male culture, and we possess an entire fiction into which we project ourselves and which is already a possible reality. It is our fiction that validates us.[56]

Without denying the force of ideology, one might reply that it is not the fiction of female resistance which validates our struggles, but its reality.

As this essay has attempted to show, the construction of the Amazon myth cannot be separated from a context of patriarchal dominance. But the context has developed to generate women's resistance. Much as it inspired feminist struggle, was not Victorian matriarchalism also its product, an acknowledgement of the female power already manifest in the new economic formation? The same, I think, can be said of present searches for a militant female past. The findings may, as in the case of the Amazons, be ultimately inappropriable. But the project itself encourages. Would it have commenced without our genuine identification with women in struggle – a new will to power born of the unease of our own patriarchal era?

Lianna and the lesbians of art cinema

In 1977, Caroline Sheldon's pioneering study of 'Lesbians and Film' noted that art cinema had gone 'relatively unexplored by feminists given that feminist film culture emerged at a time when Hollywood was the cinema being assessed'.[1] Interestingly, this remains true, despite (or perhaps because of?) that cinema's increasing deployment of feminist and lesbian themes and its consumption by feminist audiences. (Contemporary examples might range across films with specifically lesbian themes or implications, like *Another Way* [1982] or *The Bostonians* [1984], to the broader considerations of female friendship in those directed by von Trotta.)

In the face of this neglect, I want to argue here that if lesbianism hadn't already existed, art cinema might have invented it. To a cinema which affects an attitude of high seriousness in matters sexual, the lesbian romance affords a double benefit. It provides a sufficient degree of difference from dominant cinematic representations of sex and sexuality to be seen as 'realistic', 'courageous', 'questioning', '[saved] from Hollywood fudging', 'true to itself' (all terms from reviews of *Lianna*). Yet it does this by offering – quite literally – more of the same (the same being that old cinema equation 'woman = sexuality'[2] which art cinema, despite its differences with Hollywood, has rarely forsaken).

Narrative cinema has traditionally looked to the figure of the woman to signify sexual pleasure, sexual problems, sexuality itself – placing her 'as erotic object for the characters within the screen story, and as erotic object for the spectator within the auditorium'.[3] And none of those differences upon which art cinema founded its fortunes (realism, cultural specificity, authorial expressivity, episodic narratives structured by symbolic congruence or psychological re-action rather than linear ones driven by a protagonist's activity) precludes the eroticization of the female body.[4] If anything, art cinema heightens that effect. Its ancestry in movements like the French avant-garde of the 1920s provided connections (notably via the interventions of Dada and the Surrealists) with the erotic conventions of fine art, including the female nude. Thus Man Ray's 1928 *Etoile de Mer*, which intercuts the phallic regalia of skyscrapers, chimneys and starfish tentacles with the figure of a woman seen naked on a bed through frosted glass. (The compositions and conventions of European oil painting persist in art films as varied as Bertolucci's *1900* and Godard's *Passion*. *Coup de foudre* presents its nudity largely in terms of representation: Madeleine is an amateur artist whose studio is filled with figures of naked women. In an intriguing reversal of the film's recurring use of an onlooker in scenes of sexual intimacy, her sculptures seem to watch the characters.)

These high culture values were available for invocation in the debates which surrounded European cinema between the Wars. At a time when the Hays Code forbade representations of nudity and sexual activity in Hollywood films, the French cinema, for instance, found a defence from censorship on the grounds of the 'adult' and 'realistic' nature of art. When the resumption of international trade and the anti-trust suits of the 1940s relaxed Hollywood's grip on US exhibition, European films were able to capitalize on their reputation for an aesthetically defensible explicitness in the American market. By the mid 1960s to mid 1970s, much of this work – from *Last Tango in Paris* to *The Night Porter* to sundry Pasolini films – had coalesced into an explicitly erotic form: the soft-core art film.[5]

It isn't surprising, then, that art film titles (*Les Biches, Rome Open City, The Conformist, Les Stances à Sophie*) figure extensively in Caroline Sheldon's filmography. Not surprising either, given the period's interest in positive images and female authorship, are her objections to the institution for its stereotypically 'mysterious or childlike' women and 'the male-defined world' of its narratives. But where Sheldon decries this cinema in favour of women's experimental work (Oxenberg, Deren, Dulac, the scripting of *Céline and Julie Go Boating*), other lesbian critics of the late 1970s sought the naturalism urged by Susan Griffin:

> This is from a film I want to see. It is a film made by a woman about two women who live together. This is a scene from their daily lives. It is a film about the small daily transformations which some women experience, allow, tend to, and which have been invisible in this male culture. In this film, two women touch. In all

ways possible they show knowledge of what they have lived through and what they will yet do, and one sees in their movements how they have survived. I am certain that one day this film will exist.[6]

With its penchant for the 'real' and its low-budget bias towards small casts and intimate settings, art cinema has an awful tendency to grant such wishes – and seven years later [1984] close approximations of this description have arrived in our cinemas. *Coup de foudre/At First Sight* (France, 1983, directed by Diane Kurys) might have been tailored to Griffin's design, while *Lianna* (USA, 1982, directed by John Sayles), though more problematic in its male writer-director, has the advantage of an explicitly lesbian narrative. (Reviewers tend to deal with the physical ambiguity in *Coup de foudre* by citing the director's own statement that 'it was a little more than a friendship and a little less than a passion between them'.[7] This extra-textual 'evidence' itself reflects the conventions of art cinema, guaranteeing the film's realism with the biography of the director's mother; placing it as a 'prequel' to the also autobiographical *Diabolo Menthe* in the director's canon; and directing us towards a 'broad' – non-lesbian – reading of the film.)

By contrast, *Lianna* – as a product not only of the United States but of a writer-director with a considerable background in Hollywood exploitation (*Piranha, Alligator, The Howling*) – may seem a perverse example of a cinema which originated as an alternative to American dominance. However, subsequent events, notably the importation of art elements into Hollywood's New

American Cinema and the development of independent production elsewhere in the USA, have seen the rise of indigenous American art cinema(s). But even had *Lianna* lacked clear national precedents, its narrative, style and publicity strategies are markedly within the art cinema tradition.

The chief of these may be the sort of realism which tends to produce the plaudits cited above, particularly the film's very knowing dialogue about sex. Where *Coup de foudre*'s 'honesty' resides in its correspondence with an 'actual' unspoken desire, that of *Lianna* is emphasized by the extent to which it is voiced. From her first tentative recollections of teenage homosexual experimentation, the heroine's speaking of her desires becomes an important part of the story, with her candour positively contrasted to others' euphemisms. This has endeared *Lianna* to critics who regard *verbal* sexual explicitness as a crucial part of the practice of 'coming out'. Penny Ashbrook, for example, remarks on:

> Lianna's recognising and embracing her lesbian sexuality in a process of experiment, excitement and discovery, encapsulated in the moment of comic shock when we see her announcing to the mirror, 'Lianna Massey eats pussy', immediately after her night with Cindy, trying the words out and pleased by the result. It's another reminder of the physical reality of sex – none of the obscure tickling of *Personal Best* here – and an assertion of the film's recognition of the importance of naming.[8]

The paradox that this very naming, this speaking of sex, historically made 'possible a strong advance of social controls into this area of "perversity"', to cite Foucault,[9] remains an important problem for gay politics. My own point is merely that both this politics and art cinema are constituted within discourses which privilege the body, particularly its sexual functions, as a source of truth about social relations in general. The connection which Ashbrook suggests between these moments of 'physical reality' in *Lianna* and 'lesbian experience' *per se* participates in the art film's general impulse towards allegory – in which everything tends to mean something else.

The result is to assign that cinematic convention, the love scene, a particular symbolic function: the ability to represent 'lesbian experience'. (If this seems completely natural, consider whether cinema's heterosexual embraces function in the same way. . .) Ironically, critics like Penny Ashbrook, and Ruby Rich before her, reject readings of lesbian scenarios which treat them as 'a metaphor, a coded text about something else, something other than what appears on screen'.[10] Yet Rich, in her assertion that *Maedchen in Uniform* 'should have been a warning to lesbians then living in Germany', and Ashbrook, when she suggests that 'a film can be about lesbianism and also throw light on universal aspects of human experience',[11] produce their own extrapolations on film texts. And how can they avoid doing so? For a film, like any other representation, is *always* a coded text about something other than what appears on screen.

Art cinema both intensifies and reveals this process, foregrounding its own encoded status. In its suppression of action in favour of visual style, in its display of authorial signatures of technique and theme, and in its deployment of enigma in everything from narrative to spatio-temporal codes to diegetic ontology (is this really happening or is she dreaming it?), this cinema positively incites allegorical readings. As we emerge from the Gate or the Plaza or the Screen, interpretation goes into overdrive (to the sound of loose ends being tied): what was the director's message? What did such-and-such symbolize? What did it all really mean? Indeed, these acts of exegesis are one of the chief pleasures art cinema offers, especially to audiences schooled in traditional literary criticism, with its own emphasis on authorial expression and textual unity – and also to the similarly trained reviewers of our newspapers and magazines.

Thus, Philip French in *The Observer* (5 February 1984):

The film's subject is only superficially lesbianism and sexuality. It could have been a religious experience or the discovery of a new vocation that made Lianna take the vital step. What the picture is about is the sudden confrontation of a highly responsible person with the demands of self, the problem of being forced to establish an independent life after years of emotional dependency and the acceptance of our essential human loneliness.

Cynthia Rose in the *New Musical Express* (3 February 1984):

It's not a 'gay film' or a 'feminist film' or a 'low-budget cult film'. It's just a modest and realistic portrayal of the costs which can be inherent in decision-making.

David Castell in the *Sunday Telegraph* (5 February 1984):

> The result is a delightful, gentle and quietly
> questioning film, more about starting over – in a new
> flat, a new relationship, a new sexual role – than
> about homosexuality *per se*.

Phillip Bergson in *What's On and Where to Go in London* (2 February 1984):

> *Lianna* is a humane and courageous focus on the
> endless mystery of love and sex.

and Virginia Dignam in the *Morning Star* (10 February 1984):

> Ostensibly the film is about lesbianism . . . Under the
> superficial story of a wife and mother of two leaving
> her husband to live with another woman, is a whole
> minefield of emotions.

The extraordinary unanimity of these responses undoubtedly owes a great deal to the reviewers' aversion to lesbianism, but it is also a product of art cinema, which characteristically solicits essential humanist readings founded on psychologistic saws and authorial (i.e. the director's) declarations of a given film's general relevance.

John Sayles is not only credited as writer/director/ editor on *Lianna*; he also performed in it (in the not-really-reflexive role of a lecherous lecturer in film- making). Furthermore, Maggie Renzi, with whom he lives, functioned as co-producer and played the role of Sheila. This personal investment in the film was literalized by financial backing from both Sayles's and Renzi's mothers; but low budgets (here $340,000) are anyway understood as indicators of individual artistry in the cinema – no Hollywood assembly line for *Lianna*. The film was presented in the press as Sayles's 'personal statement', and his own interpretative comments were granted considerable weight. And as he frequently observed, 'I chose *Lianna* because people I knew, both gay and straight, have been through the same experiences.'[12]

Art cinema's emphasis on character and psychology (often manifested in narratives which deal explicitly with breakdown and therapy, such as Bergman's *Persona*) tends to focus attention on the individual protagonist rather than groups or classes. The realism of such films is measured in characterological terms – motivation, consistency, depth. Thus Penny Ashbrook praises the scene in which Lianna recalls her adolescent love for a camp counsellor as giving the character 'a personal lesbian history that is echoed later when we are told that she feels she has always felt "that way" without having realised it',[13] while *Jump Cut* reviewer Lisa DiCaprio criticizes the film's 'one-dimensional characters lacking in emotional depth'.[14] Where reviewers fail to discover the appropriate degree of motivation for Lianna's sudden romance with Ruth, their explanations switch – in typical art cinema terms – from the individual to 'humanity': 'why Lianna loves women isn't any more explicable than why some women love men – anyone loves anyone, for that matter . . .'.[15] As David Bordwell observes:

> The art film is non-classical in that it foregrounds deviations from the classical norm – there are certain gaps and problems. But these very deviations are placed, re-situated as realism (in life things happen this way) or authorial commentary (the ambiguity is symbolic).[16]

These readings of Lianna may also be encouraged by the film's deployment of its academic *mise en scène*. As Tom Ryall has argued, the art cinema reverses 'the subordination of formal qualities to narrative clarity which characterises the classical cinema'.[17] Here, the college setting – with its background of campus, lecture rooms, playing fields and faculty parties – is particularly emphasized. Lianna, the once and present student, leaves a male lecturer for a female one – a childless child psychologist whose subject suggests a related process of maturation on the part of her lover/pupil/would-be research assistant. Furthermore, Lianna's (homo)-sexual initiation (set off, remember, by her own recollection of adolescent experimentation) is paralleled by scenes in which her children read about sex together and by one in which her son discusses the sexual behaviour of *his* teacher. The film's linking of sexual initiation to teaching in general is underlined by Ruth's pointed parting remark to her evening class (and a reverse shot of Lianna): 'You can learn from plenty of other people'.

To present a woman's inauguration into lesbianism

171

under the aegis of the sentimental education is to evoke the sort of 'live and learn' aphorisms cited above. Stories about the initiation of a younger lover by an elder often suggest more about the power of age and experience than that invested in gender or sexual norms. Flaubert's young lover, after all, was a heterosexual man . . . In *Lianna*, the parallels with heterosexual romance are underscored in the intercutting of Lianna's final night with Ruth and a dance sequence in which a man and woman part.

Ironically, Lianna's story can signify *everyone's* experience only by remaining peculiarly ahistorical, unspecified, thus troubling art cinema's canons of realism. The heroine seems remarkably immature, even for a coming-of-age narrative, because, despite living in the present-day USA, she – like the film – seems scarcely to have registered the gay or women's movements. The contending forces which would threaten the representative status of any single character have to be masked off: 'Lianna and Ruth's relation exists in a social and political vacuum.'[18]

But if Lianna really is 'about' learning, what does the heroine learn? To love women? (Ruth: 'You love women, Lianna, not just me.') That she always loved women? (Sandy: 'She said it wasn't new, that she had always felt that way.') That loving women won't save her from unhappiness? (Lianna: 'I thought, when I found somebody, everything would be all right.') These are the lessons recited in the dialogue, but they ignore another one: the heroine's induction into the film's own voyeurism. From her first, wide-eyed gaze at the moonlit posterior of the woman student she discovers with her husband (a sight which she later reprises to Ruth in her story about watching the camp counsellors: 'we could see his bare bottom shining white in the moonlight') to her eager gaze at passing women the morning after her first visit to the lesbian bar, Lianna learns to look. As in *Coup de foudre*, with its strongly marked looks (stares, in the case of Madeleine) between the two women when they first meet after the school recital, Lianna's romance with Ruth is conducted through emphatically visual exchanges (in the classroom, in the coffee bar, after their first dinner, at the pool, in bed).

Both films match this diegetic perspective to that of the spectator in mirror scenes, in which the characters turn their backs to the camera and look with us at their own semi-clad bodies (Lianna, when considering whether to discard her bra for her first date with Ruth; Lena and Madeleine while dressing after *their* swim). Both films also write public spectacles of femininity into their narratives: Lena and Madeleine watch women model fashions in a Paris salon; Lianna watches the woman dancer as she cues the lights.

In a similar way, the sexual curiosity incited by both films is rendered innocent by their use of children as both fascinated onlookers and auditors. Lena's husband – who experiences the film's one, very displaced, primal scene when he interrupts Madeleine and her art teacher dressing after sex – may 'wonder who's kissing her now', the soldiers may spy on Lena's seduction on the train, but then so do the little girls when they watch the maid kissing her boyfriend ('Look, they're licking tongues!'). And Lianna's husband Dick asks *his* question ('How was it? Like a drugstore paperback?') only after we've seen her children consult a variety of texts on what appears to be the film's unseen revelation – oral sex: 'Lianna Massey eats pussy . . .'.

It is this legitimation of the feminine spectacle which makes lesbianism such a gift to art cinema. When Lianna complains that 'everybody's staring at us' in the My Way bar, she's right: not only because the film cuts repeatedly from her own fascinated gaze to pairs of eyes in extreme close-up, but also because *we're* staring. The scene's upbeat rock accompaniment displaces other, more diegetic sounds without adding the distraction of contradictory or particularly preoccupying lyrics – thereby permitting us to concentrate solely on the sight of women dancing together.

Lianna: learning to look at the My Way bar (production still).

This displacement of diegetic sound occurs whenever Lianna and Ruth make love. Their first sex scene runs the gamut of display techniques, and is also the most 'arty', the most redolent of certain European films: blue filter, slow motion, montage cutting, bodily fragmentation. Nor does the soundtrack disturb the spectacle (as it does, for instance, by its volume in the bed scene of Akerman's *Je, tu, il, elle*). Instead, a soft murmur of dubbed endearments is voiced over (under, really) in English and French. (The unsuitability of the latter for sex in New Jersey led one reviewer to conclude that Ruth must teach, not psychology, but modern languages!) If, as Tom Ryall remarks, '"foreignness" [is] perhaps the most generalised characteristic' of art cinema, this may explain its use here.[19] In any case, the soundtrack's low level of volume and intelligibility again enables the visual register to assume pre-eminence.

It can be argued that both the bar and bed scenes integrate the relay of looks in the first instance and the mannered style of the second into an overall theme of initiation, as experienced from the viewpoint of the central character. Thus, the first sequence of glances in the bar seems unfriendly, even menacing to the anxious initiate. But when Lianna relaxes into a swaying *pas de deux* with one of the previously staring strangers, the looks are reprised – with smiles. A similar case can be made for the stylistic devices so fulsomely employed in the first love scene. Their emphatically arty connotations may convey suggestions of an extreme, almost disorientating ecstasy, as well as a certain ritual character (slow purposeful gestures, incantation, low light).

My purpose here is not to rule out such interpretations,

but to remind readers that such switches between omniscient and subjective perspectives are characteristic art cinema fare; and that arguments which fit such scenes into an overall intelligibility are simply beside the point. These devices may indeed 'make sense' within the narrative – they may have been consciously intended to do so by an 'author'. But they also renew the sense, the meaningfulness, of that venerable tradition in which the woman functions as the object of the gaze both of a film's characters and of its spectators.

What are the consequences of a cinema which frees the woman's look in order to vindicate that of the spectator? In classical Hollywood, the heroine's investigations trespass the male prerogative and are punished accordingly.[20] In art cinema, lesbianism has also been punished, often by death (*Les Biches, The Conformist, Another Way*). Although Lianna, Lena and Madeleine survive, they suffer. They suffer for their stares in a way which we spectators escape: our looks are not returned by their mirrors, our curiosity is gratified without jeopardy. Ultimately, these characters suffer as the objects of a cinema which cannot come to terms with its own pleasures. (Witness Sayles's own defiance when discussing queries at the London Film Festival over why he hadn't made the film about homosexual men . . .[21]) Despite Dick Massey's classroom quotation of Heisenberg's Uncertainty Principle to debunk the 'purity' of documentary film, *Lianna* – like so much of art cinema – remains studiously unaware of the effects of its own observations.

from robot to romance

In 1976, a British literary magazine with a line in speculative fiction published a short story by the film-maker and theorist Peter Wollen. *Friendship's Death*[1] is offered as a memorial of the eponymous character and as something more – evidence of his very existence. In a disavowal familiar to the genre of the fantastic,[2] the narrator solicits our credulity by admitting that he can offer no proof – nothing but his own assertion and a document in 'Friendship's hand . . . the only trace left of an astonishing being' (p. 140).

The prologue yields to Jordan in 1970, where the narrator is covering the regime's war with the Palestinians for a radical British monthly. During one day's fighting a Palestinian commander brings an English-speaking stranger to this journalist and asks him to determine his identity. The stranger, who looks and talks American, replies that his name is Friendship, after the purpose of his visit to Earth as an ambassador 'from outside'. Furthermore, he is a mechanical rather than an organic being: 'what we would think of as a robot, with artificial intelligence and a very sophisticated system of plastic surgery and prosthesis' (pp. 142–3).

Cut off from his base and his intended destination (a

rendezvous with the radical linguist Noam Chomsky at the Massachusetts Institute of Technology), Friendship is confronted with the daunting prospect of what the narrator calls 'full autonomy'. He gratefully accepts the journalist's cover story (identifying him as a colleague deprived of his identity papers) and accompanies him to his hotel in war-torn Amman.

There the curious Englishman and the equally curious android engage in a series of synopsized dialogues, largely about that triad of 1970s concerns – politics, semiotics and psychoanalysis. Lacking (unlike the replicants in *Blade Runner*) a ready-made stock of ersatz familial memories, Friendship evidences a particular fascination with human sexuality and the unconscious. This places the journalist-narrator in the role of analyst, interpreting the scanty affectual life of this artificial American in Oedipal terms:

> Parricidal phantasies he was able to grasp without too much difficulty – after all, his own erstwhile 'controllers' could be identified with 'father-figures' and he could readily see that the 'fault' that occurred during entry could be construed as the realization of his own Oedipal desires. At any rate, his own uncertainty after the control device was inoperative had to be seen in this kind of light. He had experienced 'anxiety'. (p. 144)

True to form, the android analysand begins to regress – into a childhood he has never in fact experienced, a reaction that his mentor finds 'extremely embarrassing. All the more so, perhaps, because he was in reality dependent upon me for money, for conversation, for protection' (p. 145).

Spurred by his interest in the unconscious, Friendship pursues an eclectic inquiry into language, borrowing from the journalist's supply of books, including a crossword puzzle collection and a Penguin edition of Mallarmé, and bringing to him – as a child would to a parent – his own responses, notably an idiosyncratically punning translation of *L'après-midi d'un faune*.[3]

Friendship's associative play with signification is matched by his new political allegiances, which rapidly move from the radical American intelligentsia to a newly gained identification with the oppressed – women, Third World peoples, and the entire helot class of machines to which he belongs. (In a memorable passage he rebukes the journalist for hammering the keys of his typewriter, with which he recognizes 'some kind of kinship' (p. 146).) Having accomplished a fairly explicit transference to humankind, Friendship claims human rights for future generations of 'smart machines' who will come to duplicate their masters in every aspect except their intended instrumentality. He resolves to forge an alliance with other, human, workers and enlists on the side of the Palestinians as a 'Canadian' volunteer. As the fighting intensifies, the journalist is forced to leave the country, but Friendship refuses to accompany him. He is killed, the narrator assumes, along with his defeated comrades in the massacres of Black September. All that remains is his eccentric translation of Mallarmé's poem, and the story concludes with the text of that strange document.

* * *

179

A decade later, Wollen returned to his story to script and direct a feature-length adaptation for the British Film Institute (*Friendship's Death*, 1987). As a film, the project was transformed in a number of ways, but the one most discussed was Friendship's sex change. In interviews Wollen argued that an early script with two male protagonists threatened to turn into a buddy movie, and that the feminization of Friendship 'made the robot more *Other* for the journalist',[4] while reversing the traditionally masculine imagery of machines. But he did note three fictional precedents for the figure of the female robot: Villiers de l'Isle-Adam's 1880s novel *Tomorrow's Eve*, the Czech dramatist Karel Čapek's 1921 play *R.U.R.*, and Fritz Lang's 1926 *Metropolis*. In the last two he acknowledged similarities with *Friendship's Death* – notably the theme of the rebellious robot worker – but that of the French Symbolist, he maintained, involved 'a different kind of fantasy structure'.[5]

Wollen's reluctance to regard *Tomorrow's Eve* as a cautionary tale for his own project now strikes me as more than a little ironic. Indeed, as he was preparing his film, two noted scholars of the cinema, Annette Michelson and Raymond Bellour, produced readings of the novel which went on to describe its simulated woman as *the* figure of the medium, 'the fantasmatic ground of cinema itself',[6] 'a tangible foundation for the image's power to fascinate'.[7] After all, the inventor of *Tomorrow's Eve* will also invent the cinema, for he is none other than Thomas Alva Edison.

At the novel's opening,[8] Edison is discovered brooding in his laboratory at Menlo Park. If only, the 'phonograph's papa' regrets, if only he had been alive at the dawn of creation, he could have lurked 'behind some secret thicket in Eden' to record that most primal of scenes. And it's not just Genesis from which this jealous historian laments his exclusion – all the great events of the classics and the Testaments cry out to his passion for scientific proof, for mechanical reproduction as a positivist guarantee of religious faith. Photography too, he reflects, might have been marshalled to preserve the marvels of the Bible from atheistic scepticism.

In Villiers's novel, as in contemporary film theory, voyeurism, curiosity and the cinema all spring from the same sadistic root. Thus Edison devises the sound film to perfect his admonitory record of the 'cruel interrogations' of the Inquisition:

> The camera, aided by the phonograph (they are near kin), could reproduce both the sight and the different sounds made by the sufferers, giving a complete, an exact idea of the experience. What an admirable course of instruction for the grade schools, to render healthful the intelligence of modern young people – perhaps even public figures! A splendid magic lantern! (pp. 22–3)

To this laboratory of the cinema comes its central figure – the woman – the beautiful but unsatisfactory mistress of a Scottish laird. There she will be unknowingly duplicated and discarded in favour of her mechanical counterpart, for 'What is a mistress?' (asks Edison, echoing Swift). 'A belt and a cloak, no more' (p. 206). Her replacement is a creature of precious metals and scented fluids, powered by an electromagnet and programmed with sixty hours of recorded speech (and proportionate additional permutations) 'invented by the greatest poets, the most subtle metaphysicians, the most profound novelists of this century' (p. 131). Such is the sophistication of the software that this speech responds not only to that of its noble interlocutor, but to his very thoughts!

Yet, paradoxically, it is not Edison's 'scientific Eve' but her human original who is this story's truly Material Girl. The daughter of an *arriviste* family who has escaped via a loveless engagement to a fiancé who later abandons her, Alicia Cleary pursues her dual career as an operatic actress and Lord Ewald's mistress with all the 'careful calculations' of her class. Her dissatisfied protector describes her as one of those 'women who would cheerfully define honor as "a sort of luxury that only the rich can afford, but that other people can always buy when they have the price"' (p. 35), and he complains to Edison that she seems:

> wholly unaware of the mysterious extent to which her
> body fulfills the absolute ideal of human perfection.
> It's simply as a matter of business, of *trade*, that her
> theatrical training enables her to interpret the
> inspirations of genius into mimic gestures . . . The
> divine illusion of glory, the enthusiasm, the noble
> excitement of the audience, are nothing for her but
> an infatuation of people with nothing else to do . . .
> (p. 34)

Compared to this cynical deconstructionist, a machine might well possess a more tender soul. And in a fascinating – but perhaps not wholly surprising – reversal,

Alicia's android successor is unveiled at the very moment when Lord Ewald finally feels himself to be loved. The price of this perfect love is disavowal, the defence of an 'Ideal' (the android's literal name) against Reason. 'If you question my being,' she warns Ewald, 'I am lost' (p. 199).

Lord Ewald hesitates, then succumbs to *his* divine illusion, this fetish object, with fatal consequences. And not only he, argue both Michelson and Bellour, but the audience of Edison's cinema, soon to contemplate precisely this imagined perfection, the mechanized figure of the woman, in what Bellour describes as 'the vast commercial gaze of shared desire'.[9]

If the feminist film theory of the 1970s had a single purpose, it was to break the circuit of fetishism and the cinema which Villiers's 'great electrician' is seen to perfect. Where Edison fashions his loving android 'to stop time' at the 'ideal instant' of romance – 'to fix it, define it' (p. 136) – Laura Mulvey urged film-makers to 'free the look of the camera into its materiality in time and space'.[10] Such a programme was particularly adventurous in the mid 1970s, when modern feminism's own tendency to fetishistic idealization, to role models and positive images, was arguably at its height. As applied on film, it resulted in three works which attempted both to address and to escape this idealization – *Penthesilea* (1974), *Riddles of the Sphinx* (1977), and *Amy!* (1980) – films which were, of course, made jointly by Mulvey and Peter Wollen. *Penthesilea* and *Amy!* examined the feminist heroine in a number of guises (Amazon, Suffragette, Aviatrix), while *Riddles of the Sphinx* presented a narrative of single motherhood which might, in other hands, have developed into the feminist *Bildungsroman* of the period. (Valiant young mother comes of age by separating from husband, going out to work, fighting for workplace nursery and falling in love with independent black woman.)

From the outset, Mulvey and Wollen's investigation of the myth of the strong woman was a cautious one, guided by their reading of nineteenth-century writings on the Amazon – notably Kleist's and Bachofen's – in which the phallic and maternal implications of the figure are particularly marked. While one tendency in feminist politics had seized upon the myth as evidence of a pre-patriarchal woman's culture, *Penthesilea* emphasized its dramatization of male castration anxiety, and the woman warrior herself as a highly fetishized apotropaic to that fear:

> they carry spears and fight and ride horses, and have
> very phallic connotations. They appear like the
> idealised image a sexist society has of men/women –
> of phallic women. At the same time, the whole
> mystique Kleist goes into, of dying together, is very
> much a return to the idea of the strong woman as
> mother.[11]

To forestall classical cinema's tendency to relieve the spectator's anxiety through the perfection of a figure for narcissistic identification, a number of now-familiar formal strategies were adopted in these early films: the avoidance of the actor's body in favour of objects or images; angles and framings which exclude the face; the

184

use of a static camera at a fixed distance or in highly schematic movements (the famous 360-degree pans in *Riddles of the Sphinx*); and soundtracks which serve to confound or diminish the plenitude of the image or its sequencing.

The putative 'materialism' of these early films, their dissection of the stylistic components of the mainstream medium, was doubled by an emphatic interest in production – in literal work – within their diegeses: Louise's childcare and job as a telephonist in *Riddles*; Amy's self-taught expertise in aviation technology; and American feminist Jessie Ashley's unheeded plea to link the campaign for the vote with working-class politics in *Penthesilea*.

This last speech is delivered by an actress in medium close-up, upon whose face footage from an early silent film is superimposed. The film, produced in 1913 by the US Women's Political Union, is *What 80 Million Women Want*, in which a young suffragette aids her lawyer boyfriend in exposing a corrupt politician and is rewarded by the personal congratulations of Emmeline Pankhurst herself. Mulvey and Wollen's reworking of this narrative could be described as *effacement* – both of the individual portrait-style close-up and of the figure of the exemplary heroine, whose solution, *Penthesilea* warns us, is 'magical rather than political'.

If the first version of *Friendship's Death* was informed by the left-intellectual preoccupations of the 1970s – psychoanalysis, semiotics and Marxism – its 1980s successor took on the intellectual coloration of its decade – notably the postmodernism of Baudrillard's *Simulations*. Over documentary footage of a jet blown apart on the tarmac by PLO hijackers, a voice-over marvels:

It's an image with all the meaning drained out of it.
Completely opaque. Like a curtain between us and
history.

The map, for Baudrillard, 'engenders the territory'; for Wollen's journalist (called Sullivan in the film) it also engenders politics:

Politics has got absolutely nothing to do with people.
People are just the raw material. It's all to do with
territory. Look at the situation here . . . annexation,
partition, maps.

Paradoxically, Sullivan's new-found familiarity with the contemporary discourse of the hyperreal reconstitutes him as that most traditional figure of narrative cinema – the cynical journalist with three days' beard and a taste for Johnny Walker. (Wollen cites actor Bill Paterson's performance as a journalist in *The Killing Fields*; there's also his sadistic black propagandist in *Licking Hitler*.) Where Sullivan's predecessor evidenced a sort of taken-for-granted left politics (summarized in one telling phrase as 'nationalism, Marxism and so on'), the most he can muster is an irritable sympathy for the oppressed. In the shift from first-person literary narration to cinematic dialogue, he becomes the wisecracker to Friendship's straight woman, reacting to her bald announcement of extra-terrestial origins with lines like 'Here's to malfunction!'

As for Friendship, *her* transformation from her 1970s male prototype is quite usefully explained in the one passage from *Simulations* which the film doesn't quote. Comparing the automata of the *ancien régime* to the robots of industrialization, Baudrillard argues that the robot's central purpose is work: 'its only truth is in its mechanical efficacy'.[12] Such machines are designed to be the functional equivalents of human beings rather than their analogical semblances. The automaton, in contrast, is built to the latter specification, a counterfeiting of the social rather than the technical capacities of the species. 'The automaton', writes Baudrillard, 'plays the part of courtier and good company' (p. 93). And this, I believe, is the role both of Villiers's Eve and of Friendship, Mark II. Both are implicated in the same structure of fantasy, a fantasy which Villiers's novel foregrounds in the fetishistic disavowal demanded of Lord Ewald, but which Wollen's film never quite confronts.

In the theoretical move from Marxism to postmodernism, from Amy to the female Friendship, an ontology of resemblance, simulation, replaces that of labour, production. Where one flier travels from her bedsit to the heavens via a strict regime of aeronautical housekeeping ('Daily Drill . . . Wash engine down with paraffin or petrol. . . Grease valve stems and push rods'), the other simply arrives. Where Amy Johnson – prior to her aviation feats – has actually worked as a typist, Friendship claims kinship with the machine itself.

When pronounced by the childlike male android of Wollen's original story, this identification with a machine so lowly ('something in between tool and machine'[13]) and so culturally feminized has a certain impact. Coming from his self-possessed female successor, it merely seems coy. Where the male Friendship's femininity (at one point he describes himself as a hysteric) disturbs the journalist, the female's masculinity (her height, fearlessness, expertise) arouses his desire. So does the superficial perfection of her bodywork (in true postmodern terms, Friendship's human features are all surface and no depth), which spares her the embarrassment of inebriation (no digestive system) and, indeed, of that other cavity which portends a man's castration.

One day Sullivan discovers some brightly coloured crystals (very like an infant's playthings) in the room of the absent android, and steals them. When they begin to glow and hum in the middle of the night, the pyjama-clad correspondent is forced to seek Friendship's aid. Elaborately robed and coiffured, she comes to his room like a patient parent. In a series of shots angled to emphasize her height, she retrieves the crystals, explains their function as recording devices, and gives him one as a present. Then she bends down and kisses Sullivan on the cheek, bidding him to 'sleep tight. The Sand-Man's coming.'

This sly reference to Hoffmann's tale of the mechanical doll (which was filmed by Méliès in 1903 and by Powell and Pressburger in 1951, and provides an epigraph for *Tomorrow's Eve*[14]) is the film's sole acknowledgement of the castration anxiety which underlies its presentation of this phallic mother. The Sand-Man steals children's eyes, and the eye, Freud argues in his reading of Hoffmann in 'The Uncanny', is consistently equated in unconscious thought with the male organ. The young Nathaniel is threatened with a visit from the Sand-Man, 'who comes when children won't go to bed, and throws handfuls of sand in their eyes';[15] later he discovers that the beautiful woman he spies upon is a clockwork automaton, with ruined eyes. Freud's interpretation of the vulnerable doll as 'nothing less than a materialization of Nathaniel's feminine attitude towards his father' (p. 354), and Nathaniel's obsession for her as the narcissistic regard for a projected self, return us to Bellour's reading of *Tomorrow's Eve*:

> As with Freud's description of the idealized woman [in 'Being in Love and Hypnosis'], the Android fixes the man's narcissistic libido on the woman and absorbs his ego; she restores and metamorphoses his lost narcissism by occupying the 'place of the ego ideal'.[16]

Thus, when Lord Ewald's feminine Ideal is destroyed in a shipboard fire, her lover must also die. Not so Sullivan. He escapes with his ideal, so to speak, intact – and the crystalline image recorder given to him by Friendship. Years later in London, he reminisces about the events of Black September with a male colleague. Also present is Sullivan's teenage daughter, a budding science prodigy. Notably missing is her mother, or indeed any adult woman – a structural absence which makes perfect sense if we conclude that this is a drama of male narcissism, rather than that of the 'Other'.

At the film's end, Sullivan's daughter takes over the technocratic functions of her extra-terrestial role model

The journalist and his writing machine in *Friendship's Death* (production still).

and cracks the crystal's code. (Like Friendship's before her, her success in this endeavour is simply attributed to the sheer sophistication of her knowledge.) The playback which follows is an attempt at a video analogue of the

190

Mallarmé translation in the original short story – a computer-treated sequence of geometric and biological images, including simulated radio waves and scans of the human heart – *camera-stylo* impressions apparently recorded by Friendship back in 1970. The inclusion of the keys and carriage of a typewriter recalls her identification with things mechanical. But the typewriter is Sullivan's instrument, his writing machine. It serves as a salient reminder that this sad tale of a lost superwoman is very much the man's story, and that of a decade which could only look back to politics with nostalgia.[17]

sexual politics

the fatal attraction of *Intercourse*

'Are you afraid now?'
(Andrea Dworkin, *Intercourse*)

White linen, full bleed

The dust-jacket of *Intercourse* shows a photograph of an unmade bed. White sheets lie dishevelled in deep shadow, apparently just feet away from the viewer. Across the photograph, which is not inset or bordered but printed to the edges of the jacket, white letters are reversed out of the gloom. Horizontally and vertically they frame the tousled bedding, the author's name immediately visible across the top, the title taking more time to discern, a little *frisson* in sidelong italics. The blurb at the foot of the front cover reads:

> 'The Most Shocking Book Any Feminist Has Yet Written' – Germaine Greer

On the back this tribute is repeated, along with four others containing epithets like 'uncompromising', 'forbidden', 'unflinching' and (again) 'shocking'. The coarse-grained naturalism of the black and white photograph, low-lit and uncropped, seems to betoken the painful revelations promised within. As Mary Daly warns us, 'It strikes the main nerve of oppression in the man's world.'

Seventy years before *Intercourse*, Sigmund Freud wrote about a nightmare in white: one winter's evening, the bedroom window of a young boy suddenly opens to reveal the big walnut tree outside. In its branches sit a pack of wolves, with white fur and staring eyes, their ears pricked up in fierce attention. Terrified of being eaten, the boy awakes with a scream.

The interpretation of this dream, Freud was to report in his case study of the Russian *émigré* he called the Wolf Man, 'dragged on over several years'.[1] Its subject, he concluded, was intercourse. Not any intercourse, Freud hazarded, but that of the boy's own parents, interrupting an afternoon's siesta to engage in coitus and waking their infant son. The season being summer, they had retired half undressed: 'in white underclothes', Freud's footnote patiently explains, 'the *white* wolves' (p. 269).

The opening sequence of *Fatal Attraction* discloses the Gallagher family in their cramped Manhattan apartment. Attorney Dan Gallagher is completing some work in the living-room before going out for the evening. Housewife Beth Gallagher is in the bathroom, preparing to accompany him. Six-year-old Ellen Gallagher is clutching the family dog as she watches TV. All three wear white underclothes, in a suspended moment of familial intimacy which is broken by the arrival of the babysitter. Father and Mother are about to depart, leaving their child behind . . .

As the US cinematic *cause célèbre* of 1987, *Fatal Attraction* was preceded to these shores by a *Time* magazine cover story, a special supplement on family movies in the *Village Voice*, and sundry British notices trailing its UK opening with stories of vindictive American audiences screaming for the *femme fatale*'s final dispatch. British cinema-goers may have been slightly more restrained, but the overwhelming commercial success of the film in its first few months of UK release – together with the extensive number of previews, reviews, interviews and related press and broadcast features on the new familialism, sex in the age of AIDS, the Single Working Woman and – courtesy of the *Sunday Times* – 'the unending question of passion v. society' (17 January 1988), suggest a similar cultural centrality.

One of the most pervasive explanations for this success is the film's proffering of multiple figures for identification – Dan, the seducible but well-meaning husband, bewildered by the consequences of what he first regards as a minor fling; Beth, his shocked and angry wife, presented not as a repressed homebody but as an attractive sharp dresser capable of the odd swearword; and – most controversially – Alex Forrest, the Single Working Woman, an assertiveness-trained publisher in her late thirties, devastated by yet another emotional let-down from a married man. As Sue Heal argued in *Today*, 'The basic appeal of Fatal Attraction is that everyone can recognise themselves in it somewhere. The wronged wife, the irrational rejected woman, the happily married man who has a one-night stand' (15 January 1988). Similarly, Andrea Kannapell replied to a *Village Voice* poll of its regular contributors about the film: 'The main attraction of *Attraction* is that you can project just about any meaning you want on it. Some people see it from Alex's point of view, some from Dan's; some see feminism, others misogyny' (15 December 1987). Indeed, among the varied responses to the *Voice* poll were feminists who disputed the film's meaning from within a stated identification with Alex, Amy Taubin finding a sickening pathologization of the demands of the rejected woman, Karen Durbin celebrating a powerful representation of female rebellion and rage. In Britain the *Sunday Express* christened the antagonism to this character as 'the Alex effect', and ran a defensive explanation of her motives by 'consulting clinical psychologist' Charmian Bollinger:

> Fatal Attraction is like a nightmare and most people
> will see it as the nightmare of a more-or-less
> innocent husband like Dan and of a totally innocent
> wife like Beth. But it is also the nightmare of a
> lonely, passionate, woman like Alex and she
> deserves our sympathy every bit as much. (17
> January 1988)

Interestingly, none of the *Voice* commentators – or indeed any of the other sixty-odd British and American writings on the film in the British Film Institute's library – took their cue from a provocative aside in the original *Voice* review by J. Hoberman, who noted that the film employed 'the judicious use of a child's point of view' taking on a 'malign fairy-tale aspect' (29 September 1987). Dan and Beth and Alex – and Ellen?

The child makes a similarly surprising entrance at the end of Andrea Dworkin's *Intercourse*, when –

almost as an afterthought, since this is a book about 'ordinary' sex – she extrapolates from the violence and inequity she sees in heterosexual intercourse between adults:

> 'I felt like I was being ripped up the middle of my legs all the way to my throat,' one incest victim said. 'I was sure that if I opened my eyes and looked down, I would be in two parts on the bed.' This too is genital mutilation – with the penis doing the cutting. Perhaps incestuous rape is becoming a central paradigm for intercourse in our time. Women are supposed to be small and childlike, in looks, in rights; child prostitution keeps increasing in mass and in legitimacy; the children sexually used by a long chain of men – fathers, uncles, grandfathers, brothers, pimps, pornographers, and the good citizens who are the consumers; and men, who are, after all, just family, are supposed to slice us up the middle, leaving us in parts on the bed.[2]

Taking Dworkin at her word, I think it is worth reading *Intercourse* as though it were written from a child's viewpoint, or at least from within the youthful understandings of intercourse which erupt – like those of the Wolf Man – in the nightmares of our later lives. Such an approach suggests marked similarities with films like *Fatal Attraction*, which also deal with intercourse in the generic language of horror – 'bedroom horror', as Hoberman describes them.

The discourse of intercourse

Intercourse, like many of modern feminism's most influential polemics, begins as literary criticism. The first five chapters – 'Repulsion', 'Skinless', 'Stigma', 'Communion', 'Possession' – consider in turn fiction by Tolstoy, Kobo Abe, Tennessee Williams, James Baldwin and Isaac Bashevis Singer. The book's second half is more diffusely organized, but it too ranges across the writings of Flaubert, Bram Stoker, Proust, and Vargas Llosa, among others. Virtually every work selected (with the possible exception of Stoker's *Dracula*) makes literal reference to sexual intercourse within its narrative: Tolstoy's *Kreutzer Sonata*, a novella whose central character engages in a long critique of conjugal sex; the allegories of the Japanese writer Abe (*The Woman in the Dunes*, *The Face of Another*, *The Box Man*) in which a man is trapped in a formless world of shifting sand by the strong woman he fails to rape, or has sex in a mask because he's lost the skin on his face, or stops living in a box in order to engage in an affair of constant contact; the dramas of Tennessee Williams, in which women characters like Stella Kowalski and Blanche Du Bois enact desire as physical pleasure and psychical disaster. Then there's Baldwin's *Another Country* and *Giovanni's Room*, in which racial, national and normative boundaries may be crossed in intercourse, but not 'that quarter of an inch between us on that bed'.[3] Finally – and in a sense, summarily, because its horrors will dominate the rest of the book – Dworkin turns to Singer's *Satan in Goray*, a novel which stages demonic possession, racial pogrom and the highly elaborated torture of the central female character in a narrative of near apocalypse.

There is a huge array of contradictions in Dworkin's presentation of these fictions – beginning with her reluctance to read them as fictions at all. Again and again, fundamental questions of form – how incidents are framed within larger narrative structures, the organization of point of view and telling, differences between media (Williams's drama versus Baldwin's novels) and styles (Abe's allegories versus Tolstoy's realism) – are simply ignored, in order to elide these stories into various non-fiction commentaries on intercourse, some written by the authors in question, some not.

This combination of textual and extra-textual interests might seem appropriate in an investigation of how particular historical, national, racial or social contexts relate to writing on sex, but Dworkin shows remarkably little interest in the circumstances of these stories' production. We are left no wiser about the Japanese conventions which inform the anti-realism of Abe's stories than about the homosexual subtext of *A Streetcar Named Desire*. However, while Dworkin seems indifferent to the vagaries of race, geography, history and object choice, one variable is strictly controlled: all of the authors in Part One of her study – and virtually all of the fiction writers throughout it – are men. Despite such differences as are perceptible between the writers and texts under consideration – despite Dworkin's evident approval of the tenderness and regret she reads, for instance, in the work of Baldwin and Williams – intercourse is clearly presented as a matter of male oppression.

To establish this culpable conflation of author, text and gender there could be no better story than Tolstoy's *Kreutzer Sonata*. An object of great controversy in the Russian literary scene of the late 1880s, it was circulated in privately printed drafts until Tolstoy's wife – Sofya Andreyevna – persuaded Tsar Aleksander to lift the imperial ban in 1891. The irony of her intervention is not ignored by Dworkin. The novella's autobiographical elements were even at that time legible, and it is a story of a Russian aristocrat who murders his wife. As a typically undervalued amanuensis, Sofya transcribed and published Tolstoy's writings, as well as managing his considerable business affairs and bearing him thirteen children. Like her husband, she left journals which give his tale of desire and disgust, marital misery and fatal violence the documentary verisimilitude which Dworkin seeks in her opening chapter. Surely it is impossible not to identify the author with the murderous husband Pozdnyshev, who also regards his wife with a mixture of lust and loathing which finally ignites when he hears her and an imagined rival play Beethoven's 'shattering' sonata – as Tolstoy heard it in the spring of 1887, before impregnating his wife with their thirteenth child. (Particularly as Tolstoy awards Pozdnyshev the honours of narrating almost the entire story himself in a series of impassioned monologues during a long railway journey.)

Yet even Tolstoy's Russian contemporaries were uncertain of the story's moral, and they appealed to the author for an explanation. Similarly, we might ask how we are to understand Pozdnyshev's repentant description of his wife's murder as the result of 'debauchery'. Do the other elements of the text support his argument that sex for the sake of physical pleasure – indeed, that intercourse *per se* – is necessarily misogynist? Is wife-murder simply the logical extrapolation of the violence of the marriage bed, with Pozdnyshev's damask-steel dagger completing the penetration wrought by his penis?

In response to such questions, Tolstoy wrote a post-face to the novella, attempting to explain 'in clear, simple terms what I think of the subject of the story'[4]:

> It is necessary that carnal love be envisaged
> differently, that men and women be educated by
> their families and by public opinion in such a way that
> both before and after marriage they view desire and
> the carnal love that is associated with it not as a
> sublime, poetic condition, as they are viewed at
> present, but as a condition of animality that is
> degrading to human beings . . .

As an affirmative repetition of Pozdnyshev's arguments, the postface underlines Dworkin's equation of male author and male character, of Tolstoy the abusive husband of Sofya and the 'killer/husband' of his creation. But detached from a confession of wife-murder (where it can be read as a rather unconvincing piece of special pleading), much of the afterword seems indistinguishable from the Social Purity writings of the period, which, of course, commanded considerable feminist support. Tolstoy's opening argument against prostitution, for example, as well as his appeal to Christian belief, echoes Josephine Butler, while those arguments against the double standard, contraception as a sanction for the carnal indulgence of non-reproductive sex, intercourse during pregnancy and intercourse *per se*, appear in the writings of British feminists such as

Christabel Pankhurst, Elizabeth Wolstenholme Elmy, Lucy Re-Bartlett and Frances Swiney.

This is hardly an accident, since Tolstoy read his feminist contemporaries and feminists, indeed, read Tolstoy. (In his introduction to the Penguin edition, A.N. Wilson notes that *The Kreutzer Sonata* incorporates actual phrases from the American physician Alice Bunker Stockham's warnings against sex during pregnancy, while the British feminist Katherine Dixon's 1916 *Address to Soldiers* defends the 'slaves of the prostitution market' by citing Tolstoy's admonition that no 'human beings can exist without love and consideration'.[5] This is not to say that Social Purity was an unproblematic or uncontested feminist position, or that Tolstoy's postface can be entirely attributed to it (the passages decrying women's 'shameless' enticement of male lust do suggest a rather sinister oscillation between desire and disgust). But what is notable in Dworkin's account of *The Kreutzer Sonata* is the neglect of this important interrelation. Even more remarkably, the entire canon of late-nineteenth- and early-twentieth-century feminist writing on sex, recently re-examined in the light of current debates by historians like Sheila Jeffreys and Judith Walkowitz, is reduced in *Intercourse* to a brief reference to Victoria Woodhull's advocacy of a female-determined heterosexual congress in the nineteenth century – while only Shere Hite surfaces amongst Dworkin's feminist contemporaries. Why? Why would a new study of the relation between sex and the social inferiority of women ignore the extensive feminist literature already available on the subject? My suspicions take me back to that small boy's vision of his parents in bed.

Something uncanny

As early as his 1900 *Interpretation of Dreams*, Freud noted 'that sexual intercourse between adults strikes any children who observe it as something uncanny and that it arouses anxiety in them'.[6] Freud, who would later relate 'the uncanny' to 'what arouses dread and horror',[7] first attributed this anxiety to children's difficulty in coping with the arousal caused by this experience, particularly since it involves their parents. By 1908, he enlarged this explanation to argue that these young witnesses 'adopt what may be called a *sadistic view of coition* ... as something that the stronger participant is forcibly inflicting on the weaker'. In a passage with which Dworkin might well concur, Freud went on to note that these apprehensions could often be correct:

> In many marriages the wife does in fact recoil from her husband's embraces, which bring her no pleasure, but the risk of a fresh pregnancy. And so the child who is believed to be asleep (or who is pretending to be asleep) may receive an impression from his mother which he can only interpret as meaning that she is defending herself against an act of violence. At other times the whole marriage offers an observant child the spectacle of an unceasing quarrel, expressed in loud words and unfriendly gestures; so that he need not be surprised if the quarrel is carried on at night as well, and finally settled by the same method which he himself is accustomed to use in his relations with his brothers and sisters or playmates.[8]

The primal scene which Freud deduced from the dream of the young Russian added a further complication to this account – namely, the child's jealousy on discovering that what seems to be painful is sometimes pleasurable: 'He assumed to begin with, he said, that the event of which he was a witness was an act of violence, but the expression of enjoyment which he saw on his mother's face did not fit in with this' (p. 277).

The similarity between the child's secret viewing of the primal scene and the voyeurism entailed in the spectator's unseen observation of the cinema performance ('that simultaneously very close and definitely inaccessible "elsewhere"'[9] was theorized in the mid 1970s by Christian Metz, but it had long been acknowledged, both allegorically and explicitly, in the film melodrama and the thriller. In melodrama of the 1950s, children are the distraught witnesses of their parents' actual and apparent sexual transgressions in Minnelli's *Some Came Running*, Aldrich's *Autumn Leaves* and Sirk's *There's Always Tomorrow*. In Hitchcock's *Rebecca*, Joan Fontaine's researches into the marital violence at Manderly and the child's viewing in *Marnie* of her prostitute mother writhing frantically on the floor with a sailor are merely part of an *oeuvre* marked by narratives of anxious sexual investigation (*Rear Window*, *Vertigo*) and that classic of traumatic vision, *Psycho*: 'Norman found them dead together – in bed'.[10]

Psycho is not only a thriller (and a thematically typical melodrama of familial desire and destruction), it is also a horror film – a genre historically offered to young viewers as a collection of primal scenes:

> Those who saw, say, *Bride of Frankenstein* when they
> were twelve in 1938 do not forget it, just as those who
> saw *Horror of Dracula* when they were twelve in 1958
> seem destined to carry it around forever.[11]

Terrifying visions of sex and violence, of bodily destruction and monstrous procreation, are served up for
children's delight and, according to some critics, their
instruction. Following Bettelheim's observations on the
tutorial uses of the fairy-tale, one commentator has
argued that horror movies are a species of sex education: where the primal scene (real or fantasized) offers
children an account of their own origins, the primal
scenes of horror offer the audience the fictional enact-
ment of their desires – and the consequences thereof.
And if, as Metz has argued, the screen's proximate but
untouchable pleasures – 'precisely Oedipal in type'
(p. 64) – infantilize our desires, it is not surprising that
the preeminent desire discovered by one critic of the
horror film is that of incest.[12] The 'uncanny' (*unheimlich*
= 'unhomelike' or 'unfamiliar'), Freud argued, has a
more than etymological relation to the mother's body
('the former Heim [home] of all human beings'.[13] It
manifests the secret familiarity of repressed wishes,
including Oedipal wishes which may arouse anxious
fears of retribution.

If looks could kill
With the spurned Alex characterized as an almost
supernatural figure of vengeance, rising yet again from
the bath in a climax borrowed from *Les Diaboliques*, *Fatal*

Attraction adds a dimension of horror to the spate of recent family-in-peril movies (*The Untouchables*, *Someone to Watch Over Me*). All three films cast their patriarchs as lawmen (two cops, one attorney) whose moral transgressions are repaid by threats to their wives and children. (One cop worries that he has become as ruthless as the mafiosi he pursues; another has an affair with the witness he's meant to be guarding.) The sins of the fathers suggest that the supposedly external threat to the family, whether Alex Forrest or Al Capone, is actually located within.

Fatal Attraction introduces the Gallaghers' own Oedipal triangle as the wholesome familial norm. Although Dan's desire for his wife is clearly indicated as he caresses her at the dressing-table, the married couple are never seen to make love. Instead daughter Ellen (variously described as five and six in the script) is discovered in the parental bed after Dad returns from walking the family dog, a figure of guilty responsibility who will later accompany him to the Other Woman's apartment. There the animal is reproachfully present during their coupling – and Alex's subsequent suicide attempt. (The relation between the two acts is bloodily literalized when Alex embraces Dan with newly severed wrists.) In the classic co-ordinates of the primal scene, an act of coition is equated with an act of violence and silently witnessed by a third party.

The dog's close proximity to Ellen as she watches TV in the film's opening scene, as well as its parallel role in keeping Dan from the marital bed, should alert us to its affinity with the position of the child-spectator. But Ellen is not the only such figure in the film. In a claim which the narrative goes to some length to verify, Alex describes to Dan her own horror at witnessing her father's fatal heart attack when she was seven. This trauma of vision is offered as the major indication of a troubled psychical history in what is otherwise a notably sparse biographical background. (It is neatly paralleled by the experience of the Other Woman in *Someone to Watch Over Me*. There, another married lawman, this time a police detective, commits adultery with the witness he's supposed to be guarding – a beautiful heiress who's threatened by the gangster she saw murder a friend. Her subsequent fear and dependency lead her into the arms of her police protector, who refers to his assignment as 'babysitting'. When he beds his charge during his supposed hours of watch, the cop who stands guard over the illicit couple is attacked in his stead . . .)

Alex Forrest is *Fatal Attraction*'s most visible spectator – spying on the Gallagher family in the city and the country, peering in through the windows of their new suburban home in a scene whose domestic cosiness triggers an abrupt bout of nausea. Indeed, she is introduced in her first scene as someone who can reply to the ogling surveillance of Dan's colleague with more than equal force. As she cuts his come-on stone dead, the thwarted flirt exclaims, 'If looks could kill . . .'.

But if the look is violent, it is also susceptible to violation, to horrifying sights which we nevertheless long to see. This combination of attraction and terror, so marked in the child's relation to the primal scene (and the audience's relation to horror films), is spelt out in Dan and Alex's two major physical encounters. In the first, they awkwardly couple in Alex's kitchen – gasping and staggering from the dish-filled sink to the bed. In the second, the choreography and sound effects are nearly identical – but this time an enraged Dan is trying to strangle Alex for her repeated persecutions of him and his family, and she is retaliating with the kitchen knife.

This horrifying view of adult intimacy is exactly that of the primal scene, but where is the watching child? *Someone to Watch Over Me* makes the policeman's young son an actual party to its violent climax (in which the wife shoots the gangster who has taken her family hostage) and a knowing witness to his aggrieved mother's target practice after she has discovered her husband's infidelity: 'Aren't you supposed to aim at the heart?' He is also the happily grinning onlooker at their final reconciliatory embrace.

Not so Ellen Gallagher, whose most traumatic vision is the discovery of the empty rabbit hutch. In a brief but intriguing scene, presumably meant to indicate the passage of time in the narrative, the little girl is shown reciting her lines from the school Thanksgiving pageant to her parents: 'Dear Priscilla, Miles asked me to ask you to marry him'. The romantic tenure of the drama in which she has been cast (a pilgrim parallel to *Cyrano de Bergerac*), as well as her own incursion into the parental bedroom, positions Ellen within the sexual dynamics of the larger narrative – even if, like the character she plays, she cannot speak for herself. Yet when it boils up to its final crisis, she is safely offstage. As first Father, and then Mother, attempts to kill the woman who has come between them, the child who has come between them – a child who was previously aroused from bed by raised voices – fails to appear at the primal scene. As the camera surveys the film's bloody climax, the reverse look we expect to be given, Ellen's look, is withheld. Instead, I would argue, we are invited to take up her vantage point, to watch another white-clad lover struggle and die in the intimate surroundings of the family bathroom, and to be as shocked as a child. The exaggerated and implausible horror of Alex's death (a Grand Guignol finale which displeased realist critics) is rendered psychologically appropriate by our own infantilized viewpoint, which replaces that of the little girl, seen only in the film's final, notorious close-up of the Gallagher family photograph.

Dracula's daughters

Among the many horrifying stories recounted in *Intercourse* there is one of true, generic horror: Bram Stoker's 1897 novel *Dracula*. In it two childhood friends are attacked by the vampire – Lucy Westenra, a daughter of the gentry engaged to the Honourable Arthur Holmwood, and Mina Murray, an assistant schoolmistress engaged to a young solicitor sent on a difficult conveyancing deal to Transylvania. Andrea Dworkin reads these characters in the spirit of Stoker's novel. To her, Lucy, a monied beauty who effortlessly elicits three proposals of marriage in a single day, is the Bad Girl, 'pretty, flirtatious, coy, ornamental . . .', whose 'choice of the suitor for whom she has sexual desire suggests she is not entirely good' (pp. 113–114). Conversely, Mina 'is a partner, a wife in a posture of attempted equality . . . not greedy for sex or sensually submissive' (p. 115) and thus equivalent to the New Woman of the period.

Another critic has apportioned the role of New Woman to both characters, recognizing in Lucy's restless, sleepwalking sensuality an actively desiring femininity comparable to Mina's vocational ambitions.[14] If the latter can master the word-processing technologies of her day – shorthand and typing – Lucy is the one who asks:

> Why can't they let a girl marry three men, or as many as want her, and save all this trouble? But this is heresy, and I must not say it.[15]

With views like that, it's not difficult to predict which woman will end up with a stake through her heart, and the Un-Dead Lucy bears more than a casual resemblance to Alex Forrest:

> The beautiful colour became livid, the eyes seemed to throw out sparks of hell-fire, the brows were wrinkled as though the folds of flesh were the coils of Medusa's snakes, and the lovely, blood-stained mouth grew to an open square, as in the passion masks of the Greeks and Japanese. If ever a face meant death – if looks could kill – we saw it at that moment. (p. 212)

Like Alex, this vampire steals children and must be punished, dispatched in an orgy of phallic violence. In the ultimate literary primal scene, her own fiancé drives the three-foot stake through her writhing body as her other suitors look on:

Alex Forrest confronts Dan Gallagher in *Fatal Attraction* (production still).

The body shook and quivered and twisted in wild
contortions; the sharp white teeth clamped together
till the lips were cut and the mouth was smeared with
a crimson foam. But Arthur never faltered . . . His
face was set, and high duty seemed to shine through
it; the sight of it gave us courage, so that our voices
seemed to ring through the little vault. (p. 216)

'The sight of it.' Andrea Dworkin attributes *Dracula*'s
fin-de-siècle visualization of sadistic coition to a rising
culture of pornographic voyeurism: 'a new kind of sex
too, not the fuck but *watching* – watching the women die
. . . an oncoming century filled with sexual horror' (p. 119).
What I would ask is whether *Intercourse*, despite its critical
intentions, is not itself a part of this culture, generating, as
its principal product, sexual horror. Where are all those
troublesome literary counter-examples – from station

bookstore bodice-rippers to Monique Wittig and Kathy Acker – which would complicate its vision of violent sex as a uniquely male fantasy? Where, outside the book's irritatingly selective bibliography, is an acknowledgement of the contemporary feminist discussion about how, and indeed whether, intercourse can be reformed – let alone all the preceding decades of debate between our historical predecessors? If these views had been included, if the history of specific campaigns against rape, child abuse, domestic violence and heterosexism had been detailed instead of dismissed, would *Intercourse* have been so shocking? And if it hadn't been so shocking, would it have been so successful?

No way out

The problem of how audiences derive pleasure from the representation of 'the most painful experiences' was one of the questions which prompted Freud's 1920 revision of his theory of the pleasure principle. In a discussion which compares the recurring nightmares of shell-shocked soldiers to children's games of disappearance and return, he argued that the restaging of overpowering experiences, be they the trauma of war or of parental absence, offers the subject the psychical compensation of apparent activity and even revenge.[16]

At times *Intercourse* reads like a large-scale exercise of this repetition compulsion, in which a succession of violently misogynist narratives seem destined to circulate in perpetuity. In an account which flattens the material variations of textual origination and design, history evaporates, leaving us in an immutable present of male oppression. This sense of an endless round is in part a product of Dworkin's circular account of causation, in which intercourse constructs male power and male power constructs intercourse (pp. 127–8). In such a closed circuit sexual reformers like Woodhull and Hite are necessarily dreamers, useful visionaries but useless analysts.

'It is not that there is no way out if, for instance, one were to establish or believe that intercourse itself determines women's lower status', Dworkin concedes, and then takes it all back by noting that men's sexual contempt for women is easily expressed outside of bed (p. 138). Since women's analysis, organization and indeed intercourse (there is no mention of lesbian sex in this study) is granted so little efficacy, the only possible recourse seems to be an appeal to the male conscience:

> Men too make choices. When will they choose not to despise us? (p. 139)

In the politics of moral reproach, horror is a frequently employed, if much-debated, tactic. (The representations of the Holocaust which Dworkin often cites stand out as highly controversial examples, as do the mainstream television approaches to the recent African famines.) It is worth remembering that such strategies can call up the infantile fantasies that Freud described – fantasies based on powerlessness, on purely vicarious experience, on the voyeur's fascinated gaze at the horrifying scene. One of the chief fictional delegates of this infantile position is the Cassandra figure, the unheeded prophet, doomed to warn an unlistening public of some imminent catastrophe. Or as James Twitchell says of the audience at a horror movie, 'You can occasionally hear the young audience, especially the girls, squealing, "watch out! be careful!" to the female protagonist' (p. 70).

But the characters never hear those warnings, and in the difference between our knowledge and their ignorance lie both the pathos of the narrative and the security of the audience – frustrated, frightened, but fundamentally safe from the events portrayed. Such a story giveth and it taketh away – flattering our intellect, denying our agency. It can indeed be pleasant to be scared like that, but the political consequences of *Intercourse*, of feminism's most shocking study, may ultimately be less attractive.

More of a Man: gay porn cruises gay politics

In the long-running debate on sexual representation, gay men's pornography has proved as controversial as its heterosexual counterpart, if only because the two have so often been equated. Yet for every attempt by someone like Andrea Dworkin[1] – or, more recently, her ally John Stoltenberg[2] – to assimilate gay porn to a genre of allegedly unremitting patriarchal oppression (phallocentric, male-supremacist, sadistic, homophobic) come replies defending its crucial affirmation of homosexual identity, fluid role-reversals, multiple eroticism, subversive humour and educational necessity in the age of AIDS.

One way of resolving this dispute is to follow Tom Waugh's exhaustive taxonomy of gay and straight male pornographies[3] and declare everyone right. Gay porn, like other forms of representation, includes work distinguished by misogyny, racism and homophobia, as well as invitations to non-macho identifications, satires of heterosexuality and safer-sex information. To these defences Tania Modleski adds the genre's challenge to the general '*under*representation' of the eroticized male body, but at the potential expense of its lesbian counterpart:

> since the female body is most commonly figured as object of desire, the problem for women seems to be one of *over*representation.[4]

One needn't accept this corollary to Modleski's argument – and the problem it presents for an even less represented sexuality, albeit one also figured by female bodies[5] – to take her primary point. But merely to agree that gay male pornography diverges from the traditional gendering of specularity is to maintain the level of generality at which so much of this discussion is conducted.

As Linda Williams complains in her pioneering study *Hard Core*, feminist considerations of pornography have typically divided into two very broad approaches: an anti-porn stance which regards it 'as the extreme case of patriarchal power' and an anti-censorship stance which focuses 'on a continuous pornographic tradition that runs throughout dominant culture'.[6] This has historically left us stranded somewhere between the mandated ignorance of the first position and the grand generalities of the second (generalities which echo across film studies from Laura Mulvey's 1975 ascription of masculine voyeurism to the narrative cinema *tout court*[7] down to Fredric Jameson's recent observation that 'the visual is *essentially* pornographic . . . Pornographic films are . . . only the potentiation of films in general, which ask us to stare at the world as though it were a naked body.'[8])

Hard Core marked an important attempt to escape this antinomy by looking at naked bodies as though they *weren't* the world, but components of a cinematic genre designed to arouse its viewers. This is not to say that

Williams found that genre innocent of feminist import. Pornography, she concludes, is a 'genre [that] wants to be about sex', but always 'proves to be more about gender' (p. 267). Heterosexual porn, that is. *Hard Core* relies upon a definition of the form as the masculine investigation of the pleasure of the 'other' sex (although the apparent gendering of these positions is, by the book's conclusion, open to reversal). Meanwhile, lesbian and gay pornographies ('not aimed primarily at me') are deferred for the consideration of 'those who can read them better'. But as Williams is quick to admit, this exclusion clause raises more problems than it resolves, notably the latitude she allows herself 'to interpret pornographic texts aimed primarily at [straight] men' (pp. 6–7), as well as the re-establishment of heterosexuality as the norm from which other practices deviate.[9] Even more importantly, this segregation of sexual representations risks conceding the larger questions which pornography, including its extensive gay variant, can pose to the overwhelmingly heterosexual narrative cinema of which it is the supposed *telos*. As Williams later writes:

> Under the banner of the critique of a perverse
> masculine visual pleasure, feminist film critics once
> condemned the 'norm' of masculine heterosexual
> desire as manifested in narrative cinema.
> Pornography was usually assumed to be the extreme,
> and grossly explicit, instance of this perverse,
> voyeuristic, fetishizing pleasure.[10]

To reconsider these assumptions, Williams has now lifted her self-denying ordinance and gone on to examine 'other' pornographies – lesbian, gay, bisexual and sado-masochistic. (Not the least interesting of her discoveries is their apparent blurring of any 'specific and unitary sexual or gender address'.[11]) Her brief overview of the gay male genre postulates neither a profound break with heterosexual pornography nor its simple replication: 'Part of the pleasure of gay male porn would seem to reside in its play of both similarity and difference from this "norm".'[12] And indeed it would be difficult to maintain, particularly in regard to a movie entitled *More of a Man*, that gay pornography is never 'about gender'. In considering this product of a crucial moment in gay representation, my argument is that it may also be 'about sex', and (homosexual) sex's relation to both politics and the cinema itself.

More of a Man starts as it means to go on, with the hero on his knees. To the sound of church bells, the titles dissolve against a blur of votive candles. Then the camera tilts upward – revealing the first of many naked male figures, the crucified Christ suspended from the rosary of a young man at prayer. Vito's voice-over discloses his petition: that he be rid of 'all these crazy thoughts . . . all these *impure* thoughts'. In the intensity of his repentance he concludes his confession with a provocative undertaking (particularly in a scene emblematized by the limit case in sacred submission): 'You name it, I'll do it.'

Impure thoughts, of course, are what videos like this one exist to impart. And Vito's conflict – between moral intention and sexual temptation – is also that of *More of a Man*. In the ensuing scenes this Catholic construction worker will have sex in a public toilet (and then queer-bash his partner); complain of homosexual harassment to an understanding older woman (who turns out to be a drag queen); meet a Dodgers fan named Duffy (later revealed to be a member of the AIDS activist organization ACT-UP); get a formidably macho tattoo to match Duffy's (and go down on the tattooist); pick up a woman prostitute (and fantasize that she's Duffy); timidly attend the drag queen's debut at a local gay club (and then engage in an acrobatic orgy with other members of the audience); and finally consummate his relationship with Duffy, and with the condom, inside a moving float proceeding through Los Angeles during a Gay Pride parade.

Like so many of its competitors, Jerry Douglas's 1990 feature promises 'more' – a comparison which traditionally refers to the endowment of its stars (in the venerable tradition of such titles as *The Young and the Hung* and *Like a Horse*) and the extent of the 'action'. In a fascinating calculus based on 'three points for an insertion shot, one point for a wet shot, two points for coupling with segued insertion',[13] the gay magazine *Manshots* awarded this video 34 points, twice the average score for 1990. And that was the least of the plaudits. *Advocate Men* named it the Best Feature Video of 1990, Jerry Douglas Best Director and Joey Stefano, who plays Vito, Best Performer.[14] *The Windy City Times* described it as 'one of the top tapes of 1990'[15] and *Adult Video News* hailed its screenplay as 'what may be the best . . . in the 20 year history of gay adult features'.[16] Meanwhile, police officer Thomas F. Bohling and his colleagues entered Chicago's Bijou Theatre on St Valentine's Day evening 1991, arrested its manager and confiscated *More of a Man* in the first bust there since the mid 1970s.

Despite Officer Bohling's bizarre synopsis of the video in his application for a search warrant[17] (in which central characters are misidentified and whole scenes – including the crucial first two – eliminated), his seizure of *More of a Man* seems to have been the culmination of a campaign of harassment against a gay cinema rather than a test case on pornography. In the wake of the October 1990 prosecution of the Cincinnati Contemporary Arts Center's Mapplethorpe exhibition, the Bijou complained of repeated police trawls for indecency offences (i.e. masturbating customers) and even a citation for displaying the previous year's cinema licence. But their attorney was optimistic in the face of Bohling's obscenity charge. For *More of a Man* might have been designed to repel accusations of prurience, offence to community standards (particularly if that community were, like Chicago's Gold Coast, a largely homosexual one) or the lack of 'serious literary, artistic, political or scientific value'. As one local gay paper put it:

Unlike most pornographic films, More of a Man delves into serious social issues. It is a coming out story, and the main character wrestles with his religious beliefs and his fears about his masculinity. Interspersed are discussions of stereotypes and even of AIDS activism. The film also promotes safer sex.[18]

The arguments for this allegedly exceptional text were never tested in the courts. (Faced with a vigorous gay protest campaign on the eve of local elections, the Chicago prosecutors quickly abandoned the case.) I raise them here in a rather different context – not to establish *More of a Man*'s innocence of 'obscenity' but to consider its experience of dominant cinema, as well as the unique political situation in which gay pornography now finds itself.

Made on video for rental, sale and – more rarely – theatrical exhibition, with a virtually all-male cast ushered through a narrative designed to produce a set of sexual episodes punctuated by external ejaculation, *More of a Man* is readily identifiable as a piece of gay porn. As such it is, as one critic remarked of its setting, 'very L.A.'[19] – not so much Hollywood as West Hollywood (the gay-identified township which is its specified location as well as the actual residence of so many of this industry's personnel). Here, in the shadow of the studios, freelance directors turned out most of the 282 feature-length gay male tapes released in the USA during 1990 by distributors like Falcon and Catalina and Vivid. Here a video may be shot with a cast of two, or indeed one (thirty 'solo' tapes were released in 1990[20]) in the director's living-room on a schedule of three days for a total budget of ten thousand dollars.

By the end of 1990, when *More of a Man* was released, the stylistic predictability of this mode of production – a limited repertoire of 'televisual techniques',[21] including mid-shots, flat lighting and interior settings – combined with a rising volume of production, competitive cost-cutting and a wave of federal and local prosecutions like that in Chicago, led to an atmosphere of crisis in the industry. It was in this context that *Advocate Men* congratulated companies like All Worlds Video, distributors of *More of a Man*, for 'not only continuing traditions of quality' (a nostalgic reference to the more expensive theatrical features of the pre-video 1970s) 'but actually investing bigger money into fewer and better productions'.[22]

At a cost of $47,000, *More of a Man* did indeed represent a blockbuster investment in its field, enabling its producers to assemble eleven leading performers (ranging from Joey Stefano to Chi Chi LaRue to Mike Henson), plus extras, and to shoot on a variety of Los Angeles locations. In other hands (notably those of LaRue as director) these added production values might have gone for fantasy or pastiche. (See LaRue's takeoff of John Waters's *Hairspray* in *Danny and the Cruisers*.) In Douglas's the money bought into three of the most legitimating modalities of contemporary gay culture – the bravura performance of the Broadway musical, the Catholic chic of the Madonna video, and the realism of what one review called 'old fashioned movie making'.[23]

Porn movies traditionally offer one claim to realism – the actual performance of intercourse in the pro-filmic event – at the expense of any other – in the narrative, characterization, dialogue, acting, *mise en scène*, continuity editing, sound, you name it. But the ambition to get it all right persists nevertheless, and scholars have expended a great deal of ontological argument explaining why it can't be done. In Andrew Ross's view, the scenarios of most porn movies (timed and narrated to the phantasmatic demands of a masturbating male spectator) defy 'discussion among film theorists about the visual pleasure afforded by narrative in the classical realist cinema . . . pornography is like fantasies . . . no one would dream of recounting the narrative form of either.'[24] More recently, the Lacanian theorist Slavoj Žižek has argued 'that harmony, congruence between the filmic narrative (the unfolding of the story) and the immediate display of the sexual act, is structurally impossible: if we choose one, we necessarily lose the other.'[25]

To demonstrate this, Žižek offers an illustration, an imaginary sex scene added to *Out of Africa* – ten minutes of hard core performed by Streep and Redford:

> details of their aroused sexual organs, penetration, orgasm, etc. Then, after the act, the story goes on as usual, we return to the film we all know. (p. 111)

Such a scene, Žižek insists, would destroy our belief in the diegetic reality of the film by introducing a different and wholly incompatible reality, the Lacanian 'Real', 'the rock upon which every attempt at symbolization stumbles, the hard core [*sic*] . . .'.[26]

But why should a sex scene function in this disruptive manner? Setting aside the conventions of this admittedly 'old-fashioned, nostalgic melodrama' (p. 111) and its extremely metaphorical representation of sexual intimacy between the principals (climaxing when Redford shampoos Streep's hair – the film's undoubted 'come shot'), Žižek's answer seems to equate the unrepresentability of the sexual act with the unattainability of the sexual object, insofar as it is identified with the impossible object of desire:

The unattainable/forbidden object approached but never reached by the 'normal' love story – the sexual act – exists only as concealed, indicated, 'faked.' As soon as 'we show it,' its charm is dispelled, we have 'gone too far.' Instead of the sublime Thing, we are stuck with vulgar, groaning fornication. (p. 110)[27]

For all its Lacanian underclothes, this observation has a remarkably realist precedent, in André Bazin's strictures against 'showing everything' in the cinema. Again, it is argued that 'actual sexual emotion' is unrepresentable in the narrative film, owing to sex's demand for 'secrecy' and art's for 'imagination'.[28] Not only would real sex be 'unaesthetic and therefore out of place'[29] (in Williams's paraphrase of Bazin's argument), it would be downright immoral:

If you can show me on the screen a man and a woman whose dress and position are such that at least the beginnings of sexual consummation undoubtedly accompanied the action, then I would have the right to demand, in a crime film, that you really kill the victim – or at least wound him pretty badly.[30]

Bazin's equation of the *petit mort* of filmed orgasm with actual death inevitably arises when the subject turns to pornography in the age of AIDS. As Linda Williams points out, the Meese Commission headed its warnings on the risks to performers in pornographic 'photographs, films and video tapes' with an epigraph from Bazin's observations on 'the objective nature of photography':

> The photographic image is the object itself, the object freed from the conditions of time and space that govern it.[31]

A similar ontology gripped the Washington, DC gay health clinic which published this 1988 advertisement calling for visibly safer sex in pornography:

> Are we getting off watching men kill each other?
>
> How many times have we watched a video showing unprotected anal sex?
> And how many times have we actually seen another porn star becoming infected with the AIDS virus?
> Who can doubt the result of all this. More sickness very possibly leading to death.
> The difference here is that the transmission of the AIDS virus is in a sense witnessed by every viewer, every purchaser of the video.[32]

Here the equation is again that of 'watching porn with watching murder',[33] in Cindy Patton's phrase, a displacement of moral responsibility for the HIV epidemic on to the gay spectator, whose look establishes a retrospective complicity with the fatal spectacle. Patton debunks this equation comprehensively: the ejaculation – pornography's chief evidence of pleasure – is visible in so far as it is not infectious, i.e. outside the body; and infectious in so far as it is not visible, i.e. within a closed space like the vagina or the anus. The 'spectacle' of HIV transmission is simply impossible. But if AIDS activists have rejected this ascription of infection to spectatorship, they have nevertheless campaigned extensively for the industry to adopt a variety of devices – from extra-diegetic health warnings and safer-sex commercials, to non-penetrative sex and the visible use of condoms (including their application) in the 'action' – with some success. Gay porn producers now confidently assert that they protect their talent in a way that their heterosexual counterparts do not, whether we see that protection or – more commonly – do not.

The question prompted by *More of a Man* is how these hard-won warnings of possible infection might be read – not in the perennial way that it's posed (the issue of mimesis, of whether the spectator then practises safer sex, although that remains salient) but as an issue of genre. Must the inclusion of these *mementi mori* inevitably transform such videos into a species of elegy? If it is common enough to equate heterosexual coitus with death, how much more susceptible is homosexuality to what Jeff Nunokawa calls 'the lethal characterisation'?[34]

This morbidity seems particularly threatening in the face of *More of a Man*'s continual allusions to death: the effigy of the dying Christ on Vito's rosary, the flowers and candles which decorate the bedroom where Duffy and his older lover finally part, the skull tattoos worn by the two leads, the intimations of an afterlife in the name of the gay club ('Another World').

To the funereal cast of this iconography may be added the play with life and death which Bazin perceived in the photographic image. Video, that supremely temporal recorder, may surpass even cinema's ambitions to 'embalm time',[35] but its consoling illusion of some motive presence is here dispelled – first by the introduction of a still photograph (of the drag queen's absent child) and finally by the freeze-frame on which *More of a Man* concludes. Conventionally, this suspension of movement is said to remind us both of the contingency of the apparatus ('its cancelled succession, its negation as moving picture'[36]) and of its performers ('the photograph tells me death in the future'[37]). Reading Barthes's intimations of his own mortality in the photographs of his dead mother, Anne Banfield conceives of a third contingency, that of the observer, whose continued perceptions become:

> superfluous, unnecessary, the instant the shutter is released; the image separates itself irrevocably from those simultaneous thoughts to assume a separate, unthinking, existence.[38]

All three threats – to actor, audience and apparatus – were perfectly apparent to at least one reviewer of *More of a Man*. Writing in San Francisco's *Bay Area Reporter*, Marc Huestis reflected on the casting of 'a trio of porn superstars after a leave of abstinence, Rick Donovan, Butch Taylor and Mike Henson':

> As I grow older, it's refreshing to see that aging is no longer the porno taboo it once was. These days, those of us on the precipice know that it's a gift just to stay alive.

> Maybe that's what I liked most about this tape.
> It's about survival. The survival of a community,
> and indeed the survival of porn.[39]

If – as *Advocate Men* suggested in its praise for this tape's enhanced production values – *More of a Man* does contribute to the survival of gay pornography, it is not by abandoning religion, but by embracing it. The aura of redemption hangs heavily over this project – not only in the 'redeeming social value' claimed by its legal defenders in Chicago – or what Leo Bersani would undoubtedly reject as the 'pastoralizing, redemptive intentions'[40] of its attempt to infuse homosexuality with self-esteem – but most markedly in its association of religion with both gay sex and politics. In the former case, there is the comic relation between Vito's erotic and devotional fervour ('You name it, I'll do it'), as well as the juxtaposition of sacred and profane (the rosary trailing from the hip pocket of Vito's frequently lowered jeans). This leads to the recurring figure of the crucifix, which (in case anyone has forgotten) Madonna has said she reveres 'because there's a naked man on it'.

That nudity, Leo Steinberg argues in his famous study of Renaissance art, is precisely the point. The naked display of the chaste body of Christ can be said to supplant the pagan symbol of power with a new phallus, which triumphs over death by grace rather than generation: 'it obviates the necessity for procreation since, in the victory over sin, death, the result of sin, is abolished'.[41] Similarly, *More of a Man* attempts to sunder the association of gay sex with sin, and thus fatality, by redeeming both it and the hero (not incidentally named 'Vito') through a love which is non-procreative yet incarnate.

How, then, are we to understand the tape's repeated shots of the most famous ACT-UP slogan, SILENCE = DEATH? This legend is first seen on a sticker on the wall of the men's room where Vito goes to cruise. As he removes the wad of toilet paper blocking the glory hole, a reverse shot discloses him through its iris. And next to this insistent reminder of sexual spectatorship (the hole as eye and orifice) is another circle, the black sticker with its lethal warning.

When this slogan is reprised at the beginning of the next sex scene (this time in a pan from the poster in Duffy's bedroom to the candlelit catafalque on which he and his older lover lie), exactly what silence is deadly becomes more apparent. This is not – *pace* ACT-UP – the official silence which has ordained so many needless deaths, nor is it the suppression of information about safer sex. (In that regard this video is not wholly exemplary, with its only intermittent display of condoms, as well as scenes of unprotected sucking and rimming.) The silence here, which is literally broken by the incessant ringing of the telephone, is that of political non-identification, the disengagement which leads Duffy's lover to reproach him for being 'a professional homosexual', and – when Duffy finally answers the activist call – to douse him with a gush of champagne, the come shot which concludes both the scene and their affair.

'You know, Duffy,' his departing lover complains, 'you're so goddamn busy being a professional homo-

sexual it's a miracle you find time to suck cock at all.'
If *More of a Man*'s project is to reconcile gay politics
with gay pornography — a historical conflict which is
hardly one of *time* — that reconciliation is accomplished
on pornography's terms. In the crewcut figure of
Duffy the Dodgers fan, activism is assigned the youth
and muscularity of contemporary videoporn, with
added details of class and ethnicity — touches which
both enhance the masculinity of the character and
elaborate it in realist terms. These traits enable Duffy
to offer Vito — gay politics to offer gay pornography —
the virile identification which its multiple eroticization
of the male body (penile *and* anal, active *and* passive)
both troubles and requires. Thus *More of a Man* — as
Andrew Britton once complained about Stephen
Heath's equivocal reading of Lacan — has its phallus
and eats it too.[42]

Over this union presides the tape's Tiresias, the
drag queen Belle Zahringen, who pronounces the
movie's official politics and performs its title song (a
show-stopper in the 'I Am What I Am' mode):

Until you face hostility
With total visibility
You'll never know tranquillity
Or real respectability.
So join the passing parade.
Come sing this sweet serenade . . .

And folks, you can take it from me.
This incredible creature you see
Has the best of both worlds,

Yes siree.
I'm more of a woman
Than you'll ever have
And more of a man
Than you'll ever be.

Despite Belle's cross-sexual identification (figured most strikingly when *her* turbaned head turns to reveal *him* shaving), traditional gender asymmetry remains undisturbed. Women are still what men 'have' – the phallic complement which enables them to 'be'. As the only central character in the story to remain sexually inactive, Belle watches over the proceedings like the plastic virgin on Vito's dashboard. But unlike that queen, she functions to reassure – offering the phallic femininity of sexuality without lack ('the best of both worlds, yes siree'[43]) and a new political legitimacy to the revels which follow. Her coming-out anthem (in what could be an *hommage* to Linda Williams's account of pornography's affinity with the musical) is reprised in the bar-room orgy. The club's customers, like chorus boys, surround Vito in an elaborately choreographed concatenation of bodies and initiate him into a public homosexuality whose utopian energy and abundance (the club, remember, is called 'Another World') are now explicitly linked with the politics of gay self-acceptance ('cuming' to terms with yourself, in the words of one review[44]). And gay porn – with its recurrent theme of the ordinary man who discovers the joy of gay sex – offers an obvious opportunity for such a narrative, seduction elided into the kind of conversion experience which here signifies political affiliation. (We never learn what ACT-UP campaigns

for or what these 'faggot trouble-makers' do, except
to promulgate an openly gay identity.)

Nor do I use the term 'conversion' lightly. Vito's
seminal baptism in the club yields to the tape's concluding sequence, at the LA Gay Parade, where he
happily climbs aboard the Another World float, decorated with camera, tripod, stars and a go-go dancing
Belle. The finale sees him united with Duffy at last
in a sex scene memorably staged inside the supposedly moving float. As the two men ready themselves for union (in a carefully balanced position
which allows Vito the honours of first penetration,
but Duffy to be on top), Duffy asks Vito to don
protection. When the latter protests that it's 'against
my religion', Duffy tersely replies, 'Well, it's not
against mine.' In the eerie blue light of the float's
plastic-lined interior (which itself suggests the inside
of a giant condom) sex and religion finally come
together. To the sounds of applause along the
parade route, the couple consummate their romance
and rejoin the march, leaving behind a used condom
juxtaposed in a final freeze-frame with the abandoned rosary.

That applause reminds us of this tape's ambition:
to reconcile porn with cinematic narrative as well as
politics. The irony of this enterprise is that the narrative is eminently achievable, but at the expense of the
politics. Despite the axioms of film ontology, it seems
remarkably easy to fuse sex with story. The problem
is *what story*. *More of a Man* turns gay activism into a
religion – the sequence of confession, conversion and
profession which narrates so much of identity politics

so problematically. That story may be a blessing to gay pornography, but to gay politics I fear it will prove a Trojan Horse.

the feminist ethics of lesbian s/m

When, in her influential account of feminism's 'Sex Wars', B. Ruby Rich assigned 'political correctness' the role of *casus belli*, she matched it with an equally notorious opponent. 'Nowhere', she argued, 'has this Manichean struggle between updated bourgeois respectability and its opposite become more attenuated than in the debate over lesbian sadomasochism.'[1] As Rich herself notes, that sexuality is a rather odd choice for the 'bad girl' part in these conflicts. Heterosexual sadomasochism seems a far more prominent practice, and lesbian feminists have been outspoken in its condemnation, seeing in it the inherent condition of all heterosexuality.

Nevertheless, the perception of some intimate connection between feminism and lesbian sadomasochism persists, posed in terms of their successive historical emergence, unacknowledged ideological complicity, or in the psychodynamics of feminism as a family romance. Rich, for example, employs all three explanations to describe lesbian sadomasochism as part of a 'daughters' revolt' against the sexual legislations of their feminist predecessors, but enacted within understandings of subjectivity, fantasy and 'health' shared by both sides.

In reviewing these arguments, what lesbian sadomasochism *is* becomes less and less clear. If the discussion concurs at all, it is not in the definition of specific sexual acts (in which most commentators seem to have remarkably little interest) but in a range of wider concerns over genders and generations, power and proper conduct. Gilles Deleuze, who regards sadism and masochism as two very different structures, describes 'sado-masochism' as 'one of those misbegotten names, a semiological howler'.[2] Perhaps it is best expressed here by the familiar abbreviation 's/m'. Like Barthes's *S/Z* (and its feminist successor, the title of the late British journal *m/f*), s/m suggests opposition without fixed content, content which the appropriately termed 'slash' both stands in for and cuts out. In the case of lesbian s/m, one interesting question is how feminism has read this opposition – how it has, in effect, read itself into it.

I

They show less sense of justice than men.
   (Sigmund Freud, 'Some Psychical Consequences of the
            Anatomical Distinction between the Sexes')

The question of content is not fortuitous, since I want to begin with a commentary by Parveen Adams, an editor of *m/f* who has written at length on 'the form/content of masculinity/femininity' within psychoanalytic theory.[3] 'Of Female Bondage' is her continuation of that project, which discovers in lesbian s/m a unique separation of sexuality from gender.

  Adams's inquiry begins with the resolution of the Oedipus complex for the girl – a resolution which, she argues, is bound to be unhappy, no matter how it turns out. Following the account of the Lacanian analyst Catherine Millot[4] (who is following Freud's 1924–34 writing on femininity and the Oedipus complex), Adams traces four possible fates for the girl who has discovered the fact of her own castration. Driven from her mother to her father by her desire for the male organ, she takes refuge in the Oedipus complex for much longer than her brother. From there her dissatisfaction with her own genitals may lead her to renounce sexuality altogether; to continue demanding the phallus from the father (and therefore remain under his Oedipal sway); to seek a baby instead of a penis (and therefore detach from the father in pursuit of a man who might give her one); or to deny her castration and identify with the father (the masculinity complex, which also allows the subject to emerge from Oedipality into desire – often, but not inevitably, homosexual desire).

These outcomes obviously vary in their consequences for the girl's sexuality, but all of them, Millot maintains, are disappointing. The girl leaves the Oedipus complex as she entered it, under the sign of the paternal phallus. If she opts for femininity and a baby, she is subject to her own demand for the love of a father-substitute. If she opts for masculinity and identification with the father, she is subject to the demand of others for the phallus. And that, Millot concludes, 'leaves no possibility for the woman of a straightforward post-Oedipal identification with the woman' (p. 314). Or as Adams puts it: 'the Oedipus complex pathologizes femininity'[5] – not occasionally, not incipiently, but inherently.

This announcement is just the beginning of Adams's

inquiry, which then proceeds in search of a female sexuality which is not Oedipally organized. However, it marks the end of Millot's essay, which is largely preoccupied with another theme – Freud's famous claim, in the teeth of what he recognized as feminist objections, 'that for women the level of what is ethically normal is different from what it is in men'.[6]

Freud's distinction sets Catherine Millot off on *her* course – to investigate the consequences for the feminine superego of the various Oedipal trajectories described above. If I digress in that direction, it is because I believe that the source texts on lesbian s/m (notably *Coming to Power*), and the feminist debates which they address, are similarly preoccupied with ethics.

Millot begins with 'Some Psychical Consequences of the Anatomical Distinction between the Sexes', in which Freud argues that castration for the girl is not a threat but a reality: she enters the Oedipus complex when she discovers that she has nothing left to lose. Unlike the boy, who has a considerable incentive for breaking off his Oedipal attachments, the girl lacks 'a powerful motive' to do any such thing. She can linger in her Oedipal refuge, waiting for her father to give her the phallus/baby, or eventually transfer that demand to another man. Where the boy makes good his deprivation by identifying with and internalizing the parental prohibition in the form of a paternal superego, the girl assuages hers through a demand for love. The boy's superego is installed inside him; the girl's (such as it is) outside – in the place of that Other 'in a position to subject her to ultimately limitless requirements' (p. 299). The loss she fears is that of love.

The commensurate formation of the superego is the

ego ideal, which functions as the positive term (the role model or badge of identity) to the superego's negative. As Millot puts it, the superego is the source of a demand (the paternal prohibition) and the ego ideal is the object of one – the rejected Oedipal demand which precipitates the subject from desire to identification.

But the girl's demand for paternal love – or at least its surrogate – need not be rejected, and in so far as it isn't, no compensatory identification will occur. And there she will remain, without the internal mechanisms of criticism and self-love which the superego and the ego ideal provide for the boy.

But if these mechanisms are a consequence of identifying with the father, what happens to the girl who does so? After all, a girl may also convert her demand to the father into an identification with both his negative and positive manifestations, and emerge with a superego and an ego ideal in their paternal form. But the price of this insistence on an 'illusory organ' is severe anxiety, Millot argues, since the girl is now vulnerable to a double threat – of castration *and* exposure as an impostor. Her consequent need to keep up appearances may manifest itself in the conspicuous achievements of the professional woman, feats which inevitably call to mind the public eloquence of Joan Riviere's 'Masquerade' patient and her fears of paternal retribution for appropriating the phallus.[7]

Millot's final option for the girl – and the only one to valorize femininity – occurs first in the subject's chronological development. Until she believes in maternal castration, the girl will not enter the Oedipus complex but will instead address her demands to the mother.

This phallic mother is seen as omnipotent, and identification with her is said to produce both a feminine ego ideal and the menacing maternal superego which Melanie Klein attributes to the destructive projections characteristic of this stage of infantile development.[8] Of the three prospects under consideration, this pre-Oedipal maternal attachment is singled out to corroborate the Lacanian observation with which Millot opens her paper: that women seem no less vulnerable than men to an 'obscene and ferocious' (p. 294) superego.

The question of the pre-Oedipal returns us to Adams's inquiry into the vicissitudes of those sexualities organized in a different relation to the phallus – sexualities which are, by definition, perversions. Among them she cites the traditional perversions of fetishism, sadomasochism and male homosexuality, all of which are said to share the disavowal of maternal castration. Following Deleuze, Adams identifies this strategy of disavowal in the formal devices of masochism. Its fantasy scenarios entail a disavowal of reality. Its emphasis on delay, suspense, 'the frozen moment' (itself a fetish of fixed perfection) disavows sexual pleasure. Its demonstrative features solicit the onlooker's complicity in the disavowal of the social order.

Such disavowals give rise to a series of detachments culminating in the possibility that – in the perversions, at least – 'the form desire takes will be freed from the penile representation of the phallus and freed into a mobility of representations' (p. 258). But if this might be so, it is not in the case of the classic pervert of the literature, the heterosexual male masochist. In his compulsion, rigidity, impotence and castration anxiety, this figure reveals anything but the plasticity of desire. Behind his elaborate disavowal of maternal castration Adams discerns a sneaking devotion to the paternal phallus, and this ordains a heterosexual regard for traditional gender demarcations which serves as a compensation for the non-genital nature of his pleasures. Perverse, pathological *and* heterosexual, the clinical male masochist defies the Oedipal law only to confirm it. As the obverse of the subject who would escape both pathology and the social order, he is the villain of this piece.

For opposition's sake, if no other, the logic of Adams's argument leads to a figure who is neither male, nor heterosexual nor simply masochistic – a figure unknown to the clinical literature – the lesbian sadomasochist. Like the heterosexual male masochist, she too stages scenarios involving:

> fetishes, whipping, bondage, all that goes with the
> factor of fantasy and suspense; the differences are
> that lesbian sadomasochism appears not to be
> compulsive, can just as easily be genital or not, and is
> an affair of women. (p. 262)

Unlike her neurotic sisters, hetero- and homosexual, whose sexuality is still organized around the paternal phallus, the lesbian sadomasochist exercises the pervert's prerogative and constructs a fetish. But unlike other perverts – for whom constraint is often a psychical as well as physical fact – she is said to construct many fetishes, many pleasures, many fantasies, which she tries on 'like costumes'. For hers is a fetishism freed from all fixed reference, maternal as well as paternal. Here Adams employs a definition of fetishism which – in principle, at least – 'recognises that no one has the phallus':

> So the difference necessary for sexuality and sanity has to be constructed on some other basis. The axis of this difference will come to be represented by all sorts of other differences. (p. 258)

Lesbian s/m literature is read to describe a practice of 'choice', 'mobility', 'consent', and 'satisfaction': 'a play with identity and a play with genitality' (pp. 262–3). The power of the maternal phallus (along with the ferocious superego described by Millot) is eluded, and the paternal phallus which rules the male masochist functions as the object neither of desire nor of identification. With it, femininity and its discontents are left behind – hence Adams's conclusion that the lesbian sadomasochist, while undoubtedly perverse, escapes the pathology which besets her sex.

Adams calls this a 'new sexuality',[9] for whose development she can offer no historical or psychical explanation. Indeed, in a previous essay she complains that neither Freud nor his successors attempt to 'account for the appearance of this specific perversion in our culture, for this masochism of the bedroom which is such a recent phenomenon':

> reality is underdetermined by the psychical and that reality remains to be theorized.[10]

As for sadomasochism in its specifically lesbian form, Adams concludes her observations by proposing the paradox that a sexuality so transgressive of the social order can nevertheless come into existence only through its relation to 'some fledgling piece of external reality'. What this reality is, or how it might – in her description – 'press forward and make possible a change' (p. 250), is left to the disciplines of sociology or psychology to explain. But even at this level of abstraction, Adams's allusion to an external order of being which might enable psychical change would seem to refer most obviously to the opposing title of the volume in which her essay appears – feminism.

II

The scenario we would enact is sadomasochism pure and simple.

(Sarah Lucia Hoagland, *Lesbian Ethics*)

'Of Female Bondage' is published in a 1989 collection which attempts to rethink the relationship *Between Feminism and Psychoanalysis*. Its thirteen essays represent an effort to breach the impasse in the way this relationship has been theoretically articulated, notably by restoring certain debates to – as Teresa Brennan puts it – 'their specific political *or* psychoanalytic contexts'.[11] Despite these intentions, there is relatively little in this collection about specific *feminist* contexts. That is not to say that it isn't concerned with 'power relations between women and men' (p. 15), or how these manifest themselves in various forms of gendered subjectivity. Nor, in a welcome innovation, are the sexual politics of the host institution – the academy – left unexamined. But feminism itself, as a movement, affiliation, 'affair of women' (to borrow Adams's phrase) – with its own power relations, its own psychodynamics – is not investigated in anything like the same detail.

Still, the collection makes some moves in this direction which need to be noted. In an essay on psychoanalysis in the university, Alice Jardine characterizes the theoretical dichotomies which the volume repeatedly addresses – '(1) construction vs. deconstruction; (2) the drive to name vs. disarticulation; (3) unity vs. heterogeneity; (4) the Cartesian "I" vs. complex subjectivity; (5) Anglo-American vs. French; and increasingly (6) a return to literary history vs. literary theory'[12] – in terms of a generation gap between the feminist academics trained in the decade 1968–1978 and those who came after them. To their relationship (whose mother–daughter dynamics are contrasted with the father–daughter transferences of Freud's female disciples) Jardine attributes the full complement of affect – desire, dependency, 'demands for recognition and love'. But most relevant to my purposes are the reproaches hurled between the two generations:

Accusations fly about on both sides as to who is really feminist or not; who has been recuperated or not; who is just miming the masters (is it the often more history-minded mothers or more theory-minded daughters?); whose fault is it that there is a general perception that feminism has become facile, tamed

while, precisely, the humanities are being feminized?
(p. 77)

Now this is more like it. Not only is feminist academic discourse itself submitted to analysis, but its theoretical disputes are revealed to exhibit an intensely moralizing character – 'a politics and an ethics', in Jardine's phrase.[13]

In a further contribution to *Between Feminism and Psychoanalysis*, Gayatri Spivak warns against 'the quick shift' from identification to prescription in feminism, from a recognition of oneself as 'woman' to a political programme based on an unproblematic unity posited by that identity. Not only, she cautions, does this elision disenfranchise those women unimagined in that naming; it risks 'the kind of ploy that Nietzsche figured out in *The Genealogy of Morals*'[14] – the invocation of a subordinated identity to legitimate personal vengeance. How, then, do feminists construct what Spivak distinguishes from the category 'woman' – 'a constituency of anti-sexism'? Her reply returns us to Nietzsche (via the philosopher Thomas Nagel) and the need to investigate political subjectivity 'through the history and psychology of morals'.[15]

In her introduction to this collection, Teresa Brennan adds a Freudian footnote to this incipient psychology of (feminist) morals. To explain how oppositional thinking is possible in the face of arguments for the effective internalization of patriarchal norms, she postulates an 'ego-ideal identification with feminism' (p. 10). This feminist ego ideal is said to work both positively (facilitating identifications with new political values) and negatively (enforcing its prohibitions with the threat of social disapproval). Since such group identifications are necessarily multiple and often contradictory, they are not – in Freud's description – rigidly determining. Instead they offer what Brennan describes as 'a non-reductionist account of the relation between psychical and social reality' (p. 11).

This, of course, is where we left Adams's model of lesbian s/m: as an unexplained example of just that relation. I want to return to this sexuality, bearing in mind Brennan's admonition to consider both its psycho-analytic and its political contexts. Adams's sources are texts which emerged from the US women's movement in the early 1980s, a period of fabled conflict over the politics of sexual practice ('the Sex Wars') signalled by the 1980 National Organization of Women's resolution condemning sadomasochism, pornography, public sex and pederasty; the 1981 'Sex Issue' of *Heresies*; and the 1982 Barnard conference 'Towards a Politics of Sexuality'. The introduction to one of these texts, *Coming to Power* (a 1981 combination of fiction, poetry, autobiography and polemic compiled by the lesbian sadomaso-chist group Samois), notes:

> The intense political battle over S/M is increasingly polarizing members of the lesbian-feminist community. Is S/M good or evil? Is it 'feminist'? Anti-feminist? Or should we even be bothering to discuss it at all?[16]

Whether or not we choose to historicize lesbian s/m as a 'new' sexuality emerging out of some as-yet-unidentified conjuncture of the psychical and the social, it seems crucial to remember that its literature was composed in the circumstances (and the terms) indicated above. These discourses are as available for psychoanalytic readings as any other, but they are as unlikely as any other to be transparent representations of that of which they speak.

In her own contribution to the s/m debate in the early 1980s, Judith Butler noted a strong resemblance between lesbian s/m argument and the 'moral feminism' it purported to oppose:

> Sm seems to have some fundamental faith in the rightness of desire: Pat Califia says that sexual desire is 'impeccably honest'. Sm also believes in the wrongness of conscience, and seeks the radical inversion of the Judeo-Christian ethic which is renowned for its contempt for desire. They accuse moral feminists of continuing this anti-sex tradition. In turn, moral feminists charge that sm has merely appropriated patriarchal power relations and brought them into lesbianism in faintly disguised form.
>
> As these two voices work themselves out, it seems increasingly clear to me that they have more in common than it seems. They can each be seen as an attempt to find a legitimate way of relating lesbian feminist theory and practice.[17]

This similarity is most vividly apparent in the erotic scenarios of *Coming to Power*, whose conclusions seem remarkably alike – to each other and to their 'vanilla' predecessors:

Then she floated secure and safe in her lover's arms. Both womyn tender and connected.[18]

I fell asleep in her arms, all problems and decisions placed aside for another time.[19]

I draw her body around mine, she plants soft kisses at my throat, we drift off into free dreaming, soaring.[20]

Meg nestled into Carole's shoulder, feeling safe and more secure than she had in months.[21]

These are four different narratives by four different authors. Their similarity may have been preordained by the ethos which governed Samois's selection of manuscripts:

We talked about whether the fiction portrayed S/M lesbians as strong, self-defining women. Was a caring interaction shown between the characters? How was consensuality (covert or implied) shown?[22]

The conscious project of idealization here should alert us to the secondary revisions in Adams's source material. But why should a group so dedicated to speaking the truth about sexuality (indeed, to sexual desire as a form of truth) revert to a positive-images policy? Why operate within a feminist ethos at all? One explanation is simply circumstantial: lesbian feminism was where many of *Coming to Power*'s contributors first discovered an erotic community, with which most remained involved. Another sees their support for sexual diversity

as a return to the movement's initial liberationist premisses, a 'corrective to the lesbian feminist tendency in
recent years to legislate politically correct and incorrect
behavior'.[23] This last phrase is Butler's, and her own
analysis of the moral communality of pro- and anti-s/m
positions could be extended to note how this legislative
drive is both challenged and duplicated in the highly
formal *mise en scène* of lesbian sadomasochism (how-to
manuals, handkerchief codes, safety rules, as well as its
scenarios of 'discipline' and 'correction').[24]

Lesbian s/m is often described by its proponents in
similar terms – as a theatricalization of ordinary lesbian
relations, particularly their unacknowledged power
plays:

> I have never known lesbians to say to each other
> something like 'Let's start a relationship & hurt each
> other a lot, OK? You be needy & demanding &
> fearful & manipulative, & I'll be cool & tough &
> withdraw farther from you while meanwhile
> becoming completely dependent on you. Then you
> fall in love with someone else & leave me with no
> warning. We'll both be broken for months by grief &
> guilt. Sounds like a good time?'[25]

It's equally possible to see this practice (with its groups,
demonstrations and pamphlets) as a blasphemous
parody of feminism, a black mass of the women's
movement[26] – but its followers resist excommunication.

Indeed, the introduction to *Coming to Power* describes
the collection as a call 'for a re-evaluation of existing
lesbian-feminist ethics, saying, "You must own your

'illegitimate' children"'.[27] Again, the moral tenor of
this debate is stressed, in a reproach to 'you', the (even
then) familiar figure of feminism as Symbolic Mother.

III

Ah, Mother dear, you cry, you scream, scream when
your daughter fucks you.

(Sade, *Philosophy in the Bedroom*)

In her comments on the 'impassioned confrontations'
in feminist theory, Teresa de Lauretis – like Judith
Butler before her – argues that both sides of the
lesbian s/m debate are bound together by shared
values which unite even these antagonists against
non-feminists.[28] The result is that intensity of both
identification and aggression which Freud has
described, in 'Civilization and its Discontents', as 'the
narcissism of minor differences'.[29] Refusing what she
regards as fruitless accusations of essentialism, de
Lauretis plots these intra-feminist differences as a
succession of displacements – with the debate over
lesbian s/m, for example, 'recasting' an earlier opposition between lesbians in the women's and gay movements.[30]

Beneath these shifting oppositions, de Lauretis discerns 'two concurrent drives' in feminism's self-
representation: '*an erotic, narcissistic* drive that
enhances images of feminism as difference, rebellion,
daring, excess, subversion, disloyalty, agency,
empowerment, pleasure and danger . . . and *an ethical*

drive that works toward community, accountability, entrustment, sisterhood, bonding'. This 'twofold pull' of feminist affirmation and critique is attributed to political necessity, most especially in the case of lesbian feminism, 'where the erotic is as necessary a condition as the ethical, if not more'.[31]

How these apparently contradictory, yet closely related, drives might work together is the subject of Julia Creet's recent inquiry into the function of feminism in the phantasmatic economy of lesbian s/m. Like Butler, Creet pursues the disciplinary implications of a community ethic which regulates sexual conduct in the name of politics. She further observes how this regulatory power is displaced on to the previous generation to equate morality with maternity, and both with feminism. In a footnote tracing maternalist psychology (Dinnerstein, Chodorow, Kristeva) back to its precursors in late-nineteenth-century social welfarism, Creet's feminist mothers surpass Alice Jardine's. Where the latter were merely 'history-minded', Creet's feminist forebears are *history*.

In Creet's account, this principle of maternal authority, like its paternal counterpart, may survive Oedipalization in the superego. (Here she cites Freud's description of moral masochism, which acknowledges the residual influence of both parents in the formation of 'our individual ethical sense'.[32]) In lesbian s/m writing, Creet maintains, it is maternal authority which is consciously transgressed. The Law of the Father '("woman" as lack)' is 'distanced' in favour of the Law of the Mother '("woman" as morally superior)'.[33]

The tension between these jurisdictions, and the

institutional primacy of patriarchal authority, are ingeniously deployed to explain s/m lesbians' complaints against feminism. Beneath their objections to its censoriousness, Čreet discerns regret that the Symbolic Mother is *not powerful enough*. In its opposition to violence, she argues, feminism only manages to repress the instinctual aggression necessary for self-preservation. The result, according to Freud's 1915 essay on the instincts, is the 'turning around' of primary sadism into an (eventually) eroticized desire for self-punishment, masochism. But as 'The Hustler', Pat Califia's dystopian evocation of a post-revolutionary feminist society, suggests, the Symbolic Mother will not lay down the law. 'The wish for an unambiguous authority that would relieve the guilt and desire of the s/m fantasy is unfulfilled by the powers that be'; Creet concludes:

the feminist authorities are cast as unable or unwilling to specify clear laws and unable to enforce them.
(p. 155)

Restless, reproachful, unsatisfied, Creet's s/m lesbians seem a world away from Adams's playful perverts. Where the former are subjected to an authority which fails them, the latter construct their fetishes as pure simulacra, representations of a phallus which is not only disavowed but 'detached' from reference altogether. But Creet's account does supply what Adams's both requires and omits: that encounter between history and the unconscious, between the domain of feminism and that of psychoanalysis, out of which 'new' sexualities might emerge. Just how, of course, is the question.

Should we concur (as Creet apparently does) with the Samois claim that lesbian s/m is the spurned offspring of feminism, 'daughter of the movement'? Or might feminism function more ambivalently, not so much as 'a locus of [unenforceable maternal] law' (p. 138), but as a critical guide to that of the Father:

> initiating the woman into the symbolic order, but transferring and transforming a patriarchal system of gender inequities into a realm of difference presided over by women.[34]

This is Tania Modleski's description of the role of the 'top' in the lesbian s/m scene – a role which she too elaborates in terms of a Symbolic Mother who introduces the daughter to the disciplines of patriarchy while providing a critical frame of female reference and affirmation. The function of this maternal dominatrix might be identified with feminism in so far as it challenges the gendered character of the subordination it enacts – not least by replacing the father as the object of the daughter's devotion.

This gives us three psychologies of lesbian s/m: Adams's, which absolves it from the inequities of both gender (the paternal phallus) and generation (maternal authority); Creet's, which emphasizes maternal authority as the conscious focus of both desire and disappointment; and Modleski's, which counterposes maternal authority to the gender system it both transmits and contests. In technical terms, Adams's (which owes much to Deleuze) should be described as *formal* in its emphasis on the dramatic elements of fantasy and suspense rather than the moral poles of guilt and punishment or the erotogenic ones of pleasure and pain. Conversely, Creet's, with its Freudian account of guilt produced by the 'cultural suppression of instincts',[35] is *moral*.

Modleski's presents a more difficult case for categorization. Unlike both Creet and Adams, she stresses the sadism in both the paraphernalia and the practices of lesbian s/m:

whips, razors and nipple clips . . . (p. 152)

the infliction of pain and humiliation by one individual on another. (p. 154)

Yet the scene she chooses to illustrate her observations, from a short story in *Coming to Power*, is a narrative of masochism. In Martha Alexander's 'Passion Play', Meg, 'a thirty-eight-year-old professional feminist' just back from delivering a paper to the National Women's Studies Conference, is transported to tearful ecstasy by a woman who fucks her 'like a goddamn dog' after costuming her in garish makeup, a G-string, rhinestones . . . and a dog collar.[36] Modleski focuses on Meg's shock at beholding her travestied image – 'real and unreal' – in the mirror. Her ambivalent identification with this figure – 'It was her and it wasn't her' – is read in terms of woman's disavowal of her own engendered humiliation.[37] This law of gender, Modleski argues, is beaten out of Meg much as the father is said to be beaten out of her heterosexual male counterparts in certain scenarios analysed by Deleuze. In both cases the agent of punishment

255

is a woman vested with an eroticized mastery; in both patriarchal authority is expelled. Such a structure, defined by its equation of the mother with the law and a concomitant dismissal of the father from the symbolic order, identifies Modleski's account of lesbian s/m with Deleuze's description of *masochism*.

Creet's analysis displays a similar preoccupation (notwithstanding her argument for the reversibility of the instincts) since it is clearly composed as a polemic on behalf of the masochistic daughter:

> We are all too familiar with the feminist adage 'Power within not power over.' But how does it translate erotically when our first loves were people infinitely more powerful than we? (p. 155)

More controversially, perhaps, I would make the same claim for Adams's analysis, despite her best efforts to defend lesbian '*sado*masochism' from any taint of compulsion or rigidity. She herself describes the practice as 'indeed masochistic' (p. 254), and the formal elements she adduces – the fetish, suspense and delay – evoke the patient idealizations of masochism rather than sadism's sudden destruction.[38]

Where, then, *is* sadism in these accounts? (One could complain that a good top is as hard to find in the theory as it reputedly is in the practice.[39]) A few cruelties may be alluded to (and then largely in quotation from autobiography and fiction), but the subjectivity which enacts them is never examined. Nor is its philosophy. Nowhere, for example, does Adams, Creet or Modleski mention Sade.

In part, this exclusion reflects the influence of Deleuze, who assigns sadism and masochism to separate spheres predicated on the 'irreducible dissymmetry' of gender:

> sadism stands for the active negation of the mother and the inflation of the father (who is placed above the law); masochism proceeds by a twofold disavowal, a positive, idealizing disavowal of the mother (who is identified with the law) and an invalidating disavowal of the father (who is expelled from the symbolic order).[40]

If, as Deleuze maintains, masochism is the realm of female dominion, we should not be surprised to see its contours emerge in an 'affair of women'. As for the absence of the sadist, in the Deleuzean scene there is room for only a single subject (the masochist in masochism, the sadist in sadism). Hence the masochist is said to encounter the woman torturer not as his sadistic counterpart, another subject, but as the mere incarnation of 'inflicting pain'.[41] With this observation, however, the utility of the Deleuzean model for this analysis is exhausted. For unlike the configurations he describes, which both derive from the 'positive' Oedipus complex, lesbian s/m is a homosexual arrangement. To locate anything like a precedent for it in the literature of sadomasochism, we must turn to the strangely neglected Sade and his *Philosophy in the Bedroom*.

For these 'Dialogues Intended for the Education of Young Ladies', Sade assembles a cast of four: the sodomitical philosopher Dolmancé, the bisexual

débauchée Madame de Saint-Ange, her incestuous brother the Chevalier de Mirvel, and the fifteen-year-old
virgin Eugénie de Mistival. The instruction of this
young lady is accomplished by the entire group (abetted
by Madame de Saint-Ange's hugely endowed gardener
Augustin) in a series of *tableaux* which demonstrate far
more pleasures than the strictly heterosexual ones
described by Deleuze. At the commencement of the
dialogues, Eugénie has already attracted the erotic
attention of Madame de Saint-Ange, who both arranges
and participates in her defloration. By their end, this
'little monster', as Saint-Ange affectionately describes
her, will joyfully join the others in the torture and rape
of her own mother.

To be sure, the polysexual Eugénie is more libertine
than lesbian – or, as she proudly proclaims (fucking her
mother with a gigantic dildo while being buggered by
Dolmancé):

> incestuous, adulteress, sodomite, and all that in a girl
> who only lost her maidenhead today![42]

The philosophy into which she is initiated is founded on
a profound hatred of life ('this universe of woe', as Sade
writes in his introduction) and the womb that bears it.
(Among other things, *Philosophy in the Bedroom* is an
advanced textbook on contraception.) But this disdain
for maternity perversely licenses sex between women.
In the case of Madame de Saint-Ange, that sex is
accomplished by seduction; in the case of Madame de
Mistival, by attack. Both women are, in their way,
mother figures. But it is notable that Eugénie's passage

is from the mother as pleasure (the mistress of the revels Saint-Ange, with her tireless dedication to *jouissance*) to the mother as pain (the imperious Madame de Mistival, whose attempts to repress Eugénie's sexuality are repaid by the utter devastation of her own).

Angela Carter reads this transformation in terms of the daughter's double disappointment with the mother, as first love object and phallicized ego ideal. Like Catherine Millot, she turns to Klein for a description of the ferocity which informs this relationship:

> Eugénie's transgression is an exemplary vengeance upon the very idea of the good, a vengeance upon the primal 'good' object, the body of the mother. In the terms of the analysis of Melanie Klein, 'good breast' is the prototype of the fountain of all nourishment; the breast that Sade's libertines take such delight in whipping, upon which they take such derisive glee in wiping their arses, is, as Freud says, 'the place where love and hunger meet', a moving symbol of the existence and the satisfaction of the most basic of all human needs.[43]

The spectacle of lesbian s/m as an attack of this magnitude on the mother challenges the assumptions of its feminist apologists. Instead of Adams's utopian exchange of consensual acts and disengendered dildos, Creet's defence of the masochistic daughter from the maternal authority she craves, or Modleski's account of the dominatrix who prepares her daughter for the travails of patriarchy, Sade gives us the top girl. The daughter's position (the only position that these feminists, for all their talk of mothers, ever offer us) is suddenly rendered untenably cruel. And if daughters can take up torture, they might even embrace its sister vocation and become legislators.

IV

I approach my life as a series of ethical choices.

(Juicy Lucy, *Coming to Power*)

What comes first, sadism or masochism, the law or transgression, mother or daughter? Not only does Freud change his own position on this question, moving from the primacy of sadism to that of masochism as he articulates the death instinct, but his final reflections on these dualisms become positively vertiginous. Thus we read that 'guilt can turn people into criminals'[44] and that children of the most lenient upbringing are often the most conscience-ridden,[45] while civilization is said to perpetuate the very discontent it was founded to repress, an aggression which the superego simply takes over in its sadistic persecution of the ego.[46]

It is in this spirit that Lacan turns to Kant 'avec Sade', to identify the law not with repression but that which is repressed – desire. In his *Critique of Practical Reason*, Kant considers a concept of the good founded on the pleasure principle, and discards it:

the end itself, the enjoyment we seek, is not a good but only well-being, not a concept of reason but an empirical concept of an object of sensation.[47]

260

So relative a concept, it is argued, cannot serve as the basis of a universal moral law. Instead Kant proposes the reverse: that the law is not founded on the good, but the good is founded on the law.

Lacan asks us to follow this argument into Sade's *Bedroom*, where eight years later he too issues a maxim which makes enjoyment not the foundation but the object of the law:

> I have the right of enjoyment over [*le droit de jouir de*] your body, anyone can say to me, and I will exercise this right, without any limit stopping me in the capriciousness of the exactions that I might have the taste to satiate.[48]

It is threats like this one which, in 'Civilization and its Discontents', Freud lists among his grounds for doubting the commandment to love one's neighbour as oneself:

> men are not gentle creatures who want to be loved and who at the most can defend themselves if they are attacked; they are, on the contrary, creatures among whose instinctual endowments is to be reckoned a powerful share of aggressiveness. As a result, their neighbour is for them not only a potential helper or sexual object, but also someone who tempts them to satisfy their aggressiveness on him, to exploit his capacity for work without compensation, to use him sexually without his consent, to seize his possessions, to humiliate him, to cause him pain, to torture and to kill him.[49]

But as the vicissitudes of Freud's own argument (in which his neighbour is on one page a villain and on the next a victim) suggest, it is impossible to propose the general aggression of humankind without accusing oneself. Thus Lacan in 'Kant with Sade' and his seminar on the ethics of psychoanalysis:

> Each time that Freud stops, as if horrified, before the consequence of the commandment to love one's neighbor, what arises is the presence of the innate wickedness which inhabits this neighbor. But then it also inhabits myself. And what is more a neighbor to me than this heart within myself, that of my *jouissance*, which I dare not approach?[50]

And why should our *jouissance* defy approach? Because, as Lacan's Sadeian Kant explains, behind it is the law which 'makes it possible',[51] the castrating prohibition which engenders our desire for its opposite. We confront that law at the peril of our own undoing, for it is powered by nothing less than the self-aggression which Freud discovered at the root of our conscience and our bliss. Suffice it to say, our morals are as difficult to come to terms with as our pleasures, because they *are* our pleasures.

As we have seen, feminism has not remained wholly unaware of the operations of this libidinal economy in its own ethical exchanges. Even Sarah Hoagland, an avowed opponent of lesbian s/m, observes, in regard to the ostracizing of wrongdoers in lesbian communities:

> While we may find we lose respect for a lesbian at a given time as a result of something she's done, we don't

have to destroy her. Such desires involve a scenario of one lesbian saying 'fie on thee foul dyke' and the other saying 'hit me again,' while the community sits in silent approval. The scenario we would enact is sado-masochism pure and simple.[52]

Hoagland's solution to this problem (the condemnation of what could very well be lesbian s/m as its own perform-ance) is a better *Lesbian Ethics*. Conversely, Wendy Brown, while also deploring the feminist culture of reproach, calls for its replacement by an 'amoral political habitat'.[53] And in a parallel argument (which appeared in the same issue of *differences*) Joan Cocks argues against conceding 'the moral edge' to 'subjective feelings of victimization'.[54] Deconstructing, in Spivak's phrase, feminism's 'onto/epistemo/axiological confusion', they too turn to Nietzsche, elaborating his critique of 'slave morality', the vengeful negativity of the oppressed.[55]

Brown attributes this *ressentiment* to feminist argument which grounds itself in an epistemology of subordi-nation, a reverse hierarchy through which the subject claims superior knowledge (and moral standing) by vir-tue of her oppressed identity. (Precisely the 'speaking as a lesbian mother' formula which Creet locates in the femi-nist investment of maternity with morality.) Cocks pur-sues this valorization of the victim in radical feminist analyses of sex, which have enlarged to incorporate more and more practices into a politicizable sphere of abuse. Her central example, the 'condemnation of lesbian sado-masochism for being infected with the proclivities of patriarchal desire',[56] returns us to the question at hand.

As a psychical diagnosis, *ressentiment*, in which the

sadism of moral accusation clothes itself in the most luxuriant masochism, seems wickedly appropriate for a feminist ethos so deeply implicated in the sadomasochism it condemns. Challenging this morality's ontological claims, insisting that we speak from desire '("what I want for us")' rather than identity '("who I am")' are among Brown's estimable suggestions for improving the tenor (and temper) of our debates. But her closing recommendation – 'For the political making of a feminist future, we may need to loosen our historically feminised attachments to subjectivity and morality' – posed politely though it is in the subjunctive rather than the imperative, cannot elude its own logic. A new (if arguably more attractive) morality of 'explicitly postulated norms'[57] simply replaces the old guilt trip. The law can no more be escaped in feminism than it can in the Sadeian bedroom.

There Eugénie concludes her attack upon her mother by sealing up her fount of life:

> Quickly, quickly, fetch me needle and thread! . . .
> Spread your thighs, Mamma, so I can stitch you
> together – so that you'll give me no more little
> brothers and sisters.[58]

Doing so, despite her criminal intentions, the teenage libertine upholds the law. For, as Lacan points out with immense satisfaction, she succeeds in closing the very passage forbidden to the Oedipal child.

That final touch, although suggested by Madame de Saint-Ange, is appropriately authorized by the father – literally by Mistival *père*, as Dolmancé ruthlessly informs his prostrate wife, and by the Dialogues' 'leader and instructor' himself. Whether that means that the law is always on the side of the father is another question. (It will shortly become one for Monsieur de Mistival, should he – like Saint-Florent at the climax of Sade's earlier *Justine* – attempt the sadistic pleasures of penetrating an infibulated vulva. For Dolmancé has previously ordered his syphilitic servant to fill Eugénie's mother with his 'poison'.)

The wayward workings of the law take us back to Freud, and his arch dismissal of feminism and female morality in 'Some Psychical Consequences of the Anatomical Distinction between the Sexes'. Here, as we have seen, he argues that women's castrated state renders us proof against the Oedipal threat, and therefore ethically deficient:

> Character-traits which critics of every epoch have brought up against women – that they show less sense of justice than men, that they are less ready to submit to the great exigencies of life, that they are more often influenced in their judgements by feelings of affection or hostility – all these would be amply accounted for by the modification in the formation of the super-ego which we have inferred above. We must not allow ourselves to be deflected from such conclusions by the denials of the feminists, who are anxious to force us to regard the two sexes as completely equal in position and worth . . .[59]

The irony of these accusations lies not only in the vast literature of female morality rehearsed in this essay, but

265

in feminism itself. What is this movement, if not one of those 'great exigencies of life' to which women are supposed to be unequal? What does it seek, if not justice? If this is (to agree with Freud) a matter of 'submission', of bowing to our obligations, the ambitions of feminism are also more aggressive – 'to force us', he complains, 'to regard the two sexes as completely equal'. To institute (*jouissance* indeed) our own law.

The imposition of women's equality may be an odd fantasy on which to conclude these remarks about lesbian s/m. Or maybe not. The Sex Wars have taught us the error of attempting to fuse our political and sexual imaginaries, but they have also demonstrated the futility of trying to keep them apart.

Notes

Introduction

1. Mary McIntosh, 'The Homosexual Role', *Social Problems* vol. 16 no. 2 (Fall 1968), reprinted in Kenneth Plummer (ed.), *The Making of the Modern Homosexual* (Totowa, NJ: Barnes & Noble, 1981), pp. 30–49.
2. Jonathan Dollimore, *Sexual Dissidence* (Oxford: Oxford University Press, 1991), p. 120.
3. Richard von Krafft-Ebing, *Psychopathia Sexualis* (1893) (New York: Stein & Day/Scarborough, 1978), pp. 52–3.
4. Havelock Ellis, *Studies in the Psychology of Sex*, vol. II, 'Sexual Inversion' (1897) (Philadelphia: F.A. Davis, 1901), p.v.
5. Sigmund Freud, 'Three Essays on the Theory of Sexuality' (1905) in *On Sexuality* (Pelican Freud Library, vol. 7, Harmondsworth, 1977), p. 62.
6. ibid., p. 155.
7. Judith Roof, *A Lure of Knowledge: Lesbian Sexuality and Theory* (New York: Columbia University Press, 1991), p. 209.
8. 'The Lesbian Museum: Ten Thousand Years of Penis Envy', at the Franklin Furnace, New York City, March 1992.
9. Judith Butler, *Gender Trouble* (New York/London: Routledge, 1990), p. 31.
10. *Webster's New Collegiate Dictionary* (Springfield, MA: G. & C. Merriam Company, 1973), p. 1301. In a similar vein, Betsy Warland introduces her collection of 'Writing by Dykes, Queers and Lesbians', *InVersions* (Vancouver: Press Gang Publishers, 1991), p. xi by citing Gloria

Anzaldúa's 'critique of the common usage of the word *lesbian* as inclusive and representative . . . *InVersions*: not one but many *versions* we must learn to live with-*in*'.

11. Jonathan Culler, *Framing the Sign* (Oxford: Basil Blackwell, 1988), pp. 203–4.

12. Jonathan Culler, *On Deconstruction* (Ithaca, NY: Cornell University Press, 1982), pp. 43–64.

13. Gloria Anzaldúa, 'To(o) Queer the Writer – Loca, escritora y chicana', in Betsy Warland (ed.), *InVersions*, p. 258.

14. Eve Kosofsky Sedgwick, *Epistemology of the Closet* (Berkeley, CA: University of California Press, 1990), p. 248.

15. Daniel Harris, 'Make My Rainy Day', *The Nation*, 8 June 1992, pp. 790–93.

16. Section 28 of the 1988 Local Government Act prohibits local authorities and maintained schools from 'promoting homosexuality' or teaching it as a 'pretended family relationship'.

17. John Fletcher, 'Perverse Dynamics', unpublished paper given at the London Institute of Contemporary Arts, 24 October, 1991.

18. Donna Haraway, 'A Manifesto for Cyborgs: Science, Technology and Socialist Feminism in the 1980s', *Socialist Review* vol. 80, 1985, p. 67.

19. ibid., p. 94.

20. For a discussion of this film, see 'From Robot to Romance' in this collection.

21. Robin Podolsky, 'How Do We Look?', *LA Weekly*, 19–25 June, p. 18.

22. Richard Dyer, 'Believing in Fairies: The Author and the Homosexual', in Diana Fuss (ed.), *Inside/Out* (New York/London; Routledge, 1991), p. 200.

23. Donna Haraway, 'A Manifesto for Cyborgs', p. 65.

24. Christian Metz, *Psychoanalysis and Cinema* (London: Macmillan, 1982), p. 80. Jonathan Dollimore (*Sexual Dissidence*, p. 191) further notes: 'deconstruction is an inherently perverse procedure for which homosexuality is an eminently suitable subject.'

The train of thought in Freud's 'Case of Homosexuality in a Woman'

1. Sigmund Freud, 'The Psychogenesis of a Case of Homosexuality in a Woman' (1920), in *Case Histories II* (Pelican Freud Library, vol. 9, Harmondsworth, 1979), pp. 371–400. Sections I–IV in this article follow Freud's significant divisions of this study.

2. Ernest Jones, *The Life and Work of Sigmund Freud*, vol. II (unabridged edition) (London: Hogarth Press, 1955), p. 314.

3. See Jacqueline Rose, '"Dora" – Fragment of an Analysis', *m/f* no. 2 1978, p. 10, reprinted in Charles Bernheimer and Claire Kahane, eds, *In Dora's Case* (London: Virago, 1985).

4. Sigmund Freud, 'Fragment of an Analysis of a Case of Hysteria ("Dora",)' (1905 [1901.]), in *Case Histories I* (Pelican Freud Library, vol. 8, Harmondsworth, 1977), p. 162.

5. Jacques Lacan, 'Intervention on Transference', in Juliet Mitchell and Jacqueline Rose, (eds) *Feminine Sexuality* (London: Macmillan, 1982), p. 69.

6. Sigmund Freud, 'Three Essays on Sexuality' (1905), in *On Sexuality* (Pelican Freud Library, vol. 7, Harmondsworth, 1977) p. 80.

7. Otto Rank, 'Perversion and Neurosis', *International Journal of Psycho-Analysis* vol. 4, 1923, p. 273.

8. Ernest Jones, *Life and Work*, vol. II, p. 312.

9. Two remarks from the 1905 'Three Essays' should be borne in mind here: Freud's dictum that 'no one single aim can be laid down as applying in cases of inversion' (p. 58) and his listing of the 'overvaluation of the sexual object' as simply one of many perverse aims (p. 62).

10. Jacques Lacan, 'Intervention on Transference'.

11. Sigmund Freud, 'Some Psychical Consequences of the Anatomical Distinction between the Sexes' (1925) in *On Sexuality*, p. 334.

12. Ernest Jones, *Life and Work*, vol. II, p. 134.

13. Johan Huizinga, *The Waning of the Middle Ages* (London: Peregrine, 1965), p. 104.

14. Jacques Lacan, 'Guiding Remarks for a Congress', in *Feminine Sexuality*, p. 96.

15. Jacques Lacan argues that both Dora and the homosexual girl desire 'to sustain the desire of the father' in *The Four Fundamental Concepts of Psycho-Analysis* (Harmondsworth: Penguin, 1977), p. 38.

16. Jacques Lacan, 'Intervention on Transference', p. 68.

17. Sigmund Freud, 'A Special Type of Choice of Object Made by Men' (1910), in *On Sexuality*, pp. 227–42.

18. J. H. W. Van Ophuijsen, 'Contributions to the Masculinity Complex in Women' (1917), *International Journal of Psycho-Analysis* vol. 5, 1924, pp. 39–49.

19. Jacqueline Rose, '"Dora"', pp. 10–11.

20. Henry Havelock Ellis, *Sexual Inversion, Studies in the Psychology of Sex*, vol. I (London: Wilson & Macmillan, 1897), pp. 87–8.

21. The paraphrase is from Sonja Ruehl, 'Inverts and Experts: Radclyffe Hall and the Lesbian Identity', in Rosalind Brunt and Caroline Rowan, (eds), *Feminism, Culture and Politics* (London: Lawrence & Wishart, 1982), p. 19.

22. Helene Deutsch, 'On Female Homosexuality', *The Psychoanalytic Quarterly*. vol. 1, 1932, pp. 484 ff.

23. Sigmund Freud, 'Three Essays on Sexuality' (1905), in *On Sexuality*, p. 53.

24. Sigmund Freud, 'Mourning and Melancholia' (1917), in *On Metapsychology* (Pelican Freud Library, vol. 11, Harmondsworth, 1984), pp. 251–68.

25. Joyce McDougall, 'Homosexuality in Women', in Janine Chasseguet-Smirgel, (ed.), *Female Sexuality: New Psychoanalytic Views* (London: Virago, 1981), pp. 171–220. (But McDougall's patients exhibit much more serious symptoms – severe disorganization, phobias, self-mutilation – than Freud's patient, and she posits the paternal introject at an early stage of childhood.)

26. Sigmund Freud, 'Female Sexuality' (1931), in *On Sexuality*, pp. 371–92.

27. Sigmund Freud, 'Femininity' (1933), in *New Introductory Lectures on Psychoanalysis* (Pelican Freud Library, vol. 2, Harmondsworth, 1973), pp. 145–69.

28. Freud's periodization of the sexual stages of childhood is complicated by a number of revisions. Three years after this case study, he re-categorized these into active/passive

(at the anal stage), phallic/castrated (at the infantile genital stage, which would be clitoral for girls), and masculine/feminine only at the final organization of puberty. There, he writes, 'maleness combines [the factors of] subject, activity and possession of the penis; femaleness takes over [those of] object and passivity.' – 'The Infantile Genital Organisation' (1923), in *On Sexuality*, p. 312. (It's worth noting that the respective analysts cited propose three different paradigms of female homosexuality: phallic [Freud], oral [Deutsch], and anal-sadistic [McDougall].)

29. pp. 367–92.
30. Jacques Lacan, 'The Meaning of the Phallus', in *Feminine Sexuality*, p. 84.
31. Jacques Lacan, *The Four Fundamental Concepts of Psycho-Analysis*, p. 39.
32. Suzanne Gearhart, 'The Scene of Psychoanalysis: the Unanswered Questions of Dora' in Charles Bernheimer and Claire Kahane, (eds), *In Dora's Case*, pp. 105–27.
33. Toril Moi, 'Feminist Readings of Dora', in Lisa Appignanesi, (ed), *Desire* (London: Institute of Contemporary Arts Publications, 1984), p. 17.
34. Ernest Jones, *Life and Work*, vol. II, p. 221.
35. ibid., vol. I, (London: Hogarth Press, 1953), p. 14.

The critical cult of *Dora*

1. Charles Bernheimer and Claire Kahane, (eds), *In Dora's Case: Freud – Hysteria – Feminism* (London: Virago, 1985). Further citations will be indicated with page numbers in the text.
2. From yet another commentary on the case, Judith Roof's useful synopsis of *Dora*:

   In the year 1900, Freud saw a patient suffering from hysteria. Giving her the fictional name Dora (after his housemaid), Freud listened to her story and her dreams and analyzed them according to the precepts of his developing psychoanalytical techniques. These included not only his method of interpreting dreams, but also his understanding of the mechanisms of psychoanalytic

transference by which the patient transfers feelings of
love and hate onto the analyst. Dora felt that she was the
pawn in a romantic triangle between her father, the wife
of a friend, called Frau K., and Frau K.'s husband, Herr
K. She believed that she was being traded to Herr K. by
her father so that her father could continue his affair with
Frau K. After Dora recounted several incidents of sexual
aggressiveness by Herr K., Freud read her rejection of
Herr K.'s advances as repressed sexual desire for him, out
of which arose her hysteria. Freud's treatment of Dora
lasted less than six months; in the middle of the process
Dora announced to Freud that she was terminating her
visits. Only after she had ceased to be his patient did
Freud see that his interpretation of her symptoms had
probably been incorrect; instead of being in love with
Herr K., Dora was jealous of her father's relations with
Frau K. – not only because she was in love with her father,
but because she was repressing desire for Frau K. His
analysis a failure, Freud wrote up the case history and
submitted it for publication in 1901, but he withdrew it
soon after and did not publish it until 1905 . . . (*A Lure of
Knowledge: Lesbian Sexuality and Theory* [New York:
Columbia University Press, 1991], p. 174).

3. 'Psychoanalysis and Desire: The Case of Dora', in Lisa
Appignanesi, (ed.), *Desire* (London: Institute of
Contemporary Arts Publications, 1984), pp. 3–17.
Carolyn Steedman, *Landscape for a Good Woman* (London:
Virago, 1986), pp. 129–34. See also Mary Jacobus, '*Dora*
and the Pregnant Madonna', in *Reading Woman* (New
York: Columbia University Press, 1986), pp. 137–93.

4. Sigmund Freud, 'Fragment of an Analysis of a Case of
Hysteria ("Dora")' (1905 [1901]), in *Case Histories I*
(Pelican Freud Library, vol. 8, Harmondsworth, 1977), p.
37.

5. ibid., p. 53.

6. Parveen Adams, 'Symptoms and Hysteria', *Oxford Literary
Review*, Sexual Difference Issue, 1986, p. 178.

7. Laura Mulvey, 'Visual Pleasure and Narrative Cinema'
(1975), reprinted in *Visual and Other Pleasures* (London:
Macmillan, 1989), p. 21.

8. Sigmund Freud, 'Fetishism' (1927), in *On Sexuality* (Pelican Freud Library, vol. 7, Harmondsworth, 1977), p. 357.
9. Sigmund Freud, 'Fragment of an Analysis of a Case of Hysteria', in *Case Histories I*, pp. 96–7.
10. Sigmund Freud, 'Leonardo da Vinci and a Memory of His Childhood' (1910), in *Art and Literature* (Pelican Freud Library, vol. 14, Harmondsworth, 1985), p. 209.
11. Sigmund Freud, 'Analysis of a Phobia in a Five-Year-Old Boy ("Little Hans")' (1909), in *Case Histories I*, p. 280.

A case of AIDS

1. Judith Williamson, 'Every Virus Tells A Story', in Erica Carter and Simon Watney, (eds), *Taking Liberties: Aids and Cultural Politics* (London: Serpent's Tail with the ICA, 1989). p. 70.
2. Candia McWilliam, *A Case of Knives* (London: Bloomsbury, 1988). The page numbers in the text are from the 1989 Abacus edition.
3. Tania Modleski, *Loving with a Vengeance* (Hamden, Connecticut, Archon Books, 1982), p. 36.
4. Margaret Ann Jensen, *Love's Sweet Return: The Harlequin Story* (Bowling Green: Ohio, Bowling Green University Popular Press, 1984), p. 90.
5. ibid., p. 95.
6. Erica Carter, 'Aids and Critical Practice', in Erica Carter and Simon Watney, *Taking Liberties*, p. 60.
7. Tania Modleski, *Loving with a Vengeance*, p. 43.
8. Ann Snitow, 'Mass Market Romance: Pornography for Women Is Different', in Ann Snitow, Christine Stansell and Sharon Thompson, (eds), *Powers of Desire: The Politics of Sexuality*. (New York: Monthly Review Press, 1983), p. 260.
9. ibid., p. 261.
10. ibid., p. 263.
11. Henry James, 'The Beast in the Jungle', in *The Jolly Corner and Other Tales* (London: Penguin, 1990), p. 105.
12. Eve Kosofsky Sedgwick, 'The Beast in the Closet', in Elaine Showalter, *Speaking of Gender* (New York: Routledge, 1989), pp. 264–5.

Marilyn Monroe by Gloria Steinem, Brigitte Bardot by Simone de Beauvoir

1. For an influential use of this term, see Molly Haskell, *From Reverence to Rape* (1974) (Chicago/London: University of Chicago Press 1987), pp. 19–21. Further page citations will be given in the text.

2. Simone de Beauvoir, *The Second Sex* (1949) (Harmondsworth: Penguin, 1972), p. 578. Further page citations will be given in the text.

3. Walter Benjamin, 'The Work of Art in the Age of Mechanical Reproduction', in *Illuminations* (London: Fontana, 1973), p. 231.

4. Graham McCann, *Marilyn Monroe* (Cambridge: Polity Press, 1988), pp. 36–7. On Steinem's antagonism to Monroe, see also Dean MacCannell, 'Marilyn Monroe Was Not a Man', *Diacritics*, Summer 1978, pp. 114–27.

5. Richard Dyer, *Heavenly Bodies: Film Stars and Society* (London: British Film Institute, 1987), ch. 1.

6. Gloria Steinem, 'Marilyn Monroe: The Woman Who Died Too Soon', reprinted in *Outrageous Acts & Everyday Rebellions* (London: Jonathan Cape, 1984), p. 233. Further page citations will be given in the text.

7. For a summary, see E. Ann Kaplan, *Women & Film: Both Sides of the Camera* (New York/London: Methuen, 1983), pp. 32–3.

8. Gloria Steinem, *Marilyn* (London: Gollancz, 1987), p. 14. Further page citations will be given in the text.

9. Robert C. Allen, *Speaking of Soap Operas* (Chapel Hill, NC/London: University of North Carolina Press, 1985), p. 143.

10. Sigmund Freud, 'A Special Type of Choice of Object Made by Men' (1910), in *On Sexuality* (Pelican Freud Library, vol. 7, Harmondsworth, 1977), pp. 231–42.

11. Deirdre Bair, *Simone de Beauvoir: A Biography* (London: Jonathan Cape, 1990), p. 269.

12. Claude Francis and Fernande Gontier, *Simone de Beauvoir* (London: Sidgwick & Jackson, 1989), p. 282.

13. Simone de Beauvoir, *Force of Circumstance*

(Harmondsworth: Penguin, 1968), p. 467. Further page citations will be given in the text.

14. Simone de Beauvoir, *Brigitte Bardot and the Lolita Syndrome* (London: New English Library, 1962), p. 2. Further page citations will be given in the text.

15. Jean-Paul Sartre, *Saint Genet* (New York: Pantheon, 1963), pp. 79–80.

16. Judith Okely, *Simone de Beauvoir: A Re-Reading* (London: Virago, 1986), p. 136.

17. Jane Heath, *Simone de Beauvoir* (Hemel Hempstead: Harvester Wheatsheaf, 1989), p. 42.

18. Simone de Beauvoir, *She Came to Stay* (Harmondsworth: Penguin, 1966), p. 255. The recent publication of de Beauvoir's letters to Sartre in this period suggest that this homosexuality was more autobiographical than critics had imagined. In them, de Beauvoir discusses her affair with Olga Kosakiewitch, her former student and model for Xavière, as well as relationships with other young women, often shared with Sartre: 'the truth is, I've developed a certain taste for such relations.' – Simone de Beauvoir, *Letters to Sartre*, transl. and ed. Quintin Hoare (New York: Arcade Publishing, 1992), p. 206.

19. Sigmund Freud, 'On Narcissism: An Introduction' (1914), in *On Metapsychology* (Pelican Freud Library, vol. 11, Harmondsworth, 1984), pp. 82–3.

20. Sheryl Garrett, 'How I Learned to Stop Worrying and Love Madonna', *Women's Review* no. 5, March 1986.

'Transforming the Suit': a century of lesbian self-portraits

1. Esther Newton, 'The Mythic Mannish Lesbian: Radclyffe Hall and the New Woman', in Estelle B. Freedman, Barbara C. Gelpi, Susan L. Johnson and Kathleen M. Weston, (eds),*The Lesbian Issue: Essays from SIGNS*, (Chicago: University of Chicago Press, 1985), p. 8. Further page citations will be given in the text, unless otherwise indicated.

2. Roland Barthes, *Camera Lucida* (London: Jonathan Cape, 1981), pp. 88–9.

3. Radclyffe Hall, *The Well of Loneliness* (London: Virago, 1982), p. 9. Further page citations will be given in the text.

4. Michel Foucault, *The History of Sexuality, Volume 1: An Introduction* (Harmondsworth: Penguin, 1984).

5. Jeffrey Weeks, *Sexuality and its Discontents: Meanings, Myths & Modern Sexualities* (London: Routledge, 1985), pp. 67–8.

6. Michael Baker, *Our Three Selves: A Life of Radclyffe Hall* (London: Hamish Hamilton, 1985), p. 218. Additional page citations will be given in the text.

7. This retouching was more easily accomplished in *The Well*'s description of a Millais portrait of the child Stephen and her mother, revealing 'that indefinable quality in Stephen that made her look wrong in the clothes she was wearing' (p. 23).

8. Teresa de Lauretis, 'Sexual Indifference and Lesbian Representation', *Theatre Journal* vol. 40, no. 2, May 1988, p. 177.

9. Richard von Krafft-Ebing, *Psychopathia Sexualis* (London: Mayflower-Dell, 1967), p. 276. Further page citations will be given in the text.

10. See Roberta McGrath, 'Medical Police', *Ten.8* no. 14, pp. 13–18.

11. John Tagg, *The Burden of Representation: Essays on Photographies and Histories* (London: Macmillan, 1988), p. 37 (emphasis added).

12. Susan Butler, 'So How Do I Look? Women Before and Behind the Camera', in *Staging the Self: Self-Portrait Photography 1840s–1980s* (London: National Portrait Gallery, 1987), pp. 52–3.

13. Sigmund Freud, 'Medusa's Head' (1922), in *Sexuality and the Psychology of Love* (New York: Collier Books, 1978).

14. Emmanuel Cooper, *The Sexual Perspective* (London/New York: HarperCollins, 1986), pp. 88–9.

15. Contrast Jean-François Chevrier, 'The Image of the Other', in *Staging the Self* with Simon Watney, 'The Homosexual Body: Resources and a Note on Theory', *Public* no. 3, 1990, pp. 44–59; and Stuart Marshall, 'Picturing Deviancy', in Tessa Boffin and Sunil Gupta, (eds), *Ecstatic Antibodies: Resisting the AIDS Mythology* (London: Rivers Oram Press, 1990), pp. 19–36.

16. See Diana Fuss, *Essentially Speaking: Feminism, Nature &*

Difference (London/New York: Routledge, 1990), pp. 97–112.

17. Rosy Martin and Jo Spence, 'Phototherapy: New Portraits for Old', in Jo Spence, *Putting Myself in the Picture* (London: Camden Press, 1986), p. 172.

18. Havelock Ellis, *Studies in the Psychology of Sex, Volume II: Sexual Inversion* (Philadelphia: F.A. Davis Company, 1926), pp. 250–57. (My reference for this photo-text is *Ten.8*, 'Body Politics' issue no. 25, pp. 46–7.)

19. Judith Butler, *Gender Trouble: Feminism and the Subversion of Identity* (London and New York: Routledge, 1990), pp. 101, 140.

20. Diane Hamer, 'Significant Others: Lesbianism and Psychoanalytic Theory', *Feminist Review* no. 34, Spring 1990, p. 149.

21. Inge Blackman and Kathryn Perry, 'Skirting the Issue: Lesbian Fashion for the 1990s', *Feminist Review* no. 34, Spring 1990, p. 77.

22. Laura Marcus, '"Enough About You, Let's Talk About Me": Recent Autobiographical Writing', *New Formations* no. 1, Spring 1987, p. 92.

Portrait of a marriage?

1. Sandy Smithies, 'Watching Brief', *Guardian*, 19 September 1990.

2. Quoted in James Woudhusen, 'The Un-American Movie That Shook the Box Office', *Sunday Times Magazine*, 5 February 1984, p. 57.

3. Quoted in Mark Finch, 'Business as Usual: Substitution and Sex in "Prick Up Your Ears" and Other Recent Gay-Themed Movies', in Simon Shepherd and Mick Wallis, (eds), *Coming On Strong: Gay Politics and Culture* (London: Unwin Hyman, 1989), p. 77.

4. Simon Watney, 'Hollywood's Homosexual World', *Screen* vol. 23, nos. 3–4, September–October 1982, p. 114.

5. Mark Finch, 'Business as Usual', p. 81.

6. Simon Watney, 'Hollywood's Homosexual World', p. 113.

7. Mark Finch and Richard Kwietniowski, 'Melodrama and "Maurice": Homo Is Where the Het Is', *Screen* vol. 29, no. 3, Summer 1988, p. 73.

8. ibid., p. 79.

9. Elizabeth Wilson, 'Borderlines', *New Statesman & Society*, 2 November 1990, p. 31.

10. Nigel Nicolson, *Portrait of a Marriage* (London: Weidenfeld & Nicolson, 1973), pp. 4–5. Further page citations will be given in the text.

11. Marie Stopes, *Married Love* (London: A.C. Fifield, 1918), p. 11. Further page citations will be given in the text.

12. Quoted in Victoria Glendinning, *Vita* (Harmondsworth: Penguin, 1984), p. 99.

13. Quoted in ibid., p. 215.

14. Quoted in Nigel Nicolson, *Portrait of a Marriage*, p. 175.

15. Vita Sackville-West, *No Signposts in the Sea* (London; Virago, 1985), p. 87. Further page citations will be given in the text.

16. Sally Brompton, 'Vita, Violet and Me', *Radio Times* vol. 266, no. 3483, 15–21 September 1990.

17. 'Vita had in fact had girlfriends before, but you have to choose.' – quoted in Sabine Durrant, 'Stranger than Fiction', *Independent*, 22 September 1990.

18. Lester Middlehurst, 'Grand Passions of Women in Love', *Today*, 20 September 1990.

19. Nigel Nicolson, 'Portrait of a Love Betrayed?', *Times*, 22 September 1990.

20. Oonagh Blackman, 'Castle Ladies Face TV Backlash', *Sunday Express*, 16 September 1990.

21. 'Times Diary', *Times*, 10 October 1990.

22. See Paul Kerr, 'Classic Serials – To be Continued', *Screen* vol. 23, no. 1, May–June 1982, pp. 6–19.

23. 'White Flannel' was the title of a report examining this genre in film and television on Channel Four's *Out on Tuesday* (3 April 1990).

24. Franco Moretti, *The Way of the World* (London: Verso, 1987).

25. Nigel Nicolson, 'Portrait of a Love Betrayed?'.

26. Barry Baker, 'Will This TV Sex Scandal Be Good for Our Village?', *Daily Mail*, 17 September 1990.

27. Nigel Nicolson, quoted by Steve Clarke, 'Love Scenes Stir Passions at BBC', *Sunday Times*, 16 September 1990.

28. Lawrence Stone, *Road to Divorce, England 1530–1987* (Oxford: Oxford University Press, 1990), p. 2. Stone

notes (p. 409): 'In the twenty-seven years between 1960 and 1987, the number of divorces per annum in England and Wales has multiplied' sixfold, from 24,000 to 151,000.

29. Colin Tucker, quoted by Elaine Paterson, 'Lay Lady Lay', *Time Out*, 29 August–5 September 1990, p. 22.

30. Hugh Montgomery-Massingberd, 'Marriage Viewed from a Perverse Perspective', *Daily Telegraph*, 18 September 1990, p. 16.

31. Judith Butler, *Gender Trouble* (London/New York: Routledge, 1990), p. 122.

The Amazons of ancient Athens

1. Unless otherwise indicated, this and all other classical quotations are from the Loeb Classical Library editions of the named author, ed. T.E. Page, E. Capps, and W.H.D. Rouse (London: Heinemann).

2. Adrienne Rich, 'The Kingdom of the Fathers', *Partisan Review* vol. XLIII, no. 1, 1976, p. 25.

3. Elizabeth Gould Davis, *The First Sex* (London: Dent, 1973), p. 339.

4. Johann Jacob Bachofen, *Myth, Religion and Mother Right*, transl. Ralph Manheim (London: Routledge & Kegan Paul, 1967), p. 109.

5. Donald J. Sobol, *The Amazons of Greek Mythology* (London: Thomas Yoseloff, 1972), p. 122.

6. Mina Zografou, *Amazons in Homer and Hesiod* (Athens, 1972), p. 14.

7. Martin P. Nilsson, *The Mycenaean Origin of Greek Mythology* (Cambridge: Cambridge University Press, 1932), p. 215.

8. Proclus' work is also known to us indirectly, through the *Biblioteca* of Photius, a ninth-century-AD Byzantine scholar.

9. G.L. Huxley, *Greek Epic Poetry from Eumelos to Panyassis* (London: Faber & Faber, 1969), p. 148.

10. As cited in Florence Mary Bennett, *Religious Cults Associated with the Amazons* (New York: Columbia University Press, 1912), p. 3.

11. As cited in Mina Zografou, *Amazons in Homer and Hesiod*, p. 20.

12. Notably those of Pindar and Euripides (fifth century BC), Lycrophon (fourth century BC), Apollodorus (second century BC), Plutarch and Diodorus Siculus (first century AD) and Justin (third century AD).

13. For a detailed account of this, cf. Philip Slater, *The Glory of Hera* (Boston, MA: Beacon Press, 1971), pp. 337–96.

14. Dietrich von Bothmer, *Amazons in Greek Art* (London: Oxford University Press, 1957), p. 6.

15. John Boardman, *Athenian Black Figure Vases* (London: Thames & Hudson, 1974), p. 223.

16. Victor Ehrenberg, *The Greek State* (London: Methuen, 1969), p. 17.

17. John Boardman, 'Herakles, Peisistratos and Sons', *Revue Archéologique* vol. I, 1972, p. 62.

18. Herodotus, I, 60, as cited in ibid.

19. ibid., pp. 65–6. Boardman also notes that Pisistratus named a son of his Thessalos, the name of one of Heracles' sons in the *Iliad*.

20. John Boardman, 'Herakles, Peisistratos and Eleusis', *Journal of Hellenic Studies* vol. XCV, 1975, pp. 1–2.

21. Philip Slater, *The Glory of Hera*, p. 389.

22. T.B.L. Webster, *Everyday Life in Classical Athens* (London: Batsford, 1965), p. 102, also notes a humanizing of the mythic enemies: 'It is characteristic of the new attitude of the late sixth century that (although the Krommyan sow and the bull of Marathon are included) they conceive of danger mostly in terms not of dangerous animals but of monstrous men.'

23. Martin P. Nilsson, *The Mycenaean Origin of Greek Mythology*, p. 163.

24. The date of its building is often put after the Battle of Marathon (490 BC) because of a (probably erroneous) attribution of a dedicatory inscription by Pausanias. Both von Bothmer and C.M. Robertson argue that it probably antedates 490. Cf. Dietrich von Bothmer, *Amazons in Greek Art*, p. 118 and Charles Martin Robertson, *A History of Greek Art* (Cambridge: Cambridge University Press, 1975), pp. 167–8.

25. ibid., p. 170.

26. W.R. Connor, Ruth B. Edwards, Simon Tidworthy and

Anne G. Ward, *The Quest for Theseus* (London: Pall Mall Press, 1970), p. 41.

27. Plutarch, *The Rise and Fall of Athens*, transl. Ian Scott-Kilvert (Harmondsworth: Penguin, 1960), p. 33.

28. ibid., pp. 40–41.

29. Robert Drews, *The Greek Accounts of Eastern History* (Cambridge, MA: Center for Hellenic Studies, 1973), p. 35.

30. ibid., p. 67.

31. Plutarch, *The Rise and Fall of Athens*, p. 150.

32. Dietrich von Bothmer, *Amazons in Greek Art*, p. 200, notes a possible allusion to the Portico's original name, the Peisianakteion, in the Amazon name 'Peisianassa' inscribed on a contemporary bell-krater. Similarly, the appearance of the unusual Amazon name 'Dolope' on another krater of the period may allude to the Dolopians, traditionally held to have been expelled from Skyros by Cimon when he secured the bones of Theseus.

33. Plutarch, *The Rise and Fall of Athens*, p. 145.

34. Giovanni Becatti, *The Art of Ancient Greece and Rome*, transl. John Ross (London: Thames & Hudson, 1968), p. 148.

35. Dietrich von Bothmer, *Amazons in Greek Art*, pp. 147–8.

36. Charles Martin Robertson, *Greek Painting* (Geneva: Skira, 1959), p. 120.

37. Charles Martin Robertson, *A History of Greek Art*, p. 301.

38. ibid., p. 296.

39. C.M. Bowra, *Periclean Athens* (London: Weidenfeld & Nicolson, 1971), p. 112.

40. Plutarch, *The Rise and Fall of Athens*, p. 198.

41. W.R. Connor, Ruth B. Edwards, Simon Tidworthy, and Anne G. Ward, *The Quest for Theseus*, p. 170.

42. Joan Bamberger, 'The Myth of Matriarchy: Why Men Rule in Primitive Society', in Michelle Z. Rosaldo and Louise Lamphere, (eds), *Woman, Culture and Society* (Stanford, CA: Stanford University Press, 1974), p. 267. (Bachofen's own theory of a matriarchal stage in human history can itself be read as a justification of eventual patriarchy, refurbished on social darwinist lines. Cf. Elizabeth Fee, 'The Sexual Politics of Victorian Social Anthropology', in Mary Hartman and Lois W. Banner,

eds, *Clio's Consciousness Raised* (New York: Harper & Row, 1974), pp. 90–92.)

43. Joan Bamberger, 'The Myth Matriarchy', p. 279.

44. Lewis H. Morgan, *Ancient Society* (Cambridge, MA: Harvard University Press, 1964), p. 401.

45. ibid., p. 201.

46. Sarah B. Pomeroy, *Goddesses, Whores, Wives and Slaves* (London: Robert Hale, 1976), p. 57.

47. Perry Anderson, *Passages from Antiquity to Feudalism* (London: New Left Books, 1974), p. 38.

48. Sarah B. Pomeroy, *Goddesses, Whores, Wives and Slaves*, p. 97.

49. ibid.

50. Donald J. Sobol, *The Amazons of Greek Mythology*, pp. 111–12. The Latin historians Diodorus Siculus (2.45.3) and Justin (2.4.9–10) do record the tradition in later writings (first and third centuries AD, respectively).

51. Donald J. Sobol, *The Amazons of Greek Mythology*, p. 162.

52. Mary Kelly, review of *Penthesilea*, *Spare Rib* no. 30, p. 42.

53. Sophie Dick, review of *The Lesbian Body*, *Spare Rib* no. 41, p. 45.

54. Similarly, Lysias writes of the Amazons: 'They were accounted as men for their high courage, rather than as women for their sex; so much more did they seem to excel men in their spirit than to be at a disadvantage in their form' ('Funeral Oration', 4–5).

55. As cited by Mary Kelly, review of *Penthesilea*. For other discussions of *Penthesilea*, cf. Claire Johnston and Paul Willeman, 'Penthesilea, Queen of the Amazons', *Screen* vol. 15, no. 3, 1974, and Laura Mulvey and Peter Wollen, 'Written Discussion', *Afterimage* no. 6, 1976, pp. 30–39.

56. Monique Wittig, *The Lesbian Body* (London: Peter Owen, 1975), pp. 9–10.

Lianna and the lesbians of art cinema

1. Caroline Sheldon, 'Lesbians and Film: Some Thoughts', in Richard Dyer, (ed.), *Gays and Film* (London: British Film Institute, 1980), p. 18.

2. Laura Mulvey and Colin MacCabe, 'Images of Woman, Images of Sexuality', in Colin MacCabe, (ed.), *Godard:*

Images, Sounds, Politics (London: British Film Institute and Macmillan, 1980), p. 91.

3. Laura Mulvey, 'Visual Pleasure and Narrative Cinema', reprinted from *Screen* 1975 in *Visual and Other Pleasures* (London: MacMillan, 1989), p. 19.

4. The above equation is actually deduced from the films of Godard, in Laura Mulvey and Colin MacCabe, 'Images of Women'.

5. See Steve Neale, 'Art Cinema as Institution', *Screen* vol. 22, no. 1, 1981, pp. 30–33.

6. Susan Griffin, 'Transformations', *Sinister Wisdom* no. 3, 1977, quoted in *Jump Cut* no. 24/25, p. 21.

7. See John Gillett, 'Coup de Foudre', *Monthly Film Bulletin* vol. 50, no. 598, November 1983, p. 301.

8. Penny Ashbrook, 'Lesbians at the Movies – Who's Watching Who', (unpublished essay).

9. Michel Foucault, *The History of Sexuality*, vol. 1 (London: Allen Lane, 1979), p. 101.

10. Ruby Rich, 'From Repressive Tolerance to Erotic Liberation: *Maedchen in Uniform*', in Mary Ann Doane, Patricia Mellencamp and Linda Williams, (eds), *Re-Vision* (University Publications of America, Inc., Frederick, MD, in association with The American Film Institute, 1984), p. 100.

11. Penny Ashbrook, 'Lesbians at the Movies'.

12. Quoted in James Woudhusen, 'The Un-American Movie That Shook the Box Office', *Sunday Times Magazine*, 5 February 1984, p. 57.

13. Penny Ashbrook, 'Lesbians at the Movies'.

14. Lisa DiCaprio, 'Liberal Lesbianism', *Jump Cut* 29, p. 45.

15. Barbara Presley Noble, *In These Times*, 9–22 March 1983, p. 13, cited by Lisa DiCaprio, 'Liberal Lesbianism'.

16. David Bordwell, 'The Art Cinema as a Mode of Film Practice', *Film Criticism* vol. 4, no. 1, Fall 1979, pp. 56–64.

17. Tom Ryall, 'Art House, Smart House', *The Movie* no. 90, 1981, p. 8.

18. Lisa DiCaprio, 'Liberal Lesbianism', p. 46.

19. Tom Ryall, 'Art House, Smart House', p. 7. (The exoticization of the lesbian is parodied in the recent horror film *The Hunger*, when the Susan Sarandon

character attempts to explain the unusual attentions of vampire Catherine Deneuve: 'She's *European*.')

20. See Mary Ann Doane, 'The "Woman's Film": Possession and Address', in Mary Ann Doane, Patricia Mellencamp and Linda Williams, *Re-Vision*, p. 72.

21. See Paul Kerr, 'Web-Footed in Harlem', *Monthly Film Bulletin* vol. 51, no. 600, January 1984, p. 28, where Sayles is quoted: 'And finally, I don't give a shit. In *Secaucus Seven*, the men were naked and the women weren't, and there was a point to that.'

From robot to romance

1. Peter Wollen, 'Friendship's Death', reprinted from *Bananas* (Spring 1976) in *Readings and Writings: Semiotic Counter-Strategies* (London: Verso, 1982), pp. 140–52. Unless otherwise indicated, further page citations will be given in the text.

2. See Tzvetan Todorov, *The Fantastic* (Ithaca, NY: Cornell University Press, 1975).

3. In this non-literal, phonemic strategy, Mallarmé's *touffus* – 'tufted' – becomes 'Japan' via its resemblance to 'tofu'.

4. Peter Wollen, quoted in 'Waldo Off Screen', *Time Out*, 18–25 November 1987.

5. Peter Wollen, quoted in Simon Field, 'Two Weeks on Another Planet', *Monthly Film Bulletin* vol. 54, no. 646, November 1987, p. 325.

6. Annette Michelson, 'On the Eve of the Future: The Reasonable Facsimile and the Philosophical Toy', *October* 29, Summer 1984, p. 19.

7. Raymond Bellour, 'Ideal Hadaly', *Camera Obscura* 15, 1987, p. 130.

8. Villiers de l'Isle-Adam, *Tomorrow's Eve*, transl. Robert Martin Adams (Urbana, IL: University of Illinois Press, 1982), p. 9. Further page citations will be given in the text.

9. Raymond Bellour, 'Ideal Hadaly', p. 131.

10. Laura Mulvey, 'Visual Pleasure and Narrative Cinema', reprinted from *Screen* 1975 in *Visual and Other Pleasures* (London: Macmillan, 1989), p. 26.

11. 'Penthesilea, Queen of the Amazons', Laura Mulvey and

Peter Wollen interviewed by Claire Johnston and Paul Willemen, *Screen* vol. 15, no. 3, Autumn 1974, p. 122.

12. Jean Baudrillard, 'The Orders of Simulacra', *Simulations* (New York: Semiotext(e), 1983), p. 94. Further page citations will be given in the text.

13. Martin Heidegger, *Parmenides*, cited in Friedrich Kittler, 'Gramophone, Film, Typewriter', *October* 41, Summer 1987, p. 113. (See also Raymond Bellour, 'Ideal Hadaly', p. 128, on how Edison's creation 'is, in effect, a "writing machine"'; and Mark Selzer, *Bodies and Machines* (New York/London: Routledge, 1992), pp. 195–7, on writing and technologies.) Seltzer notes the nineteenth-century identification of the typewriter with its female operator (also originally called a 'typewriter'), an identification which Wollen's film, and its phallic heroine, both announce and disavow.

14. 'Ah! said I, opening my eyes wide in the dark, it is the Sand-Man!' R Hoffmann, *Night Tales*, epigraph in Villiers de l'Isle-Adam, *Tomorrow's Eve*, p. 8.

15. Sigmund Freud, 'The "Uncanny"' (1919), in *Art and Literature* (Pelican Freud Library, vol. 14, Harmondsworth, 1985), p. 349.

16. Raymond Bellour, 'Ideal Hadaly', p. 122.

17. See Frederic Jameson, *Postmodernism, or the Cultural Logic of Late Capitalism* (Durham: Duke University Press, 1991), pp. 279–96, on a different, but not unrelated, genre of 'nostalgia film'.

The fatal attraction of *Intercourse*

1. Sigmund Freud, 'From the History of an Infantile Neurosis' (1918), in *Case Histories II* (Pelican Freud Library, vol. 9, Harmondsworth, 1979), p. 263.

2. Andrea Dworkin, *Intercourse* (London: Secker & Warburg, 1987), p. 194. Further page numbers will be given in the text.

3. James Baldwin, *Another Country*, quoted in Andrea Dworkin, *Intercourse*, p. 61.

4. Leo Tolstoy, *The Kreutzer Sonata and Other Stories* (Penguin: Harmondsworth, 1985), p. 268.

5. Katherine Dixon, *Address to Soldiers* (1916) in Sheila

Jeffreys (ed.), *The Sexuality Debates* (London: Routledge & Kegan Paul, 1987), p. 205.

6. Sigmund Freud, *The Interpretation of Dreams* (1900), (Pelican Freud Library, vol. 4, Harmondsworth, 1976), p. 742.

7. Sigmund Freud, 'The Uncanny' (1919), in *Art and Literature* (Pelican Freud Library, vol. 14, Harmondsworth, 1985), p. 339.

8. Sigmund Freud, 'On the Sexual Theories of Children' (1908), in *On Sexuality* (Pelican Freud Library, vol. 7, Harmondsworth, 1977), pp. 198–200.

9. Christian Metz, *Psychoanalysis and Cinema* (London: Macmillan, 1982), p. 64. Further page numbers will be given in the text.

10. See Donald Greig, 'The Sexual Differentiation of the Hitchcock Text', *Screen* vol. 28, no. 1, Winter 1987, pp. 43–6.

11. James B. Twitchell, *Dreadful Pleasures* (New York: Oxford University Press, 1985), p. 67.

12. ibid.

13. Sigmund Freud, 'The Uncanny', in *Art and Literature*, p. 368.

14. See Geoffrey Wall, '"Different from Writing", Dracula in 1897', *Literature and History* vol. 10, no. 1, 1984.

15. Bram Stoker, *Dracula* (London: Oxford University Press, 1983), p. 59. Further page numbers will be given in the text.

16. Sigmund Freud, 'Beyond the Pleasure Principle' (1920), in *On Metapsychology* (Pelican Freud Library, vol. 11, Harmondsworth, 1984), pp. 281–7.

More of a Man: gay porn cruises gay politics

1. Andrea Dworkin, *Pornography: Men Possessing Women* (New York: Putnam, 1981).

2. John Stoltenberg, *Refusing to Be a Man* (Portland, OR: Breitenbush Books, 1989), esp. pp. 132–3.

3. Tom Waugh, 'Men's Pornography: Gay vs. Straight', *Jump Cut* no. 30, 1985, pp. 420–25.

4. Tania Modleski, *Feminism without Women* (New York/London: Routledge, 1991), p. 146.

5. While agreeing that cinema generally eroticizes the
   female body far more than the male, I would maintain
   that the narratives and conventions of current US
   'lesbian-made' pornography (e.g. the videos of Blush
   Productions) make it less assimilable to the traditional
   significance of femininity-as-spectacle than, for example,
   art cinema. (See '"Lianna" and the Lesbians of Art
   Cinema' in this collection.) Meanwhile, critics like
   Christine Holmlund ('When Is a Lesbian Not a Lesbian?',
   Camera Obscura 25–26 [1991], p. 173) have reasonably
   challenged that article's failure to consider the lesbian
   audience.

6. Linda Williams, *Hard Core: Power, Pleasure and the Frenzy of
   the Visible* (London: Pandora, 1990), p. 29. Further page
   citations will be given in the text.

7. Laura Mulvey, 'Visual Pleasure and Narrative Cinema',
   reprinted from *Screen* 1975 in *Visual and Other Pleasures*
   (London: Macmillan, 1989), pp. 14–38.

8. Fredric Jameson, *Signatures of the Visible* (New York and
   London: Routledge, 1990), p. 1.

9. 'It will be enormously important in our generic study of
   pornographic texts to challenge such contradictory
   categories of "normal" and "abnormal" on all levels.' –
   Linda Williams, *Hard Core*, p. 7.

10. Linda Williams, 'Pornographies On/Scene', in Lynne
    Segal and Mary McIntosh (eds), *Sex Exposed: Sexuality and
    the Pornography Debate* (London: Virago, 1992), p. 235.

11. ibid., p. 263.

12. ibid., p. 245.

13. Jack Monroe, 'More of a Man', *Manshots*, February 1991,
    p. 25.

14. See *Advocate Men*, May 1991, p. 90.

15. Peter Pica, 'Vid-X', *Windy City Times*, 3 January 1991, p.
    25.

16. Sid Mitchell, 'More of Man', *Adult Video News*, November
    1990, p. 72.

17. Police Officer Thomas F. Bohling, Complaint for Search
    Warrant, Circuit Court of Cook County, Illinois, 14
    February 1991.

18. David Olson, 'Film Seized in Police Raid at Bijou
    Theatre', *Windy City Times*, 21 February 1991, p. 18.

19. Marc Huestis, 'The Way We Are', *Bay Area Reporter*, 2 May 1991, p. 39.

20. Statistics compiled by *Advocate Men*, May 1991.

21. Cindy Patton, 'Visualizing Safe Sex: When Pedagogy and Pornography Collide', in Diana Fuss, (ed.), *Inside/Out* (New York/London: Routledge, 1991), p. 377.

22. *Advocate Men*, May 1991.

23. John Rowberry, *The Adam Film World 1992 Directory: Gay and Adult Video*, p. 115.

24. Andrew Ross, *No Respect: Intellectuals and Popular Culture* (London: Routledge, 1989), p. 196.

25. Slavoj Žižek, *Looking Awry* (Cambridge, MA/London: MIT Press, 1991), pp. 110–11. Further page references will be indicated in the text.

26. Slavoj Žižek, *The Sublime Object of Ideology* (London/New York: Verso, 1989), p. 169.

27. Here, I think, Žižek elides Lacan's observations on the unrepresentability of the phallus, which 'can only play its role as veiled', with those on the mythical nature of the sexual relation. See Juliet Mitchell and Jacqueline Rose, eds, *Feminine Sexuality* (London: Macmillan, 1982), esp. pp. 46, 82.

28. André Bazin, 'Marginal Notes on Eroticism in the Cinema', in Hugh Gray, (ed.), *What Is Cinema?*, vol. II (Berkeley, CA: University of California Press, 1972), pp. 169–75.

29. Linda Williams, *Hard Core*, p. 186.

30. André Bazin, 'Marginal Notes', p. 173.

31. 'The Use of Performers in Commercial Pornography', *Final Report of the Attorney General's Commission on Pornography* (Nashville, TN: Rutledge Hill Press, 1986), p. 224. (This edition, the only one on sale in London in 1991, is a commercial reprint of the two-volume Government Printing Office edition. It offers itself as 'a more affordable and available' tool to fight 'the spread of pornography' while trailing its 'extremely explicit content'.)

32. 1988 advertisement of the Whitman-Walker Clinic, Washington, DC, quoted in Cindy Patton, 'Visualizing Safe Sex', pp. 379–80.

33. Cindy Patton, ibid., p. 380.

34. Jeff Nunokawa, '"All the Sad Young Men": AIDS and the Work of Mourning', in Diana Fuss, (ed.), *Inside/Out*, pp. 311–23.

35. André Bazin, 'The Ontology of the Photographic Image', in Hugh Gray (ed.), *What Is Cinema?*, vol. I (Berkeley, CA: University of California Press, 1967), p. 14. See also Kristen Brooke Schleifer, 'Physical Evidence: Imaging Death', *The Print Collector's Newsletter*, vol. XXII, no. 6, January–February 1992, pp. 193–5; and Raymond Bellour, 'The Pensive Spectator', *Wide Angle* vol. 9, no. 1, 1987, p. 10.

36. Garrett Stewart, 'Photo-gravure: Death, Photography and Film Narrative', *Wide Angle* vol. 9, no. 1, 1987, p. 19.

37. Roland Barthes, *Camera Lucida* (New York: Hill & Wang, 1981), p. 96: 'Whether or not the subject is already dead, every photograph is this catastrophe.'

38. Anne Banfield, 'L'Imparfait de l'Objectif: The Imperfect of the Object Glass', *Camera Obscura* 24, September 1990, p. 79.

39. Marc Huestis, 'The Way We Are'.

40. Leo Bersani, 'Is the Rectum a Grave?', *October* 43, Winter 1987, p. 215.

41. Leo Steinberg, *The Sexuality of Christ in Renaissance Art and in Modern Oblivion* (New York: Pantheon, 1983), p. 46. Marlon Riggs's short video *Anthem* (1991) deploys a startlingly similar iconography – the rose, the crucifix, the (black) male embrace, the Silence = Death slogan – to rather different effect, since these are intercut with the Stars and Stripes. The result is to question the assimilability of straight and gay cultures which *More of a Man* asserts.

42. Andrew Britton, *Katharine Hepburn: The Thirties and After* (Newcastle upon Tyne: Tyneside Cinema Publications, 1984), p. 41.

43. Carole-Anne Tyler, 'Boys Will Be Girls: The Politics of Gay Drag', in Diana Fuss, (ed.), *Inside/Out*, p. 52.

44. Marc Huestis, 'The Way We Are'.

The feminist ethics of lesbian s/m

1. B. Ruby Rich, 'Feminism and Sexuality in the 1980s', *Feminist Studies* vol. 12, no. 3, 1986, p. 529.

2. Gilles Deleuze, *Masochism: An Interpretation of Coldness and Cruelty* (New York: George Braziller, 1971), p. 115.

3. Parveen Adams, 'Per Os(cillation)', *Camera Obscura* 17, 1988, pp. 28–9.

4. Catherine Millot, 'The Feminine Superego', in Parveen Adams and Elizabeth Cowie, (eds), *The Woman in Question* (Cambridge, MA: MIT Press, 1990), pp. 294–314. (Reprinted from *m/f* no. 10, 1985.) Further page citations will be given in the text.

5. Parveen Adams, 'Of Female Bondage', in Teresa Brennan, (ed.), *Between Feminism and Psychoanalysis* (London/New York: Routledge, 1989), p. 314. Further page citations will be given in the text.

6. Sigmund Freud, 'Some Psychical Consequences of the Anatomical Distinction between the Sexes' (1925), in *On Sexuality* (Pelican Freud Library, vol. 7, Harmondsworth, 1977), p. 342.

7. Joan Riviere, 'Womanliness as Masquerade' (1929), in Victor Burgin, James Donald and Cora Kaplan, (eds), *Formations of Fantasy* (London: Methuen, 1986), pp. 35–44.

8. See Melanie Klein, 'The Early Development of Conscience in the Child' (1933), in *Contributions to Psycho-Analysis* (London: Hogarth Press, 1950).

9. A term reminiscent of Joyce McDougall's description of the perversions as reparative 'neo-sexualities'. See her *Theaters of the Mind* (New York: Basic Books, 1985).

10. See Parveen Adams, 'Per Os(cillation)', p. 26.

11. Teresa Brennan, 'Introduction', in *Between Feminism and Psychoanalysis*, p. 1. Further page citations will be given in the text.

12. Alice Jardine, 'Notes for an Analysis', in Teresa Brennan, (ed.), *Between Feminism and Psychoanalysis*, p. 75. Further page citations will be given in the text.

13. ibid., p. 82.

14. Gayatri Chakravorty Spivak, 'Feminism and Deconstruction, Again: Negotiating with Unacknowledged Masculinism', in Teresa Brennan, (ed.), *Between Feminism and Psychoanalysis*, p. 217.

15. Here Spivak is quoting from Thomas Nagel, *Mortal Questions* (Cambridge: Cambridge University Press, 1979), p. xiii.

16. Katherine Davis, 'Introduction: What We Fear We Try to Keep Contained', in Samois (ed.), *Coming to Power* (Boston, MA: Alyson Publications, 1982), p. 7.

17. Judy [*sic*] Butler, 'Lesbian S & M: The Politics of Disillusion', in Robin Ruth Linden, Darlene R. Pagano, Diana E.H. Russell and Susan Leigh Star, (eds), *Against Sadomasochism* (East Palo Alto, CA: Frogs in the Well, 1982), p. 171.

18. Solo Weaves, 'On the Beam', in Samois (ed.), *Coming to Power*, p. 20.

19. Janet Schrim, 'Mirel' in ibid., p. 124.

20. Holly Drew, 'The Seduction of Earth and Rain', in ibid., p. 131.

21. Martha Alexander, 'Passion Play', in ibid., p. 242.

22. Katherine Davis, 'Introduction', p. 11.

23. Judy Butler, 'Lesbian S & M'.

24. Similarly, B. Ruby Rich, 'Feminism and Sexuality', argues that neither the pro- nor anti-s/m factions 'seems to recognize fantasy as a sphere apart, shaped by social and psychological factors but lacking any inherent linear relationship to action itself' (p. 533). And Inge Blackman and Kathryn Perry, 'Skirting the Issue: Lesbian Fashion for the 1990s', note the similarity between radical feminist and s/m lesbian arguments for a '"real" sexual being underneath', *Feminist Review* no. 34, Spring 1990, p. 70.

25. Juicy Lucy, 'If I Ask You to Tie Me Up, Will You Still Want to Love Me?', in Samois (ed.), *Coming to Power*, p. 33.

26. My favourite denunciation in this vein is Ti-Grace Atkinson, 'Why I'm Against S/M Liberation', in Linden *et al.*, (eds), *Against Sadomasochism*, p. 92: 'The twisting of c-r into a proving ground for the prevalence of sexual masochism among women, and by implication its acceptability as a static condition, is outrage almost past expression.'

27. Katherine Davis, 'Introduction', p. 13.

28. Teresa de Lauretis, 'Upping the Anti [*sic*] in Feminist Theory', in Marianne Hirsch and Evelyn Fox Keller, (eds), *Conflicts in Feminism* (New York/London: Routledge, 1990), pp. 255–70.

29. Sigmund Freud, 'Civilization and its Discontents' (1930), in *Civilization, Society and Religion* (Pelican Freud Library vol. 12, Harmondsworth, 1985), p. 305.

30. On this history of oppositions, see also Katie King, 'Producing Sex, Theory and Culture: Gay/Straight Remappings in Contemporary Feminism', in Marianne Hirsch and Evelyn Fox Keller, (eds), *Conflicts in Feminism*, pp. 82–101.

31. Teresa de Lauretis, 'Upping the Anti', p. 266.

32. Sigmund Freud, 'The Economic Problem of Masochism' (1924), in *On Metapsychology* (Pelican Freud Library, vol. 11, Harmondsworth, 1984), pp. 422–3.

33. Julia Creet, 'Daughter of the Movement: The Psycho-dynamics of Lesbian S/M Fantasy', *differences* vol. 3, no. 2, 1991, p. 145. Further page citations will be given in the text.

34. Tania Modleski, *Feminism without Women* (London/New York: Routledge, 1991), pp. 156–7. Further page citations will be given in the text.

35. Sigmund Freud, 'The Economic Problem of Masochism', in *On Metapsychology*, p. 425.

36. Martha Alexander, 'Passion Play', in Samois (ed.), *Coming to Power*, pp. 228–42.

37. I read Meg as the lesbian version of Riviere's masquerader, another public speaker who guiltily surrenders the purloined phallus after a display of professional competence. See Joan Riviere, 'Womanliness as Masquerade'.

38. See Gilles Deleuze, *Masochism*, ch. 6, pp. 61–70.

39. Thus Pat Califia, 'The Limits of the S/M Relationship', *Outlook* 15, Winter 1992, p. 17: 'It's a truism in the S/M community that bottoms outnumber tops about ten to one.'

40. Gilles Deleuze, *Masochism*, p. 60.

41. ibid., p. 38.

42. Marquis de Sade, *Philosophy in the Bedroom* (1795), in Richard Seaver and Austryn Wainhouse, (eds), *The Marquis de Sade* (New York: Grove Press, 1966), p. 359.

43. Angela Carter, *The Sadeian Woman* (New York: Pantheon, 1978), p. 134.

44. Sigmund Freud, 'The Ego and the Id' (1923), in *On Metapsychology*, p. 393.

45. Sigmund Freud, 'Civilization and its Discontents' in *Civilization, Society and Religion*, p. 323.

46. ibid., p. 321.

47. Immanuel Kant, *Critique of Practical Reason*, transl. Lewis White Beck (New York/London: Macmillan, 1956), p. 64.

48. Jacques Lacan, 'Kant with Sade', transl. James B. Swenson, Jr, *October* 51, Winter 1989, p. 59. This is Lacan's paraphrase of the 'Sadeian maxim' advanced at length in the pamphlet read aloud in *Philosophy in the Bedroom*. 'Jouissance' carries the sense of both orgasmic enjoyment and the seigneurial right to enjoy the property of others. These combine in *Philosophy in the Bedroom*, p. 318. See also Frances Ferguson on Sade and the reformulation of French property rights in the 1780s, 'Sade and the Pornographic Legacy', *Representations* 36, Fall 1991, pp. 13–14.

49. Sigmund Freud, 'Civilization and its Discontents', in *Civilization, Society and Religion*, p. 302.

50. Jacques Lacan, *Le séminaire Livre VII: L'éthique de la psychanalyse* (Paris: Editions du Seuil, 1987), p. 219, transl. James B. Swenson, Jr, 'Annotations to "Kant with Sade"', *October*, p. 102.

51. Immanuel Kant, *Critique of Practical Reason*, p. 66.

52. Sarah Hoagland, *Lesbian Ethics* (Palo Alto, CA: Institute of Lesbian Studies, 1988), p. 270.

53. Wendy Brown, 'Feminist Hesitations, Postmodern Exposures', *differences* vol. 3, no. 1, Spring 1991, p. 77.

54. Joan Cocks, 'Augustine, Nietzsche, and Contemporary Body Politics', *differences* vol. 3, no. 1, Spring 1991, p. 155.

55. Friedrich Nietzsche, *On the Genealogy of Morals*, transl. Walter Kauffman (New York: Vintage, 1967), esp. the first and second essays, pp. 15–96.

56. Joan Cocks, 'Augustine, Nietzsche', p. 154.

57. Wendy Brown, 'Feminist Hesitations', pp. 80–81.

58. Marquis de Sade, *Philosophy in the Bedroom*, p. 363.

59. Sigmund Freud, 'Some Psychical Consequences of the Anatomical Distinction between the Sexes', in *On Sexuality*, p. 342.

index

Also of interest

SEX EXPOSED
Sexuality and the Pornography Debate

Edited by Lynne Segal and Mary McIntosh

Over the past twenty years debates about pornography have raged both within feminism and the wider world. Throughout the 1970s feminists increasingly addressed the problem of men's sexual violence against women, and many insisted that men's sexual coercion was the bedrock of male power, thus reducing the politics of men's power over women to questions about sexuality. By the 1980s the issue had become more and more focused on pornography, making it harder to think clearly about either sexuality or pornography – indeed, about feminist politics more generally.

This provocative collection of sixteen essays by British, American and Australian feminists aims to open up the debate by looking at such issues as: the improbable alliance between the right and pro-censorship feminists in the USA and Britain; the displacement of heterosexual desire and its discontents on to pornography and the female nude in 'high' art.

Contributors include Elizabeth Cowie, Harriett Gilbert, Robin Gorna, Jane Mills, Mandy Merck, Lynda Nead, Carol Smart, Carole Vance, Linda Williams and Elizabeth Wilson.